Probing the Mind to Free the Soul

Probing the Mind to Free the Soul

Toward a Psychoanalytic Protest Theology

STEPHEN G. FOWLER

WIPF & STOCK · Eugene, Oregon

PROBING THE MIND TO FREE THE SOUL
Toward a Psychoanalytic Protest Theology

Wipf & Stock
An Imprint of Wipf and Stock Publishers
199 W. 8th Ave., Suite 3
Eugene, OR 97401

www.wipfandstock.com

PAPERBACK ISBN: 978-1-5326-1808-6
HARDCOVER ISBN: 978-1-4982-4333-9
EBOOK ISBN: 978-1-4982-4332-2

Manufactured in the U.S.A.   APRIL 26, 2017

Unless indicated otherwise, all Scripture quotations are from the New Geneva Study Bible, New King James Version, Nashville, TN: Thomas Nelson, 1982.

To my parents,
Dorothy and Frederick

When someone worth listening to speaks, the word
will be cryptic enough to be meaningful, which is to say
that it will be cryptic enough to be misunderstood.
There is no teleological guarantee.[1]

1. Delay, *God is Unconscious*, 129.

Contents

Introduction

THE IMPETUS FOR WRITING this work came from my own pressing need to reconcile my prior Christian understanding of the human mind with the many elements of psychoanalytic models of the mind upon which I took notes over several years of reading texts pertinent to my training in the discipline of psychoanalysis. As features of the mind became illuminated for me from psychoanalytic texts, I contrasted and compared a theological perspective on those features, both from biblical and from typical Christian practice (as I have understood them) viewpoints. It has been an immensely valuable personal exercise to attempt in this way to synthesize, hopefully in a coherent way, my thoughts from compiled notes independently recorded over years of study. My observations and arguments are my own, or those of other authors (in which case annotation is duly provided) and I acknowledge that my views are, as are all views, biased by my own experience, my particular exposures to Christianity and to psychoanalysis, and by the unique configuration of conflicts and distortions, either conscious or unconscious, that unavoidably occupy my mind. It is my hope that material in this volume, while in no way purporting to serve as the final word on any particular area of consideration, will stimulate thought in the reader and perhaps provoke some to engage with these ideas further within their own communities of discourse, whether professional, faith-based, or academic.

I have written this text with a general, educated, and curious readership in mind, and not for either psychoanalytically or theologically specially trained readers. Therefore, some of my attempts at clarification of terms may seem contrived or awkward to either of the latter groups.

A word of caution: at times, graphic language may be used either in the service of my efforts to be linguistically precise, or in the context of quotations either of source materials or of patients who have consented to my use of clinical material from their analytic work with me.

Perhaps questions as to why I, a medical doctor who practiced general family medicine and emergency medicine for thirty years before studying psychoanalysis, chose the path I did can be anticipated and deserve some answers. It is importantly relevant that I grew up within a very conservative, fundamentalist Christian environment that laid great emphasis upon the achievement of personal piety (Google dictionary: "a belief or point of view that is accepted with unthinking conventional reverence") and holiness. Mine was a working class family, in which I did not find much resonance for my questioning of assumptions regarding faith, or beliefs about life or the mind or the body. Consequently, and for many reasons, I suffered my own existential crisis in early adult years that set me on a quest for truth that would satisfy both my desire and my need to understand. Both matters of the validity or sensibility of faith-claims, and those of the complex interface of mind and body as people experience them (myself included) in their efforts to live life as well as possible were challenges for me. Cliches and simplistic answers that in no way adequately addressed the complexity of human experience no longer sufficed for me.

As for my personal "existential crisis," I call it this because for days, and a few times for weeks on end, I struggled with questions about reality, how one could confidently attest to the on-going existence of anything, and most particularly, I questioned my own sanity and whether I could reasonably expect to surpass my crisis and engage in "normal" life again. To be clear, these were times of very intense anxiety, more adequately described as terror, and not, in any way comfortable philosophical musings about reality and existence. Having lived to my late teens within a rather protected and puritanical environment that was at least skeptical and at worst paranoid about the ideas and philosophies that were considered counter to our particular conservative Christian worldview, I clearly felt threatened at the prospect of pursuing my aspirations for knowledge in the wide world of the university. I also, now, from today's perspective can see that I was, and for a number of years had been, in the Freudian sense, feeling threatened by my own repressed libidinally[1] invested memories ("the return of the repressed"[2]), the expression of which felt dreadfully and fearfully unacceptable.

Over a period of about three years, during which I managed to persist in my undergraduate studies, despite these variably intense struggles with

1. Libido is the term employed by Freud and in much of psychoanalysis since to indicate psychic energy that is thought to arise from the id, has a distinctly sexual aspect to it, and/or manifests as desire.

2. Freud, *Further Remarks on the Neuropsychoses of Defense*, 168.

anxiety, insomnia, depression, and despair, I remained steadfast in clinging to, albeit questioning, a faith in God; perhaps it was more that God clung to me. It is of relevance that the girl I was dating, and had been for nearly a year, and who was well-apprised of my strange and disturbing thoughts, and who was a Christian believer like myself, had refused my invitation to leave me to find someone who seemed to have a future. She remained committed to me, avowing that she loved me and that she was not daunted. There came a point in the spring of the third year, on a beautiful bright Sunday morning, when I was home from church, allegedly studying for exams, that I found myself once again agonizing over my despair and crying out to God for deliverance, when I had a new realization of something I had never before seen in myself. I had dated many girls through my teen years, after the manner of conservative Christian dating (i.e., quite strict avoidance of explicitly sexual touching and behavior), and had repeatedly sought to get an attractive girl to like me, at which point, soon after, I would drop her to pursue the next one. On that Sunday morning I had the powerful insight that I had been using girls' affections and emotional attachments to me to gratify my own selfish needs without regard for them. I acknowledged this to God as sin; there was a deep confession. Within an hour, the feelings of despair, terror, and what I have described as the dark clouds of depression had disappeared.

Readers who have known depression of a major character, or those who have known the (seemingly) unexplained terror that can accompany depression, with its sense of loss of personal moorings (depersonalization) or who have seen in the eyes of others the haunting that can typify what I have tried to convey here personally, will recognize that to have that subjective experience gone is like going from darkest night to the bright of day. For me, this was a deliverance that has endured, virtually without relapse, until now, age sixty-seven.

I have speculated many times as to what really transpired in that experience, both before and after having studied psychoanalysis. At the time, I believed that God had led me to discover some egregious narcissistic fixation (biblically, that which constitutes sin) in myself that stood in the way of me loving others the way a Christ-follower is to love. When I saw that fact, and acknowledged it, he was pleased to clear my mind of the anxieties and fears. In effect, I had come to know that he loved me and that love and fear cannot coexist.[3] So, was this one of those unanticipated occurrences of numinous experience, of the mystery of God, that so many people have, but can never be entirely sure about? I have also thought about more prosaic

---

3. 1 John 4:18.

explanations, of a psychological nature, such as finally letting God's claims of unconditional love penetrate my mind in such a way as to displace my own persisting fears of parental (or as will be seen in the chapters of this book, of the internalized and embellished parental representations, in the form of my superego, that populated my mind) disapproval, or the fears of rejection from the community of my childhood should I begin to expand my worldview beyond their's. Did the love of my girlfriend (who became and still is my wife) play a part in convincing me of the existence of value in me despite my insight as to glaring flaws? Did I experience the beginning of a process of superego transformation that was to become life-long? Had I been suffering from crises of superego condemnation, exceptionally sharpened and provoked by the sexual drive derivatives that I had been experiencing all my teen years (and even earlier) that had been sufficiently crushing to almost snuff out my life (I had considered suicide)? At the point of that clear insight into my narcissistic failing, and my confession of guilt before God, did I transition into the realm of conscience from the domination of superego over my mind? In fact, I believe that all of the above are valid and illumine what transpired that spring day forty four years ago.

One might wonder if I had the benefit of any professional psychological intervention at that time. I did, to a very limited extent, and certainly not of the intensity or depth of psychoanalysis, but nevertheless I was inducted into the process of acquiring a stance of observation regarding the content of my own mind, a stance of being able to think about how one thinks, and to reflect upon my emotions. At every turn throughout all of the experiences of those three years, I was encouraged and supported in my determination to gain access to medical school, and did receive acceptance to begin sixteen months later.

For reasons of needing to prove to myself that I could function adequately in the demanding and competitive world of medical practice, as well as satisfying the approval criteria of my immediate (family and Christian) community for a worthy vocational pursuit, and my own practical need to provide well for my wife and four children, I practiced in the field of physical medicine for thirty years. Notwithstanding truly enjoying my medical career, during those years, I anticipated longingly the opportunity for pursuit of further study in the later part of my professional life. I settled upon the study of psychoanalysis because it was the only clinically-based approach to the mind that held promise of probing beyond the surface, i.e., beyond that which can be accessed by conscious intention and by measurement, using standard scientific methodology. I had long experience of learning that the many distresses of my patients (and my own) whose problems clearly were rooted in the non-organic, i.e., in their mind, were not amenable to instructional approaches. By this, I mean that being counselled in better ways of thinking or of behaving, or of living more healthfully, accomplished little that would endure. It was increasingly apparent to me that the hidden matters of the mind that were beyond conscious awareness held great sway over the lived experience of many, perhaps all people.

Psychoanalysis as a body of theory and as a clinical discipline appealed to me as holding potential power for overcoming or at least elucidating a lot of the mental blockages that serve to interfere with people achieving reasonable contentment, productivity, relational success, or measures of happiness. In addition, training in psychoanalysis afforded me the opportunity, out of necessity, of undergoing my own analysis, something that I had perceived to be anathema to the cloistered community of my childhood and youth (not that I had actually known then what it was that might have satisfied my quest). It was only upon immersing myself in psychoanalysis that I was able to perceive that an approach which had seemed beyond reach held the potential to address a lot of my own long-held dilemmas. But I have alluded to a discomfort between psychoanalysis and conservative Christianity, a matter which I will now address.

CHRISTIANITY AND PSYCHOANALYSIS: BED-FELLOWS OR ENEMIES?

When it comes to considering the relationship between psychoanalysis and Christianity, the roles of fox and chicken in the proverbial battlefield have been adopted by either and interchangeably. Each has been guilty of seeking to devour the other. While both psychoanalysis and religion, specifically in the form of Christian religion, purport to seek out and articulate truth as embedded in the infinite variety of experience in what it is to be human, both cause great offense to conventional human narcissistic sensibilities. Judaeo-Christianity (Christianity is built upon the foundation of Judaism, and Christians perceive Christianity to be its logical and predicted outcome) portrays persons as flawed, or broken image-bearers of God. Persons then, according to the Christian worldview, are derivative (derived from God), subordinate beings, who, instead of possessing complete independence, autonomy of thought, and unfettered right to pursue whatever they desire, are subservient and answerable to their creator, who claims to have made adequately known, his own being as well as his ideals for the creatures he made after his own image.[4] Various expressions of Christianity,[5] i.e., the denominations, sects,

4. Genesis 1:26, 27; Romans 1.
5. Denominations, characterized by certain emphases lifted from Scripture, and by

and communities that have evolved from adherence to the biblical account of the life, death, meanings, and implications for humanity of Jesus Christ, have laid emphasis upon differing elements. Overall, however, their emphases have in various ways served to constrain human freedoms for self-expression. Perhaps the central offense which Christianity presents is the claim that all mankind is contaminated by sin.[6] To perceive oneself as sinful is to experience, first, a fundamental sense of alienation (from God, self, and fellow humans), and second, deep, inescapable guilt, along with a powerful desire to be freed or cleansed or purified from that guilt. Problematically, the diverse expressions of Christianity have variously interpreted the biblical claims for how sin can and must be dealt with, failing, all too often, to recognize the futility of persons' efforts to purify themselves of sin and its accompanying guilt.[7] While most recognize the sacrifice of Jesus Christ as necessary for salvation, there are many variances as to how that fact is to be understood and implemented in the everyday lives of regular people.

I must qualify my use of the term "Christianity." The word may be used to refer to any one or many of the various expressions of understanding and practice of communities of people who have taken upon themselves the label "Christian." Since the time of Christ, many such communities have differed wildly in terms of their hermeneutics, the particular emphasis chosen and the practices that follow from that choice. Inevitably, my own outlook has been shaped by the particular branch of Christian expression in which I developed, and by my reactions to it and to many other expressions. Nevertheless, as I hope will be evident to the reader, I have tried to shape my own ideas as they are documented here in this work, as faithfully close to what I understand the Bible to say, as I can. Clearly, however, I have my own hermeneutical biases, one of which I will be explicit about, and that is that I take the Bible's own witness to the fact that all of what scripture has to say is to be understood through Jesus[8] as the lens. I endeavour to faithfully apply a "Jesus hermeneutic."

To return to the offensiveness of psychoanalysis, which claims to be the science of the unconscious (in contrast to other fields of psychology, e.g.,

---

traditions that have grown up in support of those emphases, would include, as examples, Roman Catholicism, Jehovah's Witnesses, Presbyterianism, to name only a very few.

6. Romans 3:23.

7. See, for example, Romans 3:24, where the key biblical claim that cleansing from sin can only come about through a suitable sacrifice, is asserted. Many other references could expand upon this theme, but, for now, it will suffice to make the point that humans' own self-generated sacrifice is of no value.

8. John 5:39–40; Colossians 2:17; Luke 10:22; 24:25–27; John 1:18; 20:30–31; 1 Corinthians 2:2

cognitive psychology, behavioral psychology, etc., which focus on the products of the mind of which we are conscious), through its observations of the depths of human fantasies and wishes, of motivations or drives, of meanings to patterns of behavior previously unknown to the subject, it tells us that we are not at all what we consciously think we are. In contrast to the general preference to conceive of ourselves as fully rational beings, Jonathan Lear claims we are inevitably "motivated irrationally . . . the fundamental human phenomenon to which all of psychoanalysis is a response."[9] The confident assumption that we can and do know our own minds is offensively contradicted by the claims of Sigmund Freud and his followers that we are, in fact, governed by the unconscious realm of the mind far more than we like to acknowledge. Accordingly, regardless of just how the unconscious is variably conceptualized theoretically, it may be asserted that our conscious, manifest life, with its associated beliefs, values, and patterns of behavior that we display to the world around us is a type of veneer that is "designed"[10] to disguise (from the self as well as others) elements within that have about them that which is too disturbing to admit to conscious awareness. For example, a person's hurtful sarcasm directed toward a younger sibling might disguise a repressed, far more sinister early childhood wish to murder this usurper of parental attention, a wish too disturbing (because it was sincerely felt at the time) to ever be admitted into consciousness. Or, consider the example of the married pastor who has an affair that devastates his wife, his children, and his community; he believes he is pursuing a new "true" love, when, in actuality, he is enacting unconscious unresolved oedipal impulses to possess his mother and to defeat (eliminate) his rival father. In this example, simply put, the new woman would represent the exciting off-limits mother of unconscious memory, and the conventions of wife, children and community who are violated, are collectively representative of the (law-giving) father who could never actually be defeated in childhood, and whom the boy also loved.

Both Christianity and psychoanalysis offend, with their core claims, the sensibilities of humans who, especially since the enlightenment period, confidently assume their self-awareness to be replete and rational. We prefer to assert that we are not afflicted by guilt. Christianity asserts that we are guilty by virtue of our grasp after that which belongs only to God—sin (more on our quest to possess God's omnipotence later), while in Judaism,

---

9. Lear, *Open Minded*, 54.

10. The term "designed" suggests a conscious, deliberate act; in fact, psychoanalysis teaches that the consignment of various psychical products (thoughts, wishes, impulses, and configurations of both thoughts and their associated emotions) to the realm of the unconscious occurs, in itself, unconsciously, from early in life, onwards.

the Law was to instruct man in the particulars as to his guilt, in the form of his failure to meet standards of holiness.

Psychoanalysis, on the other hand, asserts that we are ineluctably guilty by virtue of deeply repressed wishes to violate the taboo against incest and to commit homicide, in the form of elimination of a rival parent or sibling. In addition to the guilt model, more contemporary views articulate a model of man as tragic; he is seen as the tragic victim of inadequate parenting, of failures of optimal attunement to his needs. Both Christianity and psychoanalysis offer some form of remedy to mankind's tragic, or guilt-ridden, or divided, broken state. Although the "classical" Freudian version of psychoanalysis posits a model of the mind that sees man as fundamentally guilty of wishes and impulses that are in violation of others, despite its provision of in-depth understanding of oneself and dawning awareness of consequent opportunities for reparative concern for the other, it cannot claim to achieve a deep, thorough-going erasure of that guilt. Christianity, on the other hand, does lay claim to offering the ultimate remedy for guilt, that being the acceptance of one's guilt as unalterably vile, but utterly forgiven, eliminated by the substitutionary, sacrificial death of God himself in the person of Jesus Christ. Christianity also asserts that the appropriation of this deliverance is achieved by honest acknowledgement of one's guilty state, a will to turn away from whom one has been (repentance), and an opening of the self to newly relating to the resurrected Jesus in such a way as to feel and be truly set free.[11]

The New Testament makes clear that no amount of self-improvement effort can alter one's fundamental state of sinfulness before God, and so the salvation offered is presented as a gift, extended by an infinitely gracious God. That being said, however, many Christians will attest to the fact that although they "know" (by intellectual assent) themselves forgiven and see themselves as engaged in a kind of on-going personal renovation at the hand of God and his "Holy Spirit" (the third person of the Trinity), they nevertheless find themselves repeating old, troubling (possibly sinful) patterns. They continue to feel oppressed by something like condemnation, or they cannot seem to find substantial sustained peace or happiness; or relationships continue to flounder with recrimination and counter-recrimination.

It is in response to this distressing phenomenon of failing to *feel* liberated despite a declaration of freedom, that I have wished to elaborate psychoanalytic insights that might potentially contribute to a more effective freeing of the mind (Christian and otherwise) from its bondage. Such bondage arises from residual conflicts, themselves deriving from the contents of the disturbing and mysterious unconscious, which is inherent in and from

11. John 8:32 & 36.

the fundamental conditions and situation of universal childhood. From such a perspective, Freud recognized that, disturbingly and paradoxically, "the child truly is father to the man."[12] The formative situation and experiences of childhood inevitably give rise to and indelibly "stain" the adult, who is more subject to the dictates of the child in him than he knows. While only God can ultimately repair the faults that plague humans (as per the claims of Christianity), and set a person on a radically new path, my purpose is to explore the ways in which psychoanalytic theory and practice contribute to easing one's living of life with such residual conflictual complexities here and now. In the course of so-doing I anticipate that elements of theology will similarly prove to contribute to an enrichment of psychoanalytic theory and practice.

Historically, psychoanalysis, which is only a century and a quarter old (although many of its theoretical precepts find precursors in philosophy as old as Plato and other ancient writers, as well as the Bible), has been eyed with strong suspicion by Christians, for a number of reasons. Among these are the fact that its originator, Sigmund Freud, wrote scathingly about religion as little more than the projection of infantile needs for an idealized father onto the notion of an invisible god. Freud is commonly thought to have espoused atheism (some authors dispute Freud's actual and perhaps unconscious beliefs)[13] as the natural counterpart to his rationalistic explanations for complex cognitive and emotional manifestations of the human mind. A second cause for skepticism from Christians (who have long been notoriously troubled by sexuality) has been the perception that psychoanalysis claims a central place for sexuality in the entire scope of infantile and adult psychic function. Freud has been accused of a kind of "pan-sexualism." A third source of discomfort has been the recognition that psychoanalysis, both in theory and in clinical application, places man himself at the center of his own efforts to overcome his residual infantile ways, to mature through the long and arduous journey of personal analysis. Customarily, psychoanalysis, in its theoretical formulations and traditional clinical practice has claimed no recourse to God, or any other supernatural being, although a logically correct outlook from the point of view from within psychoanalysis is to make no pronouncement at all on the validity of religion, since it has no credible epistemological authority to do so. (Its epistemology does, however, permit of a legitimate commentary on the human *praxis* of religious or theological beliefs, as did Freud.) In a sense then, psychoanalysis is seen by Christians as anthropocentric, in contrast to a faith-based stance of theocentricism, and hence a tension exists albeit, in my view, a healthy one. I say this because it is right that the focus of concern

12. Freud, *The Claims of Psycho-analysis to Scientific Interest*, 183.
13. Vitz, *Freud's Christian Unconscious.*

for the science of psychoanalysis is the unconscious of man, individually or collectively, and that the appropriate focus of Christianity is the divine; and so, as with any cross-disciplinary discourse, there rightly needs to exist tension which fosters debate, all of which has the potential to bear fruit in the form of refinements to understanding, clarification as to limits of knowledge, and integration.

Rather paradoxically, given Christianity's Jewish roots, I should highlight another unfortunate prejudice against psychoanalysis within the Christian world, one that derives from a perception that psychoanalysis is a "Jewish science." While it is true that the discipline arose from the mind of a Jew, and that many psychoanalysts are of Jewish heritage, there may be good reasons why the unconscious was recognized and observations about it systematized by Freud. Thomas Torrance, in recognizing the influence of the steady inculcation of knowledge of God into the Jewish people without the use of images (the Second Commandment), over generations, and in writing about the importance of integration between science and theology, said,

> It is significant that at these junctures in modern scientific investigation where we have to penetrate into the invisible intelligible structures [e.g. atomic particles, quantum physics, etc.] that lie behind and control all observable empirical structures in this world, it is very frequently Jewish scientists who have led the way. They have helped us to break through the screen of the phenomenalist world of appearances with which we have become obsessed in our European tradition in science and philosophy. Thus instead of interpreting the invisible in terms of the visible, or the noumenal in terms of the phenomenal, we have had to do the very opposite: interpret what is visible from what is inherently invisible[14].

While referring more specifically to the physical sciences, Torrance's remarks pertain aptly to psychoanalysis.

Torrance was remarkable for his depth of appreciation of both theology and the world of science, and for his passion for integrating the two. His works have been instrumental in inspiring me to seek for integration between psychoanalysis and theology. In his introduction of Torrance in the foreword to "Reality and Evangelical Theology," Kurt Anders Richardson said of Torrance,

> A great part of Torrance's vision has been the hope of convergence, and he has given himself tirelessly to this end. The convergence he seeks to explicate is summed up in the doctrinal

14. Torrance, *The Mediation of Christ*, 21.

convergence of creation and redemption in Christ. He argues that the knowledge of God in Christ is received according to created reality—the object of all human knowing—and that theological knowledge is always in partnership with natural and human sciences.[15]

In a similar vein, albeit in reference to his disdain for Christians' all-too-typical view of the secularism of life as a negation of worship, Alexander Schmemann decries the effects of secularism as the dichotomization into categories of profane (as devoid of any communication with the divine, of any real transformation and transfiguration) and sacred. He prefers that form of sacramentality which refers to finding the divine in the elements of the world, a kind of sanctification of all of life, and laments the replacement by secularism that dichotomously splits into natural and supernatural. "What is denied is simply the *continuity* between 'religion' and 'life,' the very function of worship as power of transformation, judgement, and change."[16] His integrative vision will be referred to later in the chapter on sexuality.

Corresponding to Christianity's suspicions, psychoanalysis has exercised wariness regarding claims based upon faith, for reasons of their assumptions being untestable empirically and therefore subject to the fault so often cited by Freud,[17] that all religious claims are based upon projections of residual childish wishes. Faith assertions claimed by Christians derive from knowledge that comes through revelation, e.g. the existence and nature of God; such were eschewed by Freud as attempts to rationalize what to him was actually being denied by those who make claim. The Judaeo-Christian God is understood by believers to be who he is because he has revealed himself to particular people, in particular ways, historically, and such revelation has been recorded in sacred texts called "scriptures." The latter, positing that Jesus was and is God, asserts his essence as "the Word, and the Word was with God, and the Word was God. . . . Through him all things were made. . . . "[18] While it is truthful and legitimate to claim that so much of "religion" (contrived by mankind) can be seen to have come into being as reaction-formation (a form of psychological defense) to a disturbingly hostile and unpredictable world, it is quite another thing to dismiss altogether all perceptions of and belief in the mysteries of the transcendent as nothing more than residual infantile fantasy-fulfillment. This would constitute a

15. Torrance, *Reality and Evangelical* Theology, xviii.

16. Schmemann, *For the Life of the World*, 133. Emphasis his.

17. Freud, *Obsessive Actions and Religious Practices;* Freud, *Totem and Taboo;* Freud, *The Future of An Illusion;* Freud, *Civilization and Its Discontents.*

18. John 1:1, 2.

throwing away of the baby with the bath water. While some factions within psychoanalysis make such pre-emptive claims, many others assert that they over-reach beyond the reasonable scope of the discipline. Wide-sweeping dismissal of belief in that which is transcendent (religious or mystical, spiritual or divine) does not arise, I believe, from a psychoanalytic outlook, but rather, from atheistic presuppositions that develop independently.

I believe that much of Freud's venom against religion, and perhaps that also of many of his followers, arose in reaction to the legalistic, authoritarian, fundamentalist certainty of belief so characteristic of many religious people, adopted in consequence of their sense of being small, weak, and vulnerable. It is a great tendency of all humans to seek to compensate for their doubts, fears, and uncertainties with claims that lean towards excess, too much certainty, or too much unwarranted dogmatism. While psychoanalysis has rightly identified and condemned this element within Judaeo-Christianity, the same criticism has been levelled at psychoanalysis, insofar as it, too, historically, has been fraught with dogmatic adherence to points of view that have only very reluctantly ceded space to alternate views based upon astute observations in recent decades.

A number of the conjunctions and disjunctions between Christianity and psychoanalysis will be highlighted and explored further in the body of this text.

WORDPLAY

The title of this volume implies that there may be a distinction between the mind and the soul. While I am not sure that there is any meaningful or necessary difference in actuality, I chose these terms, in part to engage in a bit of word-play, but also to highlight the fact that while psychoanalysis focuses on the (especially unconscious) mind, and makes as one of its clinical aims the shift of that which is unconscious into conscious awareness, Christianity, on the other hand tends to focus its sphere of concern on the soul. Translators of Freud's works from German into French have noted that he also variously used "psychic" and "soulish" to refer to the psychic apparatus, or to different elements within it.[19] Theologians may wish to parse the soul from the mind and both of them from the spirit of a person, but for my purpose, largely a functional one, the two terms, mind and soul, will essentially refer to the same thing.

The phrase in my subtitle, "psychoanalytic protest theology," I owe to Tad Delay, who says of his own writing, *God is Unconscious*:

19. Scarfone, *The Unpast, Actuality of the Unconscious.*

> This book has shied away from a constructive theology. Just as the ethics of psychoanalysis have little to say about what is ethical but much of what the ethical cannot be, a psychoanalytic protest theology can only say there must be a better way to think.[20]

Richard Rohr expresses a similar idea in referring to "'reverse theology' meant to subvert our usual merit-badge thinking."[21] His point is to focus on Jesus' assertion that the conservative loyal but indignant elder brother of the prodigal son (Luke 15:25–32) and the very properly religious, but self-righteous pharisee of Luke 18:9–14, because they miss the major point, are blinded by their loyal adherence to correctness. The major point missed is the opportunity (and responsibility) to move into an honest, thoughtful, loving, relational mode, Rohr's "second half of life.[22]"

Finally, I will point out that in referring to an unspecified person in the third person, I will use the generic male pronoun, as is common usage, and beg the forgiveness of any offended female and feminist male readers. I like to include myself in the latter group, and can only hope that such pronoun usage does not betray any lingering traces within my own mind of misogyny.

20. Delay, *God is Unconscious*, 128.
21. Rohr, *Falling Upward*, 45.
22. Ibid.

Chapter 1

Theories of Mind

TOPOGRAPHICAL THEORY

THE READER WILL BE helped to appreciate that the following remarks about the contents and activities of the topographical layers are not intended to be technically precise, but provide a rough overview for the purposes of this writing. The same applies to further remarks on models of the mind, in part because there is not unanimous agreement as to the precise categorization and mechanical functioning of mental organizational components even among psychoanalytic colleagues.

It is commonly recognized that Sigmund Freud was the founder of psychoanalysis, that his prolific, rich writings convey his sincere attempts to explore, illuminate, and rationally explain the infinitely complex workings of the human mind; but what is often not recognized by those unfamiliar with his writings is the fact that they represent a long progression over time in terms of not only theory development, but also a plurality of theories. It is more accurate to refer to his several theories than it is to presume a unitary, single conceptual framework of the mind. A refreshing experience for the reader of Freud is the frequency with which he frames his ideas in terms that speak to the awareness he had of a tentativeness to so many of his newly articulated ideas. Hewitt points out,

> As is almost always the case with Freud, his ideas are more nu-
> anced, complex and self-questioning than is often acknowledged
> by his critics. In Steven Pile's view, "one of the most outstanding

aspects of Freud's work is his readiness to challenge and reconsider his own presuppositions" (1999:206).[1]

Because of these and other features of Freud's writings, including the
obscurity of the subject matter itself, students of Freud continue to examine and debate and re-interpret his writings even many decades later. It is
not uncommon to hear a seasoned psychoanalytic colleague remark, with a
degree of wonder, that he has discovered something new upon re-reading a
previously presumed familiar Freudian text.

A brief diversion may be in order to allow the unfamiliar reader to
know a little of the historical background of Freud, a highly influential
thinker of the twentieth century. He was born to Jewish parents in the small
town of Freiburg in Moravia (now part of Poland) in 1856. His was a poor
family, holding to Jewish traditions and practices, while living in this deeply
catholic town of about forty-five hundred people. Sigmund was the eldest
child of his father, Jacob's, second family; there were two older brothers
from Jacob's late first wife. Until the age of about two, Sigmund was cared
for by a deeply religious catholic nanny, whose overt piety may have had significant influences on the formation of the young boy's unconscious mind.[2]
By the time Freud was three years of age, the family had migrated to Vienna,
where he was to spend most of the rest of his life, until 1936, when the Nazi
anti-Jewish threat was of such intensity that Freud and his family accepted
the aid of important sympathizers to exit Austria and emigrate to London,
England. Freud died in London in 1939 of complications associated with
his long battle against a form of sinus cancer. He had remained married
to his wife, Martha Bernays, of many years, and with whom he fathered
six children, one of whom, Anna Freud, followed her father into the study
of psychoanalysis, and became influential through her own writings, in
moulding theory, especially on the topic of ego defense mechanisms.

Freud was a precocious student, a voracious reader, and although
he was not especially interested in caring for suffering people, he pursued
medical training, "moved by a sort of curiosity, which was, however, directed more towards human concerns than towards natural objects."[3] After
completing medical school, he sought further training as a neurologist, and
became particularly interested in the obscure phenomena that characterized the symptoms of patients referred to as hysterical. It became a matter of
challenge to him to try to understand and explain rationally the mystifying
conversion reactions that hysterical patients display. Conversion reactions,

1. Hewitt. *Freud on Religion*, 115.

2. Vitz, *Sigmund Freud's Christian Unconscious.*

3. Freud, *An Autobiographical Study*, 8.

simply put, are physical symptoms for which no organic anatomical abnormality can be found that would neurologically explain the phenomenon observed. For example, a young woman might present as being quite nervous, but with an entirely inexplicable anaesthesia and paralysis of her right hand and wrist. Physical examination would reveal no abnormality and the distribution and character of impairment could not be explained by knowledge of the workings of the nervous system. Having been impressively influenced by his mentor, Charcot, who worked in the Paris mental hospital known as the Salpetrierre with hysterical patients, Freud began to understand that something deeply disturbing had taken place in the emotional, psychological life of such patients, forming a nucleus that was cordoned off in the psyche, so as to be unavailable to the conscious life of the person. The young lady whose hand had become useless to her was discovered, upon patient careful listening to her associations to all manner of mental products, including memories, proved to have disavowed, in effect, this portion of her anatomy because of her deep guilt/shame at masturbating. She herself was unaware of the connection between the cause and the effect, since, as was hypothesized by Freud, the memory and significance to her of the offending action had been powerfully repressed into her unconscious, and the resultant crippling of herself was achieving, in effect, a needed punishment. Both the need for punishment and the fulfillment were likewise unconscious to her. In other words, without the psychoanalytic intervention of discovering the previously concealed connection, the crippling impact of her conversion reaction might never have been overcome. Although confirming history to validate the following hypothesis is not available, one might wonder if this patient, suffering shame for her activity, had unconsciously virtually carried out Jesus' statement: " . . . if your right hand causes you to sin, cut it off and cast it from you. . . . "[4]

One can easily appreciate how fascinating to Freud such peculiar clinical phenomena was; they served as strong motivation to him to research further into the mysteries of the mind. Lest the reader think that such clinical occurrences as the case cited above were rare and hearkening only of another era, long passed, it is my own clinical experience that hysterical symptoms in the form of conversion reaction are by no means rare today. For example, during my years as an emergency physician, I once had a middle age female patient present by ambulance to the ER with apparently complete paralysis down one side of her body. For all intents and purposes, her examination findings and complaints were consistent with having had a major stroke. Following her admission to hospital, however, and subsequent

---

4. Matthew 5:30.

thorough investigation with the latest scanning technology, and full neurological assessment, no evidence for a stroke could be found, and so the diagnosis ended up being that of hysterical conversion reaction. I do not know whether she ever sought, through psychoanalysis or any other approach, to determine an underlying explanation.

While it may be true that our own apparently far more open era, educated and sophisticated about the troubling aspects of being human, such as the deep complexities that govern our sexuality, renders individuals less susceptible to such gross psychologically-caused impairments as in the cases cited, more subtle "psychosomatic" phenomena are rife in the population, no matter how sophisticated. Psychoanalytic attention given to such instances will usually shed light on unconscious underlying conflicts that contribute to manifestations of illness, e.g., anorexia, irritable bowel syndrome, various manifold musculoskeletal aches and pains that are underscored by tension, itself determined by unresolved psychic conflicts. There would hardly be a single patient in a psychotherapist's practice who does not suffer some bodily symptoms that derive from their mental conflicts.

To return to Freud, we might note that he worked in an environment of hostility to his efforts on at least two counts: to achieve academic recognition and advancement he had to overcome the prevailing anti-semitism that characterized life in Vienna during the late nineteenth and early twentieth centuries. Secondly, his time was one of scientific positivism, meaning that recognition from the established medical and scientific communities was earned on the basis of that which could be demonstrated as valid based upon the observable, "objective" scientific criteria and methodology of the time. Consequently, Freud was burdened by the need to have his new science of psychoanalysis approved and recognized by the academy that was rigidly bound to such an ideology of "scientific objectivity." He has been therefore criticized for trying overly hard to fit his new psychology of the unconscious into the medical framework that his time required.

In the early days of Freud's efforts to grasp the complexity of the human mind and to formulate a model that would reflect how it functions and provide clinicians with a conceptual framework for thinking about their therapeutic work, the so-called "topographical" model developed. According to this approach, the mind is conceived as layered, with the top layer representing conscious mental activity, and the much larger bottom layer representing the unconscious. By definition, of course, that which is unconscious is beyond the person's capacity to recall at will, and is, in effect, inaccessible. Nevertheless, features of the unconscious, such as being the location of the biologically-based drives and the sight of stored memory traces of past experience, along with their closely attached residues of powerful affects, give rise to the impulsive force for elements from within the unconscious to press forward for representation in conscious life. This topographically organized mind includes a third layer, which is termed the "preconscious," thought to exist between the other two, and to represent previously unconscious configurations of thought and affect which are not quite, but are almost present as conscious material. A very simple example of this would be the very common experience of having a person's name that we know, "on the tip of our tongue," but not quite within grasp. A much more disruptive example of pre-conscious mental activity would be the common anxiety-inducing experience of the sense of being under threat, of feeling extremely unsafe, and yet having no idea why this is so. For many sufferers of mental and emotional distress, this experience of "free-floating" anxiety, often referred to psychiatrically as generalized anxiety disorder, and commonly something that has been present life-long, is also commonly associated with depression.

If we were to suppose that an individual suffering from such pervasive and seemingly free-floating anxiety (and often its counterpart, depression) is able to affirm that the outside world around him does not really pose any specific threat to him that would account for the intense and ever-present anxiety he feels, I might request of that person to consider whether there might be any source of threat arising from within his own self. Sometimes such a person in analysis, when asked to freely associate,[5] will come to articulate some awareness of a sense of being "haunted," or of feeling as if he is "possessed" by some force or entity that exerts a kind of control over him. Freud, along with psychoanalysts since his time, by engaging in this kind of exploration with a patient (referred to as an analysand), recognized that something important and powerful was gradually coming into the the analyst's and the patient's awareness; although still not delineated in terms of its character or its shape, it was coming to be perceived as malevolent and something previously outside conscious awareness. All such a patient before engaging in this kind of work would have been able to know about himself was that he suffered from

---

5. Free association is the basic technique devised by Freud for psychoanalytic therapy and essentially means that a patient is requested to try to allow their conscious mind to be receptive to whatever occurs to them during a session, in the form of a thought which might arise as a memory, a recent dream, or that is connected to a feeling of which the patient has become aware. The patient is further requested to try to put such thoughts into words regardless of how much the patient might prefer to censor, on the basis of their thought seeming too trivial, or personal, or embarrassing, etc. Analogously, the analyst is committed to turning his own mind and ear to whatever is spoken, without judgement or censorship, and to allow himself to freely associate to his patient's material.

un-ending and debilitating anxiety.[6] At points in analytic therapy of incremental attainment of self-awareness, he experiences that which has previously been inaccessible to awareness shifting from the unconscious realm of
his mind into preconscious, and then as the work continues, preconscious
material can be made fully conscious; then the analytic couple (analysand and
analyst) may recognize change having occurred in the form of the subject's
significant gain in self-awareness. Of course, it is understood and hoped that
the shift of some disturbing unconscious mental product into consciousness
will, of itself, lead to relief of symptoms by virtue of the person gaining much
greater capacity to *think* effectively about the contents of his own mind. In
other words, there is a significant gain in the sense, usually, of true (as opposed to contrived) mastery and control—in place of feeling so emotionally
controlled by some ineffable mental entity, there comes the experience of
gaining traction and exerting agency (the sense of being able to conceive of
and effect change) consciously and deliberately. I do not mean to suggest that
this happens quickly or simply, but may take considerable time and much
meticulous analytic work. Coming to think differently, with different parameters about one's own mental life, could be likened to learning to play the
piano: long learning and acquisition of skill, such that it gets into implicit
memory is required. In the mental realm, what has been operating unconsciously, so implicitly and automatically, and giving rise to symptoms, can,
with analytic work, be shifted into conscious activity and eventually the new
mode of thinking about what is going on similarly becomes implicit, natural,
and automatic, but without the symptoms. Anxiety, for example, when first
felt, can come to serve a "signal" function, which means it alerts the mind
that some work, in the form of thinking needs to be done, instead of simply
exerting its incrementally overwhelming or debilitating effects. Of course, the
thinking type of work required may only be possible through the influence of
therapy.

Lest it be thought that psychoanalytic therapeutic efficacy derives
singularly from the movement of unconscious mental complexes into consciousness. Let it be said that there are many other factors that importantly
contribute to change. Since it is not within the scope of this writing to explore these other components in detail, suffice it to say that elements like
the experience of being deeply heard and profoundly respected regardless
of what one says, along with the impact of, often for the first time, feeling one's essential self recognized and accorded value, instead of dismissed
or worse, scorned, have enormous transformative influence. Additionally,

6. Anxiety and depression, although considered diagnoses in psychiatry, in psychoanalysis, are considered symptoms, or clusters thereof.

acquiring language to describe affects (the psychological term for emotions or feelings), discovering words that capture the essence of what one feels, but for which, often one has not previously had language, similarly effects substantial change. Furthermore, as the mechanics of how one's mind has characteristically worked are gradually brought into the light of conscious consideration, then one has opportunity to thoughtfully construct newer ways of organizing one's thoughts and patterns of thought. In so doing, one thereby can replace archaic, destructive modes with more life-enhancing modes of thinking; modifying faulty thought processes, although not in themselves sufficient to effect long-lasting change, does help to shift the associated affects as well. This latter element, which is a major component of the popular CBT (Cognitive Behavioral Therapy) is implicitly encompassed within a larger, more comprehensive psychoanalytic work.

Finally, the phenomenon of transference which will be elaborated later, but which essentially involves experiencing in relation to one's analyst, one's own unique and particular configuration of emotion-laden patterns of intimacy with someone important, especially the parents of early childhood, is itself, if handled well, transformative. Because the analysand is powerfully moved by the analyst's careful non-judgemental attention to the content of his mind, the analyst becomes an object into whom strong emotional connection is invested, as if the analyst were a parent, or perhaps a lover. Because transference involves in the present a here-and-now emotionally charged and seemingly real experience (albeit transferred from past to present), it leads to very alive explorations by the analytic couple of what is actually happening, what the patient thinks is happening, and who is doing and/or feeling what toward whom, etc. In other words, an archaic mode of experiencing other people has come alive in the room and is available for careful analysis. Transference, while in other forms of therapy may be something to avoid or minimize (since transference is ubiquitous in all relationships it cannot be avoided) or at least not address, is at the heart of psychoanalysis which is uniquely organized to maximize the opportunity to utilize transference for exploration and for its transformative potential.

DRIVE-CONFLICT THEORY

Instincts and Drives

From the beginning of Freud's theorizing about the nature of the mind of man, he appreciated the unavoidably embodied character of the human mind; perhaps his medical training and his interest in neurobiology and neurology helped to seat his perceptions of human psychological function firmly within the biological substrate of humanity. A moment's reflection will cause us to immediately recognize that however much we may wish to divorce our mind and our emotions from our body, we cannot and must not attempt to do so. We are not simply cognizant, thinking beings isolated from our bodies, however civilized we may think we are, but are deeply and intimately embedded in our bodies, such that the body-mind interface is indissolubly intertwined, giving rise to endlessly complex patterns of mutual influence, one upon the other between body and mind. Of course, all our social relations occur through the agency of our bodies also, although this claim might be contested since the dawning of the internet age.

At the risk of stating the obvious, I wish to emphasize that people in Freud's day went to him as a physician, because they were suffering. For the most part (with the exception of the occasional person who is seeking self-understanding or expansion of his creative capacities), it is still true today that people will only commit to the arduous and time-consuming enterprise of in-depth psychotherapy, of the form that is psychoanalysis because of the degree of their suffering. Commonly, they have exhausted other alternative, less demanding, seemingly more expedient, and less costly approaches to their problems. Accordingly, Freud realized that his patients were suffering from, on the one hand, varying types and intensities of impulses and wishes to satisfy biologically-based instincts or drives that clamoured for satisfaction, while, on the other hand, and at the same time, severe prohibitions against such gratifications. While the prohibitions may have had their origin in the surrounding culture or immediate social environment, they seemed to his patients to arise from within their own selves; they had typically sought, in response to the prohibition demand, to disown or disavow the disturbing impulses and so repressed them out of conscious awareness by means of the agency of their own superego, which encompassed the now internalized cultural, social, or parental mores and sanctions. This configuration of conflict between impulses and internal prohibitions constitutes the nucleus of neurosis which is, in varying measure, universal to all mankind. Of course, it might also be said that prohibitions against drive satisfaction may arise from conscience as well. I am inferring here a distinction between superego and conscience, but more on this later.

It is well known that psychoanalysis pays much attention to the early life experiences of the person, in the development and formation of that person's psyche (or, perhaps, soul). How do we understand, then, the role of instincts or drives in the early life of any individual, especially in light of what we have covered already in terms of the existence of the unconscious, and the pressures of impulses and wishes? At least since Freud's ideas came into popular usage, we have conceived of instincts and drives to arise from the seemingly dark, secret cauldron of mental life, called the "id". I will have more to say later about the id, but suffice it to say for now, that it is thought of as the source in the mind/body of powerful forces, desires, and urges that seem unruly, and which must be tamed for any individual to have a place in civilized society. Perhaps more importantly, we should understand that id forces must be managed for any individual to maintain a reasonably organized and balanced mental life, one that does not spin out of control with emotional or drive excess, yet still to be able to arrive at satisfactions in the broad areas of life that count for so much: work, play, and love.[7] Let us consider Freud's description of the term instinct—first his early definition:

> If we now apply ourselves to considering mental life from a biological point of view, an 'instinct' appears to us as a concept on the frontier between the mental and the somatic, as the psychical representative to the stimuli originating from within the organism and reaching the mind, as a measure of the demand made upon the mind for work in consequence of its connection with the body.[8]

His definition grew, if not less convoluted, to cluster around two basic instincts:

> The forces we assume to exist behind the tensions caused by the needs of the id are called instincts. They represent the somatic demands upon the mind. Though they are the ultimate cause of all activity, they are of a conservative nature [i.e. they tend toward restoring the organism to a steady equilibrium] . . . It is thus possible to distinguish an indeterminate number of instincts, and in common practice, this is in fact done. For us, however, the important question arises whether it may not be possible to trace all these numerous instincts back to a few basic ones. We have found that instincts can change their aim (by displacement) and also that they can replace one another—the energy of one instinct passing over to another. This latter process is still insufficiently understood. After long hesitancies and vacillations, we have decided to assume the existence of only two basic instincts, Eros, and the destructive instinct. . . . The aim of the first basic instinct is to establish ever greater unities and to preserve them thus—in short, to bind together; the aim of the second is, on the contrary, to undo connections and so

7. Freud's triad of life experience markers for improvement through psychoanalysis.
8. Freud, *Instincts and Their Vicissitudes,* 121–22. Emphasis his.

to destroy things. [This is the so-called "death instinct."] . . . In biological functions the two basic instincts operate against each other or combine with each other. Thus, the act of eating is the destruction of the object with the final aim of incorporating it, and the sexual act is an act of aggression with the purpose of the most intimate union. This concurrent and mutually opposing action of the two basic instincts gives rise to the whole variega-tion of the phenomena of life. . . . Modifications of the propor-tions of the fusion between the instincts have the most tangible results. A surplus of sexual aggressiveness will turn a lover into a sex-murderer, while a sharp diminution in the aggressive factor will make him bashful or impotent.[9]

Lest we think, however, in terms that would suggest that humans are very little different from animals, and that Freud thought of humans as sole-ly biologically instinctually impelled, we need to develop a more nuanced appreciation of Freud's use of the notion of instincts. For this, I will rely upon the work of two analytic authors, Hans Loewald and Jean Laplanche. Loewald took the first of Freud's statements regarding instincts, "the psychi-cal representative of the stimuli originating from within the organism and reaching the mind" and clarified that it was the mind's task to represent the stimuli, in word or in affect or in image, etc., and not to get rid of them. In effect, Loewald saw the mind as mastering the somatic stimuli and render-ing them useful as basic units of motivation.[10] So, in contrast to animals in which the impulse to act is thought to have little in the way of representa-tion in the mind, and therefore subject to minimal reflective influence, in the mature human, motivational forces in the form of instincts or drives become, through their representations, psychically, subjective experiences available for reflective consideration. Of course, as per the above quote from Freud, the net outcome of such consideration may vary considerably.

Laplanche pointed out a generally over-looked distinction of concepts in Freud's work, between "instinct" and "drive," a distinction that he believed is implicit, but is neglected because Freud himself did not emphasize it, and so the the two German words used by Freud, *instinkt* and *trieb* (drive) are collapsed into each other. Furthermore, this coalescing of terms was espe-cially manifested in the English translation. The point is that,

> . . . for Freud [an instinctual conception] is primarily appli-cable to self-preservation and to "instinct in animals," [in con-trast to] his conception of the drive. Instinct is relatively fixed

9. Freud, *An Outline of Psychoanalysis, Chapter 2*, 148–49.

10. Loewald, *Papers on Psychoanalysis*, 1980.

within the species, is largely innate, and corresponds to adaptive aims; whereas drive, the model for which remains the sexual drive, is variable from one individual to another, is contingent with regard to its aims and its objects, and is emphatically "polymorphously perverse," at least in proximity to its origins.[11]

This point takes on particular importance when one considers that the sexual drive, or libido, constitutes one of the two basic drives, and all the derivatives or variants of the sexual drive. In fact, Laplanche[12] claimed that the death drive also can be understood to have its roots in the same source as the sexual drive.

The essential thing to grasp here is that Freud never intended for the sexual drive, the drive he understood to be so foundational to human experience and especially to the vast territory of the unconscious, to be thought of as fixed and innate, like the animal instincts. Laplanche, condensing and clarifying a lot of Freud's writings, asserts that the sexual drive develops in very early life, in conjunction with a kind of "propping up" (emphasizing in so doing a claim made by Freud that has been over-looked) by virtue of the object relational nurturing attachment experiences that take place with the primary care-giver, usually the mother, and by close association with the natural manifestations of the self-preservative instincts, e.g. crying to register hunger, pain, wet diaper, etc. During those early infantile interactions with a "good enough mother,"[13] a lot of sensual contact occurs, inevitably and appropriately, in the form of bathing, cleaning, cuddling, and caressing of all parts of the infant's body. Such sensually stimulating body contact between mother and infant were recognized initially by Freud and then emphasized by Laplanche as serving to act as a form of seduction, a seduction into the formation of fantasy which is established in close connection to sensations felt in the body. Freud's original seduction theory in which he thought that his patients' symptoms had arisen from actual seductive interference by an inappropriate, exploitive older attendant or child was subsequently rejected by him because of the absence of evidence for same. He came to realize that the sexual fantasies that so pervade the unconscious came into being during the course of the normal experiences of healthy childhood up-bringing. An infinite variety of actual experiences are encountered, along with innumerable factors that influence the significance and subjective meaning (such as the subjective emotional

11. Laplanche, *Freud and The Sexual*, 32. Emphasis his.

12. Laplanche, *Life and Death in Psychoanalysis*, 96.

13. Winnicott, *Playing and Reality*, 13–14: "The good-enough mother is one who makes active adaptation to the infant's needs, an active adaptation that gradually lessons, according to the infant's growing ability to account for failure of adaptation and to tolerate the results of frustration."

tone of mother or child or the child's impression of what is happening at the time of the experience) of those experiences throughout the course of the very long human childhood (at least until puberty). It is therefore possible to comprehend why, as stated above, the human sexual drive is so polymorphously perverse. More will be said about this in a later chapter.

Let me quote Laplanche once again, at some length:

> The object of psychoanalysis is the unconscious, and the unconscious is above all the sexual in the precise Freudian sense—drive sexuality, infantile sexuality, pre-, para- or infantile-genital sexuality. It is the sexuality whose very source is fantasy itself, implanted of course within the body.
>
> And to take up again the terms instinct and drive, I shall recapitulate in just a few words:
>
> The *self-preservative instinct* exists in man, but it must be understood that (a) it is in large part affection or attachment, which is to say that it is mediated by reciprocal communication; and (b) it is from the start covered over and thus hidden by the peculiarly human and sexual phenomena of both seduction and the narcissistic reciprocity with the other.
>
> In man, there is a *sexual drive* that occupies a major and decisive place from birth until puberty. It is this that constitutes the object of psychoanalysis; it is this that is lodged in the unconscious.
>
> There is a *sexual instinct*, which is pubertal and adult, but it 'finds its place occupied' already by the infantile drive. This instinct is thus very difficult to define epistemologically-and precisely to the extent that concretely and in the real it does not appear in a pure state, but only in uncertain transactions with the infantile sexuality that reigns in the unconscious.[14]

This distinction between drive and instinct is exceedingly helpful in comprehending why the human sexual drive is so diverse, complex, and confusing, in both its large, socially binding together sense and in its more specifically genital, i.e. erotic intimate relational sense. As Laplanche contends, the drive has been formed in the crucible of childhood development, with all of that stage's intricate relational contributions, coupled with fantasies, fears, guilts, shames, etc., all while no-one is recognizing anything sexual going on. Then, when puberty brings the actual instinct into play, it has to adapt to what is already there in the character of the drive.

---

14. Laplanche, *Freud and The Sexual*, 25.

Oedipus Complex

Perhaps from what has already been said, it will be evident that conflict is inevitable between the drive-impelled wishes and desires and the environment in which we develop. The child comes to understand that his desire, however inchoate it may be, is unacceptable, and so it must be repressed, meaning it must be forced into the unconscious, outside of awareness. This brings me to another core feature of Freud's theories, that of the Oedipus Complex. According to him, the Oedipus Complex is based upon and named for its analogy to the ancient Greek myth of Oedipus Rex. In brief, Freud understood that in the ordinary course of childhood developmental life, everyone will experience a sexually-driven attraction to his opposite-sex parent, such that he will wish to displace the same-sex parent in such a way so as to become the opposite sex parent's special and intimate partner; the child experiences a powerful longing to have for himself what he perceives to exist between the two adult members of the family triad. To accomplish his aim would require the removal or elimination of the same sex parent, tantamount to the murder of that parent. Naturally, this leaves the child with a terrible dilemma since he also loves both parents and feels terrible guilt at having these horrifyingly disturbing impulses.

Picture, for the sake of example, the male child of two or three, competing with the father for the mother's affections and attentions, and to varying degrees encountering the unacceptable desires to triumph over daddy and win mommy; he somehow has to deal with such impulses and their accompanying thoughts and emotions. We might recognize the importance of potential impact on the psyche of the child by the parents' responses to the infinitely various manifestations of the little boy's struggle. Most parents will recognize the displays of these jealousies and wishes in their children as cute "childishness" and view the ploys toward accomplishing their goal as normal, enjoyable, and non-threatening components of typical childhood development. This would be so in spite of and, more likely, because of the routine fact that most parents do not conceive of these behaviors and emotions as reflecting the development of their child's sexuality, since people generally have not conceived of sexuality as beginning before puberty. According to the ordinary oedipal journey, the successful outcome will entail relinquishment of the desire-driven enterprise toward triumph, a repression of the offending urges and their component thoughts (the associated emotions may not be truly repressed into unconscious, but become dissipated and connected to thoughts that are far less offensive, yet have some links

to the original thoughts)[15] and some sort of acceptance of his inferior attractiveness to the opposite sex parent and the deferral of fulfilment of the
sexual drive until later in life, with an appropriate partner of his own (who
may nevertheless unwittingly be chosen on the basis of subtle similarities to
the unacceptably desired parent).

Mature and reasonably well (emotionally) developed parents will facilitate their child's passage through this vital phase of development with a
minimum of long-term disturbance. Consider, however, how it might be for
the child who is explicitly chastised and/or shamed by the parents (or other
close adult) for any display of sexual interest or desire, or for any manifestation of jealousy. For example, a parent who overtly chastises this little boy
with threats of amputation for displaying his penis to try and impress his
mother, may well drive all of his oedipal thoughts and wishes underground,
with attendant intense anxiety at the likelihood of castration should he feel
sexual desire in future, including in adult life. Such a future adolescent and
adult may suffer from a sexual drive that that is corrupted by intense fears
and could lead so far as impotence.

Consider also the equally damaging impact of parental responses that
are not overt, but are *implicit*, perceived intuitively by the attuned child,
but for whom the reality of what is understood is, in effect, denied by the
parent's *explicit* statements or behaviors. An example of this might be the
latency[16] age child whose parents are overtly loving of the child, and non-
critical of him, but who readily and frequently express their criticisms and
disapproval of other people's attitudes and behaviors in matters to do with
inter-personal relationships, especially sexuality. The child hears and knows
of the real attitudes of the parents, even though he is ostensibly protected
from direct assaults from those attitudes. His own internal workings feel
then to him to be dangerously unacceptable to the parents and a gulf opens
up between the parents and himself, premised upon the undeniable dis-
approbation residing in the parents, but which is displaced away from the
parents' own child. The net effect for the child may be that attitudes actually
present in the parents are denied by them; and so the child colludes in the
denial (how can he, in his immaturity, sustain a view contrary to that of
his parents?) but suffers a split in his ego, such that he knows something to

15. This phenomenon is understood to give rise to symptoms; experiences subsequently encountered in which thoughts are stimulated that somehow link to the original offending ideas stir the original emotions and lead to anxiety. Anxiety is seen as the
primary affect signalling the presence of unconscious conflict.

16. Latency is the period in childhood development between the end of the oedipal
journey, about age six, and the onset of puberty. Sexuality is thought to be quiescent
during this time.

be true, yet also "knows" it to not be true at the same time. Even if he can remain consciously aware of the parents' true attitude, he keeps that awareness a part of his own secret inner world, in which case, the formation of inner secrecy dividing him from his parents is reinforced.

Even under the best of conditions with the most sensitive of parents, the manifestations of infantile sexuality cannot typically be mirrored by the parent. Successful development of the regulation of affect is understood to require attuned mirroring of that affect by the parent. Mirroring confirms the reality and legitimacy of an affect by the parent's display of the child's perceived affect in return. How can a parent mirror to her child the affects of sexual expression without violating the incest taboo?[17]

While the responses of the parents to the child's oedipal displays are no doubt important in determining the adequacy of his resolution of the conflict, we must also consider the role of the child's own imagination in the process, and the development of fantasies associated with the experienced drives in the form of wishes and urges. The possibilities for fantasy development are infinite and polymorphous. Such fantasies become intimately connected to the sexual drive during the course of the drive's development, and are repressed into unconsciousness. The character and power of impact (i.e. the strength of the grip or the position of centrality in the functioning of the mind) of such fantasies likely also influence the adequacy of oedipal resolution. Furthermore, the fantasies that inevitably accompany the development of the sexual drive, and the oedipal experience become an implicit and vital part of the adult's sexuality, accounting, in significant part, for the unavoidable "perversity" (i.e. variety or divergence from some mythical "normal") that is universal to every person's sexuality (more will be said about polymorphous perversity in a later chapter).

A not uncommon configuration of the inadequately resolved Oedipus Complex that is encountered in psychoanalytic clinical practice is manifest in the memories of patients, who, when they were a child, were required to serve for the opposite sex parent as a kind of substitute surrogate spouse. This can transpire because of a necessary absence of the spouse, or because the spouse is considered debased and is denigrated as unsuitable to the parent. For example, the little boy whose parents, because of discord, have taken to sleeping separately, and the mother admits the boy to her bed, partly in response to pressure from the boy who is naturally in need of comforting, and partly in response to her own insecurities of which she has some conscious awareness; but perhaps also active is her (likely unacknowledged) need or desire for a substitute male presence in her bed. In this

17. Target, *A Developmental Model of Sexual Excitement, Desire, and Alienation.*

instance, the unconscious oedipal strivings of the boy are being gratified. Another example may be the girl who is inducted into the role of confidante for personal problems to either parent, again because of a disrupted parental relationship, but, by being admitted to the parent's intimate, confidential world, achieves an oedipal triumph, i.e., in some way attaining the unconscious oedipal goal of displacing the other parent. Both examples are given because of their common occurrence, and also because of the serious consequences that can be suffered by the developing child's psyche. The consequences referred to might include apparently unwarranted constant anxiety, an absence of deep, implicit security (related to feeling that the triumph was/is wrong, i.e. guilt that exceeds the normal measure of guilt inherently deriving from a "resolved"[18] oedipal journey, and from feelings of presumed responsibility for the disorder in the family) or disordered sexuality in young adulthood, such that promiscuity is pursued, out of an incessant and compelling need to master the unruly impulses that remain in the unconscious. The particular consequences of such oedipal disturbance in any affected individual are unique to that person and endlessly variable. One variant from my own practice entails Carmen, whose previously only pre-conscious constant striving to repair her aging parents' troubled relationship has meant that her own happiness has been contingent upon the successful accomplishment of this unconsciously determined demand upon herself. Given that the requirement is impossible for her to achieve, she struggles to attain the freedom to enjoy a better life than her parents. I will elaborate Carmen's story more later.

Other psychoanalytic thinkers have disputed the validity of Freud's claim of the universality of the Oedipus Complex, at least as to its central importance in the unconscious life of people, and some have cited alternate Greek myths for a different perspective on unconscious life. However we may choose to think about this whole phenomenon, we must acknowledge the potentially powerful and formative influences of the early childhood relationship pattern that has to be negotiated by all of us. Somehow, every infant must come to grips ultimately with the unavoidable fact of not remaining forever the primary focus of his mother's world, and of accepting the truth that he does not have primacy in the very intimate and especially exciting (erotic) relationship that he intuits (if not observes) exists between mother and father; in fact, from this, he is excluded. The inherent jealousy that occurs has to be overcome, and the child must "triangulate," i.e. achieve the capacity to live in a world populated by multiple others, who inter-relate; he has to learn to deal with not just *one* other, usually the mother with

---

18. It is debatable whether anyone's oedipal journey is ever fully resolved.

whom the child has had the particularly special relationship of dyadic intimacy, but multiple others (the desired parent's partner(s) plus siblings) who lay claim to her attention and affections. I might mention that the oedipal journey of the girl is considered similar to that of the boy, but more complex by virtue of the fact that she begins life with her strong attachment to her mother consisting in a same-sex relationship. Suffice to say that she has to negotiate detaching from her initial object-attachment, form an attachment to the opposite sex object, and then identify with the original object. The steps for the boy are fewer; he does not need to detach from the original object to form the new love-connection as the girl must.

Freud thought that the "heir" to the Oedipus Complex is the superego. He believed that the internalization of parental sanctions and prohibitions that constitute the formation of the superego more or less congeal in the mind of the child by the end of the oedipal journey, approximately age six. That is not to say that he perceived it to be fixed or beyond being malleable throughout life. It may be important to recognize that other theorists, including object relations psychoanalysts, beginning with Melanie Klein, have understood the superego to form at a much earlier point in life.

THE STRUCTURAL THEORY

By the latter portion of Freud's life, he had settled upon a so-called structural conception of the mind: three "structures" were conceived of comprising three different functions within the mind. We have mentioned the id as that portion that is understood as the source of the bodily-based instincts and drives which, of course, are thought of as providing energy, fuelling the system overall. The ego forms as the structure which tests reality and carries out the tasks necessary to negotiate the exigencies of life, including the management of the id impulses; it serves to provide the executive functions of the mind. Donald Winnicott, the famous British paediatrician-come-psychoanalyst said,

> [Preverbal infancy] is essentially a period of ego development, and integration is the main feature of such development. The id-forces clamour for attention. At first they are external to the infant. In health, the id gets gathered into the ego, and the ego masters the id, so that id-satisfactions become ego strengtheners. This, however, is an achievement of healthy development and in infancy there are many variants dependent on relative failure of this achievement. . . . the reason [why this can occur]

is the fact of maternal care, the maternal ego implementing the
infant ego, and so making it powerful and stable.[19]

The superego, the third structure of the structural theory, is thought to
form as a specialized portion or cluster of particular functions, from within
the ego. It might be thought of as the over-seer, and so carries out the task
of judging whether a thought or its accompanying emotion or an act is suitable, acceptable or, alternatively, worthy of condemnation and rejection. It
serves, in the positive aspect of its functions, the vital role of enabling self-
assessment, against standards and ideals which it also, in turn, formulates,
the so-called, ego-ideal.

Without getting too far into the complexities of how the mind forms,
we can readily understand that identification with important others is an
essential and potent mode of acquiring patterns of character and mind
attitudes and functions. Accordingly, an important element of identification that ostensibly serves the purpose of defending against painful affects,
is "identification with the aggressor." A young child might naturally and
unwittingly adopt attitudes and behaviors that are patterned after a person
experienced as an aggressor toward him in order to be able to manage
for himself the experience of being aggressed against, and the associated
emotions endured when this occurs. It is painfully shame-inducing to be
repeatedly reprimanded for some form of behavior; better to identify with
the reprimander him- or herself so that one can become one's own master,
administer the reprimand oneself, and potentially pre-empt the action of
the other so that no externally applied reprimand is necessary. The idea is to
assume for oneself control over whatever correctional directive is required
to avoid behavior which will invite critique. It is less painful (seemingly)
to judge oneself than be judged by another; furthermore, one develops a
sense of self-mastery which feels satisfyingly powerful, and builds toward a
sense of agency. In forming a superego, one identifies with parents, teachers,
and any others whose attitudes and opinions and judgements impinge upon
one's world, in effect, internalizing the functions of critic, prohibiter, and
assessor. The superego comes into being, therefore, by identification with
the aggressor(s); the persons or social structures that fill the role of "aggressor" may not necessarily be harsh or malicious, but in their role as guide or
corrector, they are, in effect, aggressing against the unacceptable behaviors,
attitudes, wishes, or intentions of the child.

Superego development is not quite so straightforward, however, because
the role of fantasy and of the aggressive drives from the child's id also influence
the quality and character of the identifications that occur. Such influences can

19. Winnicott, "The Theory of the Parent Infant Relationship," 587.

and often do lead to the superego acquiring a rather primitive, legalistic, punitive, and harsh character. In fact, unless there is opportunity for simultaneous adequate development of a counter-balancing conscience, then the superego is most likely to be harsh.[20] When the superego manifests features of primitive punishing harshness, it is likely also to generate and demand conformity to standards that are extreme, perfectionistic, and idealistic. For so many people who suffer from a superego of this character, life may be ordered around the simplicity of black-white and either-or, i.e. a highly polarized universe, characterized by "splitting." Splitting, separating one thing or idea from another, making distinctions, is essential for clear thinking and is healthy, unless it is adopted and heavily relied upon as a form of defense. Defensive splitting is developed with a view to relieving anxiety through a dichotomization of entities into clear categories of either-or, each of which side is represented in the extreme. It allows for little integration of opposing perceptions and thereby distorts thinking; there can be little room allowed for nuance and ambiguity or subtle gradation, all of which are causes of anxiety in a rigidly organized personality that employs a lot of splitting.

Many people who suffer from depression do so because of the persistent dominating demands and condemnations of their superego. For them, this internal powerful function that has escaped from the influence and direction of the ego, having "gone rogue" has become more or less autonomous and dictatorial, making life an oppressive, living hell. The ego is under siege. Such a superego is anything but a humane, compassionate, encouraging, and forgiving entity. These latter qualities are those one wishes to see a previously sadistic transformed superego acquire during the course of a psychoanalytic therapy.

Essentially, then, the structural theory of Freud is so-called because of the differentiation of the mental functions into the three organizational entities, id, ego, and superego. To clarify, the ego is thought of in terms of functioning as the executor or, if you will, the CEO, the decision-maker, the arbiter between reality and wishful fantasy, the negotiator between id impulses and superego sanctions. All three categories of function operate largely unconsciously. Contemporary psychoanalysts may employ any of the above theories, along with many other theoretical influences from other perspectives. I doubt any psychoanalyst today practices from within any particular theoretical framework exclusively, let lone any one of the specifically Freudian theoretical frames.

As a final comment on the structural theory, I find Carveth's effort to advocate for including a fourth structure, in the form of the conscience to

20. Carveth, *The Still Small Voice*.

be very appealing and helpful in clarifying not only theory but also clinical work with patients.[21]

OBJECT RELATIONS THEORY

Building upon aspects of Freudian theory, but laying emphasis less upon drive-conflict and more upon the early developmental influence of the relationship between the infant and its main "object" (the term used by Freud to designate the intra-psychic representation of the other, as opposed to the *actual* other as he or she is), typically its mother, analysts like Melanie Klein, Donald Winnicott, and Douglas Fairbairn elaborated a theory of the mind that focussed on the relationship. At the risk of grossly over-simplifying their important and complex theories, I will highlight elements that seem pertinent to my purposes and that I think will be relevant to the reader. Depending on the quality of the relationship between the young infant and his primary caregiver, he will inevitably internalize her in such a way as to form internal representations of her that will include her as good, i.e. comforting, reassuring, benevolent; and bad, i.e. unpredictably frightening, withholding, persecutory, and possibly even malevolent. Optimally, the good internal object predominates, but obviously, not always. It is thought that such internal representations of good and/or bad maternal objects form initially on the basis of the infant's experience of the breast, a breast that either readily dispenses comforting milk and satiates, or a breast that is insufficiently available and therefore frustrates, or deprives.

Klein developed the useful notion of part-object versus whole-object. The young infant may initially experience his mother as a breast (part-object), with a spectrum of good to bad features, but in time, assuming healthy development, the child should increasingly come to experience her as a whole object, with her own thoughts, emotions, preferences, personality, interests, etc., which include both good and bad, satisfying and unsatisfying (to the child). Klein laid emphasis upon strong affects like fear and envy along with aggressive drive intensity in the young child such that he was seen to occupy a "position" called the "paranoid-schizoid" position, which is characterized by frightened and/or rageful withdrawal and perhaps psychotic or near-psychotic ideation and perceptions. She conceived of healthy emotional developmental progression as consisting in a shift in position, toward the "depressive" position. This latter is called "depressive" because it is characterized by feelings of concern for the other, as a whole object, associated in the child with guilt for his perceived negative impact on the

21. Ibid.

(m)other. A little reflection will allow us to readily see that anyone, adult or child will shift into one or other position depending on a multitude of factors; hence the term "position." The adult who is occupying the P-S position is often not in a good place, for either himself or others. On the other hand, P-S states or perhaps the reactions in defense against them might also generate intense creativity.

For the sake of demonstrating how theories overlap and can be integrated, it is helpful to realize that most P-S functioning can also be described, especially in the adult, as that which is dominated by a savage, primitive, and authoritarian superego. By contrast, depressive position functioning can be seen to indicate the effective activity of a well-developed and operative conscience, not dominated by a severe superego.

Object relations theory promotes an appreciation of the person's internal world, populated by many important "object representations" that, because unconscious, wield profound influence on the person's emotional and mental life. In effect, the existence of these internal representations of which we are unaware, forms the basis of transference, about which more is said in other portions of this work. Transference, as it manifests in the analytic relationship, (and in all other relationships also) is charged with affect; i.e. the analyst may become the object of a powerful romantic fantasy, or become someone to be feared as ultimately hostile and rejecting. The intensity of the affect is determined by the "cathexis" (Freud's term for emotional or libidinal energy investment) formed in relation to the old, infantile object representation(s) that is/are evoked by the patient's experience of the analyst.

OTHER "RELATIONAL" THEORIES

More contemporary psychoanalytic theories of the mind have laid more specific emphasis upon the formation of a self (self psychology) or on the relational or attachment aspects of early child-parent life for understanding the development of the mind. I will briefly remark upon their distinctive features as I see them. Generally speaking, these more recent theories focus attention on the results in the developing mind of defects in or deficits from the early mother-child relationship, essentially finding an insufficiency of attuned maternal responsiveness to account for later psychological disturbance. Michael Balint named this defect the "basic fault." Attachment theory, building on the work of John Bowlby focuses on the disorder in child-parent attachment style that is thought to carry forward into future relationships and wield its influence the more intimate the relationship is. Attachment styles range from secure to anxious to avoidant to disorganized;

the tone of a person's mental and emotional life can be seen to correlate with secure, anxious, avoidant, or disorganized (i.e. chaotically anxious or angry or withdrawn, etc.) styles. Self psychology, initiated by Hans Kohut focussed on the impairments to one's sense of self as a cohesive, competent entity brought about by suboptimal experience with one's parents; so-called selfobject needs represent that which is needed for the incremental establishment of a stable sense of one's self. For example, healthy development requires sufficient mirroring from significant adults. Similarly, a growing mind needs to have sufficient opportunity to idealize, say, one's father. The absence of such suitable opportunity for idealization leads to persisting unsatisfied needs, and the way the person then relates to other people will reflect these "selfobject" needs, which if archaic, can impair the quality of the relationships. We all are seen to have selfobject needs which we may gratify suitably and maturely by virtue of interests, varieties of social relationships, career pursuits, etc. The persistence of archaic (i.e. under satisfied, leaving child-like needs and demands on other people) selfobject needs tend to stress relationships, in that the subject tends to *use* the object in ways which the object eventually despises and rejects. Furthermore, the person with archaic selfobject needs is understood to suffer from narcissistic fragility and, under especially stressful circumstances (whatever those might be for that person), will fragment. In analysis, the analyst may be able to recognize a particular selfobject need by virtue of the sense of what the patient is drawing from him; this would then be referred to as a selfobject transference that becomes a focus of important remedial work.

Further developments from self psychology have led to inter-subjectivity theory, and relational theory. The latter lays emphasis upon the actual relationship between the patient and the analyst and conceptualizes the unconscious differently from more "classical" theories. For instance, some more relational approaches would consider the implicitly learned pattern of relationships, so-called "implicit relational knowing" as the key constituent of the unconscious that is the object of clinical psychoanalytic interest. Others will lay emphasis upon "self-states," different ways of being which may reflect the consequences of dissociation, a psychic feat of checking out or removing oneself in the face of trauma, such as childhood sexual abuse. And so analytic interest might focus upon self-states that are recognized as emerging in the course of the analytic relationship. Inter-subjectivity theory lays emphasis upon the shared emotion, attention, and intention between persons as determining what occurs in the analytic experience, and perhaps in all human experience. These latter theoretical developments and emphases stress that the psychoanalytic endeavour is a "two person" effort, in contrast to their perception that the traditional Freudian approach is too much a "one person" (i.e. the analyst as the detached observer-investigator of the psyche of the analysand, and ignoring the influence of his own subjectivity) effort.

Finally, in recent years, there has grown a committed effort to invoke systems field theory to recognize the dynamic interplay both in development and in moment-to-moment lived experience, of multiple influences on psychological life. The Boston Change Process Study Group has made notable in-roads in this realm and has published work that is important for psychoanalysis to recognize.

As may be evident from the all too brief descriptions and sketchy details I have given of these more contemporary theories and approaches to therapy, I have cast more weight onto the more classical and neo-classical theories because of my personal satisfaction regarding their explanatory power for the unconscious. As much as the contemporary theories have much to offer, I lament, however, any movement to dismiss drive theory as irrelevant, since its exclusion, I fear, leaves our comprehension of the bedrock of the mind deficient. In practice, I believe I employ approaches that are influenced by all of these "schools," depending on what emerges and how it does so with any particular patient. I am of the belief that the historical internecine warfare among psychoanalytic theory groups is only destructive; I believe there is much to be gained from each theory, insofar as each is emphasizing some feature of human mental life that others may have over-looked or under-emphasized. I have felt it essential for the purposes of this volume, and particularly for the reader who is not familiar with psychoanalytic concepts, to outline the earlier foundational elements to psychoanalytic thinking, because they have such relevance to what will follow. I have undoubtedly omitted much, and possibly aspects that some informed readers would consider essential. Furthermore, I beg the indulgence of my colleagues who are strongly committed to any particular persuasion, if I have committed offense in short-changing theories precious to them.

Chapter 2

A Biblical Perspective on the Mind

SIN

> Listen to Me, all of you, and understand: there is nothing out-
> side the man which going into him can defile him; but the things
> which proceed out of the man are what defile the man . . . For
> *from within*, out of the heart of men, proceed the evil thoughts,
> acts of sexual immorality, thefts, murders, adulteries, deeds of
> coveting and wickedness, as well as deceit, sensuality, envy, slan-
> der, pride, and foolishness.[1]

THESE WORDS OF JESUS leave no doubt that the divine perspective on the nature of man is that he is sinful, defiled. Paul affirms this view: " . . . there is no
distinction; for *all* have sinned and fall short of the glory of God[2]" (NAS). Lest
we think, however, that this view of the defilement of mankind is strictly one
of Christianity and not Judaism, Jeremiah wrote that, "Thus says the Lord: . . .
The heart is deceitful above all things, and desperately wicked; who can know
it?"[3] What is this phenomenon that the Bible calls sin? And is it a matter of
behavior alone that is considered violating or unacceptable, or is it, as Jesus
states in the quote above, a matter also of the "heart," i.e. the inner man, the
thoughts, wishes, impulses, desires? And is the "heart" ancient language for
that which lies beyond conscious awareness, i.e. the unconscious, as the Lord

---

1. Mark 7:14–22. Emphasis mine.
2. Rom 3:22–23. Emphasis mine.
3. Jeremiah 17:5 and 9.

is quoted as saying to Jeremiah: "who can know it?" And what about the notion of "original sin"?

Reading the Old Testament, one acquires a sense of an undeniable dismay on the part of God for the repeated inclination of his people to turn away from him. Much of the Old Testament has to do with his efforts to turn them back to focus on and worship him, the invisible God. Original sin as a catch phrase caught on early in the Christian era, as a doctrine of the faith, beginning, according to Wikipedia, with Irenaeus, Bishop of Lyons, and then promulgated by Augustine, who may have, perhaps because of his own personal struggles with his sexuality, conflated the disobedience of Adam and Eve with concupiscence (desire, specifically, sexual) as the original sin (more on this later under Sexuality). The doctrine derives from Paul's claims in Romans 5:12-20, where he cites Adam as the entry-point of sin into the world, and sin's consequence, death, and thus were sin and death passed on to all men. Quite how this works has been the matter of much theological debate over centuries, a debate with which I am neither truly familiar nor prepared to enter. I am attracted, however, to a remark by Schmemann:

> The sin of all sins—the truly "original sin"—is not a transgression of rules, but, first of all, the deviation of man's love and his alienation from God. That man prefers something—the world, himself—to God, this is the only real sin, and in it all sins become natural, inevitable.[4]

Sin is not easily defined. What sin is not is opposition to or disobedience to the law. "The prohibition of the law is . . . revealed by Paul as that which generates the very desire to transgress the prohibition."[5] Rollins draws upon Paul's "But sin, taking opportunity by the commandment, which was to bring life, produced in me all manner of evil desire. For apart from the law sin was dead."[6] For Paul, sin is not controlled by the law, but rather is instantiated by it. Insofar as superego serves as the internal agent of law, sin, law, and the superego operate in concert, against conscience, which, as Schmemann alludes to, carries out that which transcends law, love.

SATAN'S CHOICE

If sin, as the Bible sees it is, essentially, a state of mind in which man is turned away from what was normative and intended by God, that is, for

4. Schmemann, *For the Life of the World*, 78.
5. Rollins, *Insurrection*, 104.
6. Rom 7:8.

man to have his primary focus of desire and intention upon God, then what can we make of the perversion of this? Schmemann says it is a matter of man's preference, or perhaps, his desire being turned toward himself or the creation rather than the creator.[7] One of the early tenets of Freud's theory was that the initial state of the infant is one of "primary narcissism." By this he meant that the infant's entire focus is on himself, as a matter of survival, and he rightly experiences himself as the centre of the (known) universe, his mother's attentions and affections. He will wield immense power in bending her toward the fulfillment of his needs and rudimentary wishes. (As an aside, we might ponder a moment over the disastrous impact on the infant whose mother, for a host of potential reasons, is incapable of or unwilling to engage with her infant as her "primary maternal preoccupation."[8])

Although Freud's insistence on primary narcissism (he called the infant "His Majesty, the Baby")[9] has been contested by those who see the infant's preoccupation with the mother in a dyadic relationship as trumping his primordial preoccupation with himself, I have wondered about the validity of his claim, as one views a contented infant as if a little sovereign, implicitly self-satisfied, or, alternatively, a rageful, demanding infant who insists his needs be met. However we understand the arguments to and fro on this matter, we are all narcissists in varying degrees. We all need to have a reasonably healthy narcissism, but we also know that our narcissism is not all healthy, i.e. it alienates us from others and from much of life's goodness. Sooner or later in nearly all psychoanalyses, there will emerge into view elements of the patient's strivings for omnipotence and omniscience, hallmarks of residual infantile primary narcissism. These will manifest in the person as his need to strive for maximum control over his universe. As examples, the person who insists upon arranging the items in his home with superordinate precision; the person who collects and hordes massive quantities of unused items; or the person who demands of himself that he have a *complete* set of knowledge on any given subject (an impossibility) before he can make a decision; all such strivings reflect unconscious impulses for a level of control that can be recognized ultimately as omnipotent control. Secondary narcissism may come into being as a defensive approach against intolerable feelings of weakness, vulnerability, or smallness. Perhaps primary narcissism is none other than the innate impulse to protect oneself from a seemingly hostile world. In any case, insofar as mankind is full of impulses that direct him to grasp for self will, control, determination of his

7. See Romans 1, especially verse 25.

8. Winnicott, *The Maturational Processes,* 85.

9. Freud, *On Narcissism,* 91.

universe and his future, such strivings might be considered to be after the fashion of Satan. I will try to explain.

In Luke 10:17–19, Jesus responds to his seventy followers whom he had sent out as emissaries into places he was about to go. When they joyfully returned and said, "Lord, even the demons are subject to us in Your name," he said to them, "I saw Satan fall like lightening from heaven. Behold, *I* give you the authority . . . " (Emphasis mine). It was evidently because Jesus detected the hubris (narcissism) in their proud claims that he told them of having seen Satan fall from heaven in a flash, presumably for reasons of pointing out their likeness to Satan, specifically, Satan's aspiration and presumption to be like God, and to despise his subservient status. Jesus emphasizes that he, God, is the one who gives authority, and infers that these men, displaying hubris, were victims of the satanic trap or choice.

Sin, then, may consist in narcissistic strivings to be like God, the inevitable hubris that afflicts us all, whether we can see it or not, and is of the nature of Satan's choice. The Genesis account of creation makes clear that mankind is formed in the image of God. However, does it mean our status as image-bearers is erased, if our first parents chose after the fashion of Satan and we are all heirs of the same flaw? I don't think so. If sin consists in our striving to *be* God in place of directing our preference toward him, we nevertheless retain the right and responsibility to bear the image of the creator (broken image-bearers). Perhaps in our seeking of that which is God's we can be good; evil derives, however from our seeking to become our own god. Although human striving for omnipotence is inferred in the Bible, psychoanalytic observations and insights clarify and affirm its ubiquitous existence (unconscious and in varying degrees) and are therefore entirely in accord with scripture's view of man as sinful. It is for reasons of our narcissism, along with others, like oedipal guilt, that Freud's view of the mind has given rise to the label "guilty man," in contrast to the more contemporary "relational" theories which posit parental deficiencies as cause of man's miseries, and hence the label "tragic man." This latter perspective sees man as victim, and not as guilty perpetrator.

Further support for my hypothesis that mankind is (sinfully) prone to aspire after omnipotence is found in Jesus' warning against swearing oaths.[10] He says, "But let your 'Yes' be 'Yes', and your 'No' be 'No'. For whatever is more than these is from the evil one." Essentially, he forbids the swearing of oaths because of the human impossibility of ensuring the outcome, something that belongs only to God. And so making vows presumes omnipotence, after the order of Satan's error.

10. Matthew 5:33–37.

ADAM AND EVE'S CHOICE

In light of the foregoing thoughts, what might we make of the story of Adam and Eve? In the Bible's mythical (myths are stories told in ways that reflect the time, context and idiom of the story-teller, and of the listener, but convey some abiding truth[11]) account of creation and the primordial disobedience of the first people, we see what is presumed to be Satan making an early appearance in the guise of a serpent. The serpent tempts Eve in a fashion reminiscent of his own fall to temptation, i.e. after inviting her to question the actual intent of God's edict regarding the fruit of the tree of the knowledge of good and evil, he asserts, "You surely shall not die! [a partial truth, in that neither she nor Adam immediately died] For God knows that in the day you eat from it your eyes will be opened, and you will be like God, knowing good and evil."[12] We learn then that Eve chose to partake of the fruit, because it appealed to her visual sensual desires: " . . . the woman saw that the tree was good for food, and that it was a delight to the eyes," and it appealed to her now awakened desire for that which was forbidden (to have understanding like God's regarding good and evil): " . . . and that the tree was desirable to make one wise." It should be noted that Eve's interest in becoming wise, like God, seemed to arise from the influence of the other, in this case, Satan, who we might understand had travelled this path himself.

Drawing upon Lacan's ideas and language, Tad Delay refers to the prohibition issued by God as "The entry of the big Other's injunction . . . As we have seen, the prohibition generates the desire."[13] The prohibition instantiates the superego for the couple. Yet, as Delay notes, Eve had already exceeded the actual taboo, which was not to eat of the fruit, by expanding the injunction to not permitting touch; he recognizes the innate impulse of the superego: "[once the] big Other's prohibition grafts itself into place, . . . [it] begin[s] to guard the taboo object with progressively expansive prohibitions."[14] Such self-regulatory excess pervades the history of believers, manifesting in the New Testament era and onward from there as people have striven to be more pious than Christ, more godly than God.

To take what transpired at the fall, first, there is no indication of it having anything whatsoever to do with sexual desire per se, as is so often alleged regarding the cause. One might, I suppose, recognize that illicit desire came into being with the serpent's influence on Eve, and that this might

---

11. Enns, *The Bible Tells Me So.*

12. Genesis 3:2, 3.

13. Delay, *God is Unconscious*, 68.

14. Ibid.

transfer over into sexual desire, as early Christians claimed, but, this is an unacceptable stretch, having more to do with perceptions regarding sexuality in the first Christian centuries than careful interpretation of Genesis.[15] Would we have to presume, if original sin had to do with concupiscence, that before the fall, Adam and Eve would have somehow procreated without any desire for one another and yet have had sexual intercourse?

Second, we might see in the influence that the serpent had on Eve something analogous to the enigmatic message that Laplanche[16] claims is paradigmatic of the infant-mother connection. What Laplanche means in his analysis of that primary relationship is that the correspondence between infant and mother is entirely asymmetrical in the specific sense of the mother being the one of the pair who has a sexual unconscious. He posits that the infant at the outset does not yet have an unconscious, that it develops in association with its parents (especially its mother). Because the mother's unconscious is itself sexual (i.e. came from repression of transmitted untranslatable bits of her own mother's sexual unconscious), it is infused by desire, pleasure, excitement, mystery, etc. Laplanche asserts that the mother's caregiving activities are therefore inevitably pregnant with messages to her infant, the enigmatic "sexual" fragments of which are, for the infant, untranslatable, and so can only be repressed, thereby forming the unconscious. Adam and Eve were up against the serpent, as naive innocents, without an unconscious, the deck is stacked, asymmetrical such that Eve could in no way have been able to "translate" the enigmatic elements within the serpent's suggestive discourse. Clearly Satan's approach was malicious i.e. evil, but was it also pregnant with sexual overtones? It was at least seductive. He desired to possess her, to have her (and Adam) dominated by his perspective, and under his control. In effect, he was seducing her to burn with desire for him, or at least for what he offered. Perhaps I am stretching this a bit far, but the essential point was that Eve's (and Adam's) disobedience of God, came about by a turning of primary affection or attention to an exciting other and away from God.

BIBLICAL ALLUSIONS TO A DYNAMIC UNCONSCIOUS

The Freudian unconscious, as described thus far, is considered dynamic because of the repressive forces at work to ban the unacceptable matter from awareness. Freud perceived that whatever is repressed is first, however briefly and inchoately it appears, represented consciously. Analogous to the

15. See Chapter 8, "Sexuality."
16. Laplanche, *Freud and the Sexual.*

repressive "downward" force there is an opposing force or pressure for those repressed matters to push "upward" into conscious representation again. As we have seen, both psychoanalysis and Christianity view mankind as needing and preferring to avoid certain truths regarding oneself and perhaps reality or the Real. One might perceive the unconscious repressed items or complexes to in some sense represent the truth of oneself that cannot be tolerated consciously. I will now highlight several portions of scripture that, in my opinion, point to that which is the object of psychoanalysis, the dynamic unconscious. Proverbs 26:24–26:

> He who hates disguises it with his lips, and lays up deceit within himself; when he speaks kindly, do not believe him, for there are seven abominations in his heart; though his hatred is covered by deceit, his wickedness will be revealed before the assembly.

While this proverb might refer to conscious attitudes, the deceit suggests disguise, which may be in the form of defenses; he who hates is often (self)-deceived as to the existence of his hate, by virtue of his unconscious defense mechanisms. This matter highlights an important corollary of the theory of the dynamic unconscious, and that is, that the defenses themselves which have been developed to maintain unawareness are also unconscious. In the above proverb, for example, if the subject of the proverb is unaware of his true nature, he might be employing defense mechanisms like denial, inattention, or reaction-formation in the form of excessive "niceness"; if his kindly speech is to be considered untrustworthy, he may be employing reaction-formation, which refers to an opposite display from what is being disguised, i.e. the hate is disguised as "niceness." In this example, both the hate and the mode or modes of defense (or disguise) may be repressed into the unconscious. In popular common parlance, this is called "passive aggression." Defense mechanisms will be further illustrated in subsequent examples, but it should be appreciated that the analysis of such mechanisms of self-protection constitutes a vital aspect of clinical psychoanalysis.

The previous quote from Jeremiah 17:9 ("The heart is deceitful above all things, and is desperately wicked") suggests that the deceit in the "heart" is pervasive, and if that is so, how many of us really know our own selves? There must be very powerful forces at work that serve to maintain our unawareness, forces which themselves are also concealed from conscious awareness. Else, how could we live with ourselves?

Jeremiah 9:4–6 coupled with Isaiah 30:9–11 both again emphasize the prevalence of the impulse to deception, and the fragmenting consequences of deception and refusal of the truth on community harmony, and on the people's willingness to be led by truth-speaking prophets. The people of Israel suffered gravely, as a nation for their refusal of the truth.

Miroslav Volf said of political states,

> When a "regime of truth" is imposed, however, when cultural mores, public opinion, or decrees of a totalitarian state codify what may or may not be said, saying out loud what is the case may indeed be revolutionary. If you say some things that you know are the case too loudly, you may lose not only a friend or a job, but even your life (Havel 1986).[17]

Just as regimes of truth (i.e. regimes of truth-denial) may be destructive in states, so are they deeply damaging in families. Families, too, can operate under a kind of totalitarianism when, implicit or explicit suppression or denial of truth exists.[18] When painful truth, e.g. sexual abuse of a young child by the father, is denied unanimously by all in the family, a kind of hole forms in the psyches of the participants. Silence, or forms of Volf's codification of what can be acceptably spoken about, inevitably lead to the damaging effects of shame. That which is unspeakable in families, about which there exists a code of silence, cannot but damage the psyche, and the hole in the mind is shrouded in shame.

An illustration of Jesus' unique capacity to identify concealed unconscious motivations and strivings, is found in Matthew 19:16–22:

> Now behold, one came and said to Him, "Good Teacher, what good thing shall I do that I may have eternal life?" So He said to him, "Why do you call Me good? No one is good but One, that is, God. But if you want to enter into life, keep the commandments." He said to Him, "Which ones?" Jesus said, "'You shall not murder,' 'You shall not commit adultery,' 'You shall not steal,' 'you shall not bear false witness,' 'Honor your father and your mother,' and, 'You shall love your neighbor as yourself.'" The young man said to Him, "All these things I have kept from my youth. What do I still lack?" Jesus said to him, "If you want to be *perfect*, go, sell what you have and give to the poor, and you will have treasure in heaven; and come, follow Me." But when the young man heard that saying, he went away sorrowful, for he had great possessions. (Emphasis mine)

Jesus interprets, with his "if you want to be perfect," the man's concealed craving to be perfect, an obsessional's motivation that no doubt had

---

17. Volf, *Exclusion and Embrace*, 236.

18. See Chapter 4.

determined the course of his life. Furthermore, sadly, his identity source, his vast possessions to which he clung stood in the way of him entering into a transformational relationship. The man had come to Jesus expecting to discover what he had to do to "have it all." He was a self-made, likely narcissistically vulnerable man for whom wealth was to gratify deep self-object needs (as per the self psychology model). The verses that follow this account regarding the difficulty the rich have in entering into the Kingdom of heaven, highlight that the gospel requires a relinquishing of one's grasp on the central core of sin, as discussed above, i.e. the unconscious fantasy of omnipotence, and perhaps the material expressions of that core complex, and, in its place, embrace of one's dependence, limitations, and fallibility, and the impossibility of the fantasy of having control as does the big Other.

A few further stories from the Bible will suffice to illustrate my belief that although the Bible uses different terminology and imposes a moral judgement onto that which it calls sin, its view of the mind of man is very like that of psychoanalysis. While psychoanalysis seeks to free the mind (or soul) by, among other things, conscious understanding, it can only go so far. Christianity purports to truly free the soul: "If you abide in my word, you are my disciples indeed. And you shall know the truth and the truth shall make you free" and "I am the way, the truth, and the life."[19] Somewhat analogous to treatment in psychoanalysis wherein the discovery of truth about oneself and one's relationship with the analyst, in whatever way it is construed according to the different theories, liberates the mind, so freedom for the soul as presented by Christianity similarly entails uncovering truth, only in the context of a relationship with Jesus who himself identifies as that very truth.

In Genesis chapters 37 through 45, we find the story of Joseph, who was favored by his father with a coat of many colors after tattling to his father on the bad behavior he had observed in his older brothers, who, naturally, then resented him. Because of their bitter resentment of Joseph, they deceived their father, leading him to believe that Joseph had been attacked and killed by a wild animal, when, in fact they had sold him into slavery to merchants heading to Egypt. To cut a very long, albeit fascinating story short, we are told that Joseph remained faithful to the God of his fathers, and resisted defiling himself while in Egypt. In fact, because of his integrity and his God-given capacity to interpret the dreams of the pharaoh, he ended up in a position of high leadership in the nation. We are led to see that despite all the disturbing things that happened to Joseph, he was where he was because of God's pre-ordained purpose that he would save God's people, Joseph's own family, from extinction by famine. Perhaps because Joseph has always been held up

19. Jesus: John 8:31, John 14:6.

as a righteous paragon of virtue, when one realizes that his scheme of hiding palace treasures in the luggage of his brothers, ostensibly to ensure their return, had another, more sinister motive, that of revenge on his brothers who had mistreated him, one might experience a kind of psychoanalytic vindication, discovering that even Joseph had his own (unconscious?) human flaws as well. He tormented his brothers repeatedly, subjecting them to accusations of thievery, evidently and perhaps unknowingly satisfying his envy and desire for revenge. Of course the Bible is full of flawed characters and dysfunctional families. It doesn't always, however, make everything explicit.

A further example of this is found in I Samuel chapters 1 and 2. Once again, an apparently saintly person, this time Hannah, who is desperate to have a child, but has suffered from infertility, is provoked severely by her husband's other wife. Of course this occurs because Elkanah, the husband, plays favorites by giving larger portions of food to Hannah because he loves her more. Out of her desperation to triumph over her rival, and to end her own torment, she bargains with God, promising to make of her son something like a sacrifice, i.e. to give him over to God as his dedicated servant all his days. Her motives were clearly a mix of reverence for God and self-serving revenge on her tormentor, reversing the tables, in effect. All this came about despite God's very clear abhorrence of the practice of child sacrifice (see Jeremiah 7:31, 19:5). Any sacrifice to a god is for the purpose of placating that god, or trying to win favor. Hannah, although she does not literally sacrifice her son, engages in a high-stakes maneuver for the sake of her own narcissistic injury. One can only wonder about the the impact of such maneuvering on the psyche of the child. According to the Laplanchian model of untranslatable portions of the enigmatic message coming from the mother's unconscious, Hannah's desires as they pertained to her infant boy and what he meant to her may have had grave potential impact on Samuel's mind. I have not sought at this point to examine the record of Samuel's life to see if I might find evidence of such potentially deleterious impact.

Whether evidence exists in the recorded life of Samuel or not, Avivah Gottlieb Zornberg[20] does, however, recognize the phenomenon of intergenerational transmission of the unconscious in her examination of the lived experience of several Biblical characters. I have already referred to the dysfunction evident in Joseph's family and how he participated, likely unwittingly, in its perpetuation. In Gottlieb Zornberg's analysis of aspects of Jacob's[21] (Joseph's father) life, she highlights the symmetry of Jacob being deceived by his father-in-law Laban's substitution of his far less desirable

20. Zornberg, *The Murmuring Deep.*
21. See Genesis 28 ff.

daughter, Leah, in disguise, on the wedding night of what was supposed to be the marriage of Jacob to Rachel. Rachel was indeed desired, being beautiful in form. Leah, on the other hand, is described as having weak eyes, which, I assume is to mean that she was plain. A symmetrical justice is achieved in regard to the fact that Jacob himself had analogously deceived his father, Isaac, in order to win his blessing, in place of his twin brother Esau. Gottlieb Zornberg finds, however, that:

> In Jacob's evolving sense of self, Leah plays a crucial role. She comes to him unbidden, and with her comes agitation and disorder. . . . [Rachel] was the single object of his quest, the purpose of his journey.
>
> . . . [a cited author] writes of these two types of marriage relationship as types of "helpmate that God sends a person." In one, a human being seeks out in full intentionality the object that will satisfy his desire, his sense of a coherent life. Rachel is the archetype of this mode. . . . The other mode, however, is represented by Leah: unwittingly and unwillingly, Jacob finds her lodged in his life. She has been sent by God, she comes to him; but Jacob experiences her as a grotesque disruption of his design. Such forms of "helpmate," which appear . . . as incoherent, inscrutable elements of experience, often bring a sense of moral dissonance with them. Paradoxically, writes R. Leiner, precisely this sort of relationship may later be understood as a source of vital power.
>
> . . . Jacob and Leah thus represent a turbulent matching that disrupts Jacob's world of desire. Their children, too, are problematic, the protagonists of troubling narratives. . . . But, significantly, it is from this marriage that the Davidic—and messianic—dynasty eventually emerges.
>
> . . . the clarification is the transformative later revision of the narrative, when new perspectives have become visible and when one is moved to pursue different meaning.
>
> Such reformulations of experience mobilize a vital energy around the most enigmatic phenomena. Leah comes to symbolize this power of the "hidden world," in Beit Ya'akov's kabbalistic terminology. A grotesque event—like the unveiling of the *wrong* sister the morning after the wedding—may eventually be transformed in Jacob's mind; he may even come to see beauty—a generative beauty—in this complex relationship.
>
> The use of the [clarification] has a similar function to Freud's *nachtraglichkeit*—the "afterwardness," or the "deferred action," by which "experiences, impressions and memory traces may be revised at a later date to fit in with fresh experiences or with the development of a new stage of development" (Quoted

from J. Laplanche and J.B. Pontalis, The Language of Psycho-analysis, Trans. Donald Nicholson-Smith [London: Hogarth Press, 1973]). The [clarification] retrospectively allows one to see what before was imperceptible. The new formulation does more than register meaning: it retranscribes memory, creating new possibilities for questioning, for reflecting on the "un-thought known" (From Christopher Bollas, The Shadow of the Object).[22]

I have prevailed upon the reader to persist through this long quotation for reasons of illustrating the value of recognizing the complexities visited upon human experience and relationships by the unconscious elements that operate within the mind, including the rich portrayals of storied people in the Bible. Gottlieb Zornberg has given us a picture of how we can benefit from probing into the interstices of lives, memories, accounts of experience; it is an example of how psychoanalysis can profoundly enrich and contrib-ute toward "freeing the soul."

Citing the anthropological work of Mary Douglas in her *Purity and Danger*, Gottlieb Zornberg offers us further insights into the value of the retrospective clarification and reformulation of "grotesque events." Douglas employs a gardening metaphor to make the point that dirt, defined as "mat-ter out of place" is the very thing that when allowed to be transformed into compost, enriches the soil. Gottlieb Zornberg:

Normally, dirt . . . threatens order . . . Since ordering [think here of the striving for omnipotence in the form of precise order and purity of one's self or one's world] involves rejecting inap-propriate elements, elements that make no rational whole of experience are excluded. And yet, precisely such anomalies can be fed back into the organism and be made powerful for good. The composting metaphor exploits the paradox of two opposite yet related ways of looking at an object: the weed is pollutant, dangerous, but also a source of enrichment.

Jacob's marriage to Leah can be viewed through the prism of this metaphor. Jacob first perceives Leah as, literally "out of place": an alien element in his life. . . . Two different models of beauty set up a field of tension. Immaculate purity of design occurs rarely in human experience. As against Rachel's harmo-nious beauty, which evokes a tapestry world of perfect design, Leah comes to represent the world of ambiguity that disrupts his conscious ordering. She and her children will release their power for good: weeds turned to compost strangely enrich the

22. Zornberg, The Murmuring Deep, 290–91. Emphasis hers.

garden. What has been avoided, repudiated, becomes a source of fertility, and, perhaps, of a different aesthetic. Her "[weak] eyes" evade classic norms of beauty, telling of danger and desire.[23]

Finally, Gottlieb Zornberg, citing the midrash (rabbinic for the interpretive study of the Bible; the writings that came from that exegesis) that pertains to Jacob's life, considers his concern to have his life and his offspring neatly ordered as per the prophesied family destiny:

> . . . he wishes that none of his many, varied offspring may be repudiated. His bed is to be whole. Its integrity remains his concern to the end of his life. But the ideal of integrity comes to include the work of integration. From the night when Leah is given to him, the notion of purity is constantly challenged.
>
> "Purity is the enemy of change" . . . "The yearning for rigidity [qua purity] is in all of us."[24]

Gottlieb Zornberg has not only illustrated how, in complex ways God brings about his good purposes despite the messy outcomes of human foibles, but also, she has demonstrated how productive a re-thinking of what we thought we knew can be, both in the narratives of others, and also in ourselves. Furthermore, she has caused us to appreciate that the content of the unconscious, that which has been repudiated, can and does serve as fertile ground. It may well be that if one can open oneself to his unconscious, imagination and unrealized potential might be unleashed for all manner of good.

We have journeyed through several deliberations to do with how we might see the unconscious playing out in the lives of Biblical characters, some rather subtle. A look at the life of David and his lusting after Bathsheba and subsequent arrangement of the murder of her husband might seem to suggest nothing to be learned from his unconscious. If, however, we link the episode of David, "leaping and whirling before the Lord" on the occasion of the ark of the Lord returning to Jerusalem, and his wife, Michal's, subsequent rebuke of him for "uncovering himself today in the eyes of the maids of his servants,"[25] with the episode with Bathsheba,[26] we might speculate about some unconscious impulse in David to exhibit himself. If this was so, then Bathsheba's own exhibition of herself, beyond the natural prurient interest of any man for a beautiful naked woman, might have led to a convergence of unconscious sexually "perverse" elements in these two people, leading to

23. Ibid., 293.

24. Ibid., 293–94. Quoting Douglas.

25. 2 Samuel 6:16 and 20, respectively.

26. 2 Samuel 11.

disastrous consequences. (More will be examined regarding perversity later.) Notwithstanding the disaster for Uriah, Bathsheba's husband, once again the record shows that ultimate good came from "dirt," in that, despite David's bad behavior, Christ came from his genetic line, through Bathsheba.[27]

In the New Testament, we could consider the unconscious forces at work in Peter, when he adamantly refused Jesus' prediction of his impending three-times denial of knowing Jesus, in the face of threat[28]. Clearly, Peter did not know his own mind.

When Jesus, in urging his listeners to not judge,[29] identified the plank in one's own eye as serving to interfere with seeing the speck in the eye of another, he drew attention to the elaborate systems of defense we all have against seeing the truth concerning our own selves. I might also suggest that Jesus may have been inferring that the speck in the brother's eye could, in fact, be a projection of the plank in one's own eye; the very common human trend to find that which is unacceptably egregious in oneself located in the other is projection, a kind of mis-attribution, and is universal. Projection as a defense mechanism, if relied upon heavily, signals significant psychopathology, and seriously damages interpersonal relationships.

We have already referred to Jeremiah's complaint against the deception that reigned in the people and its damaging impact on community. Paul (2 Corinthians 4:2), likewise concerned about the impact of cunning and deception on the development of community, proclaims his and his acolytes' renouncement of cunning or deception, "but by the open statement of the truth we commend ourselves to the conscience of everyone in the sight of God." Miroslav Volf notes that it is not just "minds" one encounters, but "neighbors," i.e. total persons. He says, "Of course all these people have "minds," but these are embodied minds, pulled in various directions by various desires, interests, and conflicts, and shaped by cultural [including those involved in shaping unconscious forces] and religious convictions and practices."[30] Volf, a theologian, speaks with psychoanalytic insight.

Acts 5:1–11 provides us with an example of the seriousness with which God looked upon the impact of deception on community and the degree to which he was prepared to go to prevent deception's inevitable disruptiveness. The married couple, Ananias and Sapphira, conspired to deceive the early Christian community as to how generous they were being in sharing the proceeds of the sale of property. Both were, in their turn, struck dead. Peter asked

27. Matthew 1:6.
28. See Luke 22.
29. Matthew 7:1–5.
30. Volf, *Exclusion & Embrace*, 260.

the question to which we get no answer, "Why have you conceived this thing in your heart?" Did Ananias and Sapphira harbour unconscious binding attachments to their money and possessions coupled with powerful needs to be admired for their conformity to community ideals so much so that they would lie? We cannot know what forces may have impelled them, but it reminds me of a patient, Amanda, whose strong attachment to her accumulated possessions led to a classic hoarding situation from which she has not been able to liberate herself. From Amanda's analysis, it has become apparent that the hoarded things have served, unconsciously, as extensions of her physical self, which has always been experienced as defective and deficient. This patient has come to learn that she'd always been seeking to achieve organizational perfection in these stored goods, as compensation for the perceived disorder in her body. Of course, there is a great deal of shame and secrecy regarding all of this, hence impairing her capacity to comfortably engage with her community, so that she suffers added isolation necessitated by efforts to hide that which feels shameful. Amanda's story will be amplified later.

Paul gives a quite frank account of the workings of his own unconscious: in expounding the role of the (Old Testament) law, and its ineffectuality in changing his "carnal" self, he says, "For what I am doing I do not understand. For what I will to do, that I do not practice; but what I hate, that I do."[31] He acknowledges his own conflicts, his sense of a divided self in an extended testimonial to his own experience in Romans 7, where he clearly alludes to the existence of his own unconscious; only of the consequences, the out-workings of his own unconscious activities is he aware and of which he laments. When he says, "Now if I do what I will not to do, it is no longer I who do it, but sin that dwells in me,"[32] Paul describes an experience very common to people who seek out therapy, and that is, the sense of being occupied and controlled by some seemingly autonomous agent which the person is not able on their own, to identify nor effectively modify. Much more will be said about Romans 7 in Chapter 9.

DID JESUS HAVE AN UNCONSCIOUS?

I have hesitated to include my thoughts and deliberations about the question of Jesus' unconscious because any thoughts will be necessarily highly speculative. It might be argued that even the speculations are of no value, and so why bother? The question has been particularly provocative to me because of the following claims: "Therefore, in all things [Christ] had to be

31. Romans 7:15.
32. Ibid., verse 20.

made like his brethren" and "[Christ is] one who has been tempted in all things as we are, yet without sin."[33] This was said of Jesus so as to convince us of the possibility of being able to fully identify, us with him, and he with us, as a truly effective "great high priest." As Hebrews 4:16 suggests, because he has entered into our reality, we therefore can have confidence in his mercifully gracious advocacy on our behalf. In other words, he was fully man, while also being fully God, as the doctrine holds, God incarnate. As both fully God, and fully man, and as such, he is to be emulated and identified with, how do believers understand him to have managed his sexuality? As a young Christian, I wondered about the implications for my sexuality. The Bible gives no indications of Jesus grappling with his own sexuality, at least not in the terms with which we are ordinarily accustomed. Perhaps there *is* a point in trying to address the question of Jesus' unconscious.

Insofar as Christians will insist on Jesus being fully God, i.e. omniscient, omnipotent, holy, without sin, etc., we cannot think of whatever unconscious he might have had as a "dynamic unconscious," in the ways we have thus far considered it. Freud's conceptualization of repression involved the activation of forces to counter the derivatives of id impulses that push forward for expression; e.g. the young child's wish for sexual gratification with his mother (the Oedipus Complex), or his wish to enact revenge on a sibling who has displaced him from his primary place of favor. It would defy all of our comprehension of Jesus as God to consider him having such thoughts or impulses let alone any need to deal with them by repression, because the phenomenon of repression of unacceptable wishes and impulses naturally implies division within the mind, a state of incomplete integration (Lacan's "the divided subject"). If the dynamic force impelling repression derives from feelings of guilt and/or shame, then a sinless Jesus could not have known guilt or shame arising from his own impulses. To stretch the claim of Jesus' human identity to necessarily including a dynamic unconscious of the kind we find in ourselves and in Godly characters like St. Paul, we would draw near to questioning his sinlessness since sin seems to bear a close relationship to elements of dynamic unconscious.

We could wonder about Jesus' unconscious being modeled more along the line of the object relations model wherein there are instantiated internal imagoes of the parents. This, too is problematic however, given that the flaws of the parents are as likely to infiltrate the imagoes as is their goodness, in fact maybe even more so, because of the fantasy activity of the child, and the impact on fantasy of the emotions (such as anger, hate) that are experienced in the child when the parent's failings are manifest.

---

33. Hebrews 2:17 and 4:15.

We could speculate, though, about the sense of communion that might have existed between the infant Jesus with his heavenly father, and whether the internalization of the holy father supplanted the internalization of the earthly parents. His attachment style would be recognized as secure, especially given the response he gave to his anxiously seeking parents when they found him teaching in the temple at age twelve: *"Why did you seek me? Did you not know that I must be about my father's business?"*[34] Since he had been apart from his parents for three days, and was teaching the teachers in the temple, he clearly had a secure attachment to the heavenly father, and an apparently precocious independence from his earthly parents.

Can we think of Jesus having selfobject needs and acquiring his sense of self through the adequacy of provision for those needs, as per a self psychology model? All of these speculations falter, in part because of the fact that we cannot confine our conceptualizations of Jesus as having solely earthly parents. In fact, John asserts at the beginning of his gospel that Jesus pre-existed the formation of the world, and co-existed in the beginning, with God. And so whatever developmental model we invoke for the formation of his mind, we have to account for Jesus being uniquely different, having had his mind formed in past eternity by relating to God, the father, whose mind is beyond comprehending. We seem, then, to be stuck with considering some form of admixture of influences from his trinitarian relational origins and his earthly parental origins.

Whatever model we consider, there is no getting away from the fact that the human unconscious as we know it is constituted within the psychologic-emotional milieu of an enigmatic other. This hearkens back to Laplanche's notions about the seduction of the child by the sexual unconscious of the (m)other. Gottlieb Zornberg characterizes his ideas as follows:

> The mother unconsciously transmits to her child seductive messages, which intimate aspects of her life that he is incapable of grasping. The child receives the impact of the other in all her beauty; he is dazzled by a light beyond his comprehension. The alienness of the other is registered; its unassimilable, stimulating message is locked within. From now, the child will be haunted, decentered by his unconscious life. In Freud's words, "The ego is not master in his own house."[35]

While this paragraph beautifully describes the situation for all humans, it is difficult to imagine, for reasons mentioned above, the influence of Mary's sexual unconscious on Jesus. And yet Mary was in every respect,

34. Luke 2:49.

35. Zornberg, *The Murmuring Deep,* Introduction xv.

a real woman, raised, herself by flawed parents who had their own sexual unconscious. I find myself inclined towards an idea that Jesus' pre-existing, eternal relationship with the Father and the Holy Spirit, co-existing in trinitarian wholeness even during the time of Jesus' infancy, served to mitigate, perhaps even to nullify the enigmatic, untranslatable impact of the (m) other. For Jesus, perhaps his mother's otherness never was enigmatic; perhaps there were no untranslatable messages for him, in which case there was no dynamic unconscious formed. There would then be no subsequent fantasizing in order to try to organize and manage the unconscious traces. I think I am content, at least for now, to subsume the question under the "mysterium" that surrounds Christ.

From the foregoing, it is clear that lies and falsehood serve as refuge for all of mankind. Living in harmonious community is therefore made difficult for humanity; conflicts, wars, and their consequences inevitably reflect human reliance on deception for the sake of power, and truth proves scarce. Jesus transcended the conflicts and deceptions of the world in which he lived. He was without guile[36] and those who are his followers are to be likewise, full of truth, without deceit; a tall (perhaps ultimately impossible) order for unconsciously-motivated mankind. Perhaps true community "depends on truth and the truth depends not so much on the plausibility of the transcendental conditions of its possibility, but on the struggle of the truthful warriors on behalf of the truth."[37] Accordingly, Volf contends that God establishes himself and that it is vital for us to see it so, as the "warrior engaged in the struggle for truth," and that it is more important to see this "as the prophets and the apostles do,"[38] than it is to see God as "the transcendental condition for the possibility of truthful speech."[39] The latter refers to the biblical assertion that God *is* truth (Jesus: "I am the way, the truth, and . . . ") and claims that the very essence of the human capacity to conceptualize truth as distinct from untruth inheres in the character and being of God. In the sphere of human power relations, Volf claims the importance of God and his servants actively engaging as warriors for truth, and not simply meditating on the source of truth. Yet, we cannot know a lie unless we have a gold standard for truth. Since God is truth, he cannot possibly have an unconscious. As such, the possibility exists for humans, in the experience of God's personal embrace, of transcending the very powerful human need for refuge in lies and deceit.

---

36. 1 Peter 2:22.

37. Volf, *Exclusion & Embrace,* 263.

38. Volf cites Isaiah 28:15–17.

39. Ibid, 263.

Chapter 3

Conscience, Superego, and the Gospel

CASE ILLUSTRATION

TO BEGIN TO DEMONSTRATE the differentiation between conscience and superego, I will provide some details from a real life case, with personal identifiers obscured.

Carmen is a middle age professional woman with a husband and three children who was referred to me because of debilitating anxiety that was threatening her ability to continue in her demanding profession, as well as her commitment to her family. Her family's very materially comfortable lifestyle is significantly the result of her success in her career. From the fairly abrupt onset of the anxiety, it had been apparent that the anxiety focussed very heavily on bodily symptoms, most notably limb pain. Under the direction of her family physician, she had been extensively investigated for potential causes of the pain, even to the extent of having sophisticated scanning and referral to consultants. When a scan revealed the presence of a minor abnormality that was thought to be innocuous and likely congenital and not the cause of her pain, she, nevertheless, incorporated this finding into and made it the focus of her anxiety. Specifically, she feared she was going to have some dreadful disease, most likely cancer, that would prematurely end her life and leave her children motherless.

Carmen was born to married parents who were living in a country which for years had been oppressed by an authoritarian regime. Life was difficult, and so, like many others, her parents sought a way to improve their life circumstances by working their way toward emigration to Canada. This necessitated her mother leaving the family for a few years to study abroad, leaving Carmen in the care of her father and grandparents. Immigration to Canada was accomplished when she was in her early teens. Needless to say, her parents had to endure the hardship of separation from each other in order to achieve a better life for their children, of whom Carmen was the eldest. Adapting to life in Canada was also arduous, and yet, from all superficial appearances, successful. Although Carmen had always, she discovered in analysis, felt a powerful need to care for and in fact to attempt repair of the conflictual relationship that existed between her parents, this impulse had intensified since her father has been depressed and purposeless for the six years following a relatively minor and definitely not incapacitating stroke. Since Carmen had concerns about the impact of her father's listlessness on his competence, about four weeks before the onset of her intense anxiety, she had felt it necessary to refuse her father's offer to take care of her children when the summer ended, and she would be back to her full schedule of work. Added to this disturbing struggle was a background of overt pressure from her mother (who may be impelled by her own unconscious guilt about leaving her family to study) to devote less time to her profession and more to her children; in fact, Carmen felt her mother always found fault with her parenting choices. Carmen, on the contrary, believed herself to be a good enough mother, and claimed to be content with the work-home balance that she had established, along with her husband.

Although much could be said about this case and the material that my psychoanalytic readers would no doubt wish elaborated, I will focus on what is pertinent to the topic I am about to address. Perhaps I will only add that a few months into the analytic work, Carmen had a dream: she was about to climb into the cockpit of a plane as a novice pilot, when her father appeared and deterred her from pursuing her plan, insisting she was not equipped or competent to fly.

With considerable time and analytic work, we came to discover that her anxiety was closely tied to a deep guilt she felt. There evidently had been long-standing guilt at persistently failing to effectively repair the parents (and their marriage), but the guilt had exploded, so to speak, following Carmen's refusal of her father's offer to care for her children, on the basis of his incompetence. Her father, as per the dream, had always tended to dismiss her accomplishments, and conveyed his doubt about her competence. We were then able to see that her long-standing guilt had been intensified when she engaged in doing to him what he had always done to her, by refusing his offer to care for the children, based upon his doubtful competence to do so. No doubt also, she had guilt for having exceeded her father's expectations of her, and perhaps also, the station in life which he had himself attained.

In fact, she had exceeded by considerable distance her father and mother's socio-economic status in life.

Without elaborating detail, it is nevertheless pertinent to recognize that under-girding the guilt I have outlined was guilt at having achieved something of an oedipal triumph, since her mother's departure for years of study left Carmen to occupy her place as the primary woman in her father's life. Perhaps Carmen's disturbance in response to her father's offer of care for the children, if in her unconscious, there existed this taboo oedipal connection to him, further supports her intense anxiety.

From the foregoing understandings of Carmen's thoughts and feelings, we were able to construct the following hypothesis (or, psychoanalytic interpretation) about the meanings of both her intense anxiety and her limb pain. Because of the guilt, she had unconsciously felt a need for punishment which was satisfied in the form of expected serious, life-ending illness. "For we know that every man creates and obeys his own god or gods, and that every man decrees and executes punishment upon himself."[1] Furthermore, the pain in her limbs that accompanied her anxiety could be understood as a "hysterical conversion" symptom, rather like those mentioned in chapter one. In general, such "conversions" refer to the mind-body translation of a psychic conflict into an approximately anatomically corresponding physical symptom for which no organic pathology can be found that might account for it. Carmen's limb pain correlated with the conflict she felt at having actually successfully mobilized herself ("flying," in effect, as per her dream) by achieving professional, material, and family triumph (this term is used to capture the sense of wished-for oedipal defeat of the rival) despite her father's disapprovals and non-support of her.

I have called Carmen's central disturbing affect guilt. It certainly feels to her like guilt. But is she actually guilty? If so, of what? If we understand guilt to be the emotion that we rightly feel when we have violated a moral or a legal standard, then, although Carmen felt she had violated her father's (and her mother's) view of her, she had remained a loyal and dedicated daughter (in fact, so much so that it was to her detriment). She had not violated or transgressed against another at all. What she had done was defied the inordinate expectations or standards of her actual parents, as well as those of her internalized parental representations or imagoes as they exist in her psyche. To whatever extent her parents actually impose their expectations on their daughter, we could say that *they* have violated *her*, i.e. in ways that have transgressed her inherent right to autonomous self-determination. As an aside, I might underline that there is not a parent alive who has not done

1. Menninger, Man Against Himself, 317.

this to their children in some way or degree or another; hence the inevitability of "The Lord . . . visiting the iniquity of the fathers upon the children and the children's children to the third and fourth generation."[2]

So, if Carmen is not actually guilty (or at least not in the way and for the reasons uncovered, albeit we later explored her oedipal guilt, and found legitimate the guilt felt for egregious childhood impulses of possession of and hate toward her parents) do we have nothing more to offer her than to say that she shouldn't feel what she does, that her guilt is not actually legitimate? Psychoanalysis enabled me to propose an understanding of greater depth. I helped her to see that what she more precisely was feeling was shame, that terribly searing affect we suffer when we fail to live up to the ideals of our superego. In Carmen, we could gradually discern the way in which her superego had shifted from relative quiescence as a fairly benign (although quite inhibiting) background activity previously, to taking up a very active dominating role in the foreground of her mind as a result of the episode of refusing her father because of her perception of his incompetence.

The superego is constituted by the identification with and the internalization of elements of the parents, typically those elements which are disapproving, critical, and prohibiting. Not only the attitudes, values, and ideals of the parents are internalized i.e., having much to do with the parents' own superegos, but also those of the surrounding culture, through the agency of one's teachers, etc. This may seem rather simple, but it is complicated by the role of unconscious fantasies that form in the child's early mind about their own self in relation to the other, in response to those untranslated fragments of the message from the mother (and father), that are forged into the imagoes of the parents and the superego. To complicate things even further, the innate id aggression, however unopposed it may be by libido, its opposite force, can and often does infuse the imagoes of the superego such that the character of the superego becomes especially harsh, sadistic, perfectionistic and unrealistic in its setting up of ideals. The superego may, then, be quite unlike the actual parents, and is largely aligned against the self, having come into being by virtue of identification with the (perceived) aggressors against the self. The formation of the superego, as necessary as it is to become a citizen of society, is impelled by a drive for mastery of oneself, and so can acquire the features of a tyrannical master, over the self as slave. Since it derives from identification with the aggressor, the tendency is for the subject to conclude that the more one can approximate toward perfection, the more one might be loved.

True guilt can be ameliorated through remorse and active pursuit of repair, and may especially be banished by the experience of being forgiven

---

2. Exodus 34:6, 7.

by the offended other, including the divine Other. Shame, on the other hand, the result of superego affliction, can only be ameliorated by recognizing the inordinately condemning character and activity of one's superego and, by intentional refusal to submit, along with reasoned scrutiny of its claims and values, incrementally transforming it. Such activity can entail long, difficult analytic work, and is an example of the process of making the unconscious conscious, so that work can be done. One cannot deal with an enemy that one cannot recognize or confront. A reformed superego is one that becomes benevolent, supportive, compassionate, accepting (in place of rejecting), and can reasonably allow the person (via the agency of his ego) to assess himself and his performance along any given measure. The transition from the hell of living under a primitive, sadistic superego to life with a benevolent superego is liberating indeed.

We will leave Carmen, who continues to work through the implications of these insights; she has, happily, enjoyed considerable relief from both her anxiety and the limb pain, although she, as with most patients needing to address such things, still relies on the benevolent, accepting auxiliary superego in the person of her psychoanalyst while she progresses in the work of transforming her own.

CONSCIENCE VERSUS SUPEREGO

A valued mentor in my psychoanalytic training, Professor Donald Carveth, inspired, himself, by the engaging ideas of Eli Sagan, as set forth in Sagan's book, *Freud, Women and Morality: The Psychology of Good and Evil* (1988), has taught and written[3] extensively on the important matter of distinguishing conscience from superego. Until that time, like Freud himself, and many colleagues, I had not thought of conscience as being distinct from superego. One of Sagan's theses was that Freud had conflated the concepts of superego and conscience, a blurring which led to confused thinking.

Before pursuing Sagan's insights, I will try to clarify how Freud saw things pertaining to the superego. Given the centrality for Freud of the Oedipus Complex, and the perceived id-instinctually driven object choices of mother and father for the two drives (as he saw them) of libido and aggression, respectively, he hypothesized the development of a precipitate in the ego, as an effort at resolution of conflict between these two troublesome instinctual connections to the parents, by identifying with aspects of both parents to form an ego ideal. Further, the superego, he thought would also be constituted by powerful reaction formations against the instinctual activity,

3. Carveth, *The Still, Small Voice.*

and encompass prohibitions against exceeding the father's attainments. The following will illustrate Freud's ideas:

> It is easy to show that the ego ideal answers to everything that is expected of the higher nature of man. As a substitute for a longing for the father, it contains the germ from which all religions have evolved. The self-judgement which declares that the ego falls short of its ideal produces the religious sense of humility to which the believer appeals in his longing. As a child grows up the role of the father is carried on by teachers and others in authority; their injunctions and prohibitions remain powerful in the ego ideal and continue, in the form of conscience, to exercise the moral censorship. The tension between the demands of conscience and the actual performances of the ego is experienced as a sense of guilt. Social feelings rest on identifications with other people, on the basis of having the same ego ideal.[4]

Freud's superego is formed through an identification with society's value system, albeit mediated symbolically, through the father. As Sagan points out, however, it is through another identification, that is, with a suitably nurturing mother earlier then the age of the Oedipus Complex (between three and six) that empathy for the other and a moral conscience develops that is sensitive to avoiding violation or exploitation of an other.

In order to clarify the distinction between superego and conscience, Sagan invoked the story of Huckleberry Finn, and his friendship with the run-away black slave, Jim. Huck finds Jim while he also is running away from his abusive father. Jim is trying to get to free states where he hopes eventually to buy freedom for his family. Huckleberry faces a crisis when he reflects upon his own in-grained societal expectation that he turn in any run-away slave to the authorities. His conscience, however, does not make it easy for him, since he sees Jim as deserving of human freedom and dignity as he is himself. Eventually he decides in favor of conscience and the two of them continue on their eventful journey.

The story informs of us essential differences between superego and conscience. Huckleberry's superego had been formed through identification with and internalization of parental and societal values, and of course they were values hostile toward black slaves, thereby demanding of Huckleberry similarly hostile and aggressive attitudes toward Jim. Sagan makes the point that, in large part the formation of the superego involves "identification with the aggressor." In the case of Carmen, we could see that her superego's character was aggressive toward her and had formed by identification with

4. Freud, *The Ego and the Id*, 37.

the (parental) aggressors. Classically, as per Freud's conclusions, the aggressor with whom the child identifies is the father who represents the rule of law. Attaining mastery over oneself, as considered above, even if unduly harshly, is perceived as preferable to being painfully governed by others. In this sense, the "identification with the aggressor" serves a defensive function and as such, becomes a mechanism of defense.[5]

Often contributing to the development of a harsh superego is the need on the part of the young child to preserve the perception of the parents as good. In the face of emotionally intolerable harsh treatment from the parents or other problems in the parental "containing" environment of the child, he may consign all badness to himself, in order to preserve the perception of benevolent parents, his "moral defense"[6] against a moral dilemma. Fairbairn, who coined this term, described the child's thought as follows: " . . . it is better to be a sinner in a world ruled by God than to live in a world ruled by the Devil." With a heavy-handed superego, the child, in effect, creates an internal world in which he figures as the sinner ruled by the god (superego) of his own creation, in preference to the prospect of living in a world ruled by devils, i.e. cruel, sadistic or incompetent parents. The solution is defensive because, as suggested by Fairbairn, it is aimed at achieving security; the result, however, is the creation of a pathologically severe superego built upon identification with bad internal objects (the parental imago that is unloving), a superego "designed to control the child's dangerous negative feelings toward the parent."[7]

To illustrate further his argument regarding the identification with the aggressor, Sagan cites the physicians under the Hitler regime who performed atrocities on people who were ostensibly their patients. They did so, he claims, because of their powerful identification with a charismatic, aggressive leader whose value system had penetrated the minds of so many. They were acting in accordance with their ideals; their superegos dominated over conscience, rendering conscience inactive.

As evidenced in the adolescent struggle of Huckleberry Finn, Sagan argues that conflict between superego and conscience is a healthy, maturing phenomenon:

> Such conflict entails a challenge to the corrupt values of the superego, a challenge that necessitates a subjection of the values of

5. See Freud, *The Ego and the Mechanisms of Defense.*

6. Fairbairn, *Psychoanalytic Studies of the Personality,* 66.

7. Grotstein, in his foreword to: Reiner, *The Quest for Conscience and the Birth of the Mind.*

the parents and/or society to criticism. Only in adolescence does the psyche become potent enough to generate such a critique.[8]

Very often in therapy, the work of transforming the superego (I have often referred to it as the "internal judge" in clinical practice, to get away from technical jargon) includes scrutinizing the values embedded within it and by which it generates its condemnation of the ego and thereby destroys one's sense of security or self esteem. The task becomes one of determining whether the values found are values that stand up to thoughtful scrutiny according to the conscious deliberate, secondary process form of thinking that comes with psychic maturation. It may be that many of the values found in the superego will be retained because they do accord with the worldview of the person. Not all of the values of the superego are corrupt. Part of the transforming enterprise is a re-ordering of the priority of the values found. Important to note is that the rehabilitation of the superego toward one that is moral requires the activation of a functioning conscience.[9]

From these deliberations, we can look back at the above quote from Freud and reasonably question his conflation of moral with societal values and standards. Carveth offers a helpful perspective on the differentiation:

> Conscience is fundamentally grounded in non-rational, emotional processes of attachment, sympathy, concern and love. For Sagan, whereas the superego arises through identification with the aggressor, and operates essentially in accordance with the talion law revenge ("an eye for an eye"), conscience arises from identification with the nurturer and operates through an analogous reciprocity, only one in which one feels called upon to return love for love received.[10]

A severe, sadistic superego, one that is more or less in a constant state of attack on the ego impairs one's capacity for cognitive function, because of the intense anxiety that results. We might readily recognize the poor academic performance of a school-age child arising thus, perhaps suffering conflicts in the home, and lack of a truly secure environment. Anxiety impairs the child's ability to think and to organize and integrate concepts. Similarly, the adult who is assailed by an endlessly fault-finding and accusatory superego, one that will be satisfied by nothing short of perfection, will be chronically anxious, and have little confidence in his capacity to think. Typically, his chronic anxiety will morph into associated depression as well.

8. Sagan, *Freud, Women and Morality,* 172–73.
9. Carveth, *The Still Small Voice,* 71.
10. Carveth, *Four Contributions,* 352.

Lydia

A patient of mine I'll call Lydia, has suffered under a superego such as has been described, one for which she and I long ago, for the sake of a shorthand way of speaking of it, adopted the code name "SS" (sadistic superego). We discovered that her chronic pattern of broken relationships stems from the activity of the SS, by virtue of its savage attacks on her manner of relating ("you're not worthy of loving or being loved"), or the directing of its primitive aggression against the other, instead of against herself, as the result of projecting aspects of her unsatisfactory self onto the other. If the SS does not convince her that she is not good enough to be liked as a friend, she finds her SS angrily attacking others in response to any perceived slight. In addition, we recognized that her repeated assertions that "I don't know," in reference to so many things, actually reflected an SS activity in fragmenting any "knowing" she might achieve, essentially asserting that she is not competent to know since only perfect and impossibly complete knowledge would satisfy the requirements of her demanding SS. Lydia is the only child of a highly narcissistic and critical mother, with whom, as a strategy for psychic survival she could only identify. The narcissism of her mother demanded that Lydia mirror her, i.e., she was not permitted or encouraged to have a separate self, different from her mother; she was required to be according to the ideals of her mother's own superego. And yet always, her mother had to compete with and defeat Lydia; most egregiously, out of jealousy and envy, she seduced Lydia's teenage boyfriend.

Over time, Lydia has come to want friends, to be able to love people and not attack them or perceive them as threatening to her. She also laments that she has hurt people so much, and feels she has been amoral. Together, through the course of her long analytic work, we have recognized growth in her conscience, and her wish to operate more from conscience than from superego. To be more precise about this, it is likely that conscience has not had opportunity to develop or flourish, having been so overwhelmed by the sadism and intensity of her superego.

I will try to develop ideas about the mind's capacity to think by drawing upon the work of Annie Reiner. Let me quote extensively from her introduction to her book *The Quest for Conscience and The Birth of the Mind,* in which she formulates the development of mature conscience, as distinct from superego, the latter of which in her view fosters a more primitive form of thought:

> . . . mature conscience [is] an unrealized human potential . . . a higher mental function, or even, as Kant suggested, the *highest* mental function . . . several hypotheses.

> First, that a mature conscience is predicated on an authen-
> tic or "true self." As a corollary to this, the development of a true
> self may, and perhaps in most cases does, require a psychologi-
> cal birth, by which process the individual can begin to experi-
> ence buried, unrealized, or unborn aspects of the personality.
>   . . . The second hypothesis, very much related to the first,
> reflects the direct relationship between mental birth and the de-
> velopment of the capacity to think, the development of higher
> mental functions that is dependent upon the capacity to contain
> primitive emotional states (Bion, 1962a, 1970). The capacities
> for contact with an authentic emotional self, the capacity to
> think, and the capacity for a true conscience are, therefore, seen
> as necessary to each other and constantly linked. As this kind
> of emotional containment is a function of conscious awareness,
> I hope to show to show that conscience is a by-product of con-
> sciousness, in particular the capacity to contain emotional real-
> ity. The latter has its source in the mother's capacity to contain
> the child's unconscious states of mind (Bion, 1962a).[11]

If we reconsider Lydia's challenges in light of these comments from
Reiner, and incorporate notions about Klein's "positions" (PS & D, outlined
above), we might say that Lydia, under the tyranny of her SS could only
operate much of the time, mentally speaking, in the PS (paranoid-schizoid)
position, and, as per her own assessment of her thinking capacities, could
not think effectively, being unable to contain her primitive intense emotional states which fragmented the organization of her thoughts. She had
not had a mother who was able to accurately mirror her emotional states,
nor contain and "metabolize," as Bion suggested, her unconscious states of
mind. Perhaps it could be said that her analysis has taken up the task of
mirroring, containment and metabolization of primitive affect states, such
that she has been able to recognize in herself, a birthing of her mind as she
has moved increasingly into D(depressive) position. Indeed, as per Reiner,
Lydia's gains toward mature conscience have been and continue to be matters of conscious awareness. Importantly, she realizes that she now has the
capacity to choose (not that choosing has yet become easy) whether she
will act upon evil intent (the manifestations of her SS) which she can now
recognize and reflect upon; the act of choosing is a matter of consciously
employing conscience. Reiner says:

> *I believe this detoxification through conscious thought is the founda-*
> *tion of the ongoing process of development of a mature conscience.* It
> may be fair to say then, that conscience is the knowledge, that is,

11. Reiner, *The Quest for Conscience*, Introduction xviii, xix. Emphasis hers.

containment, of unthought and potentially evil feelings, thoughts, or intentions within the light of one's conscious mind. Conscience, therefore, is always the by-product of consciousness, requiring all the attributes of higher mental functioning necessary in thinking: attention, memory, alpha function [Bion's designation of mental metabolizing of primitive feeling/thought complexes], and the dynamic interplay of container and contained.[12]

When psychoanalytic work exposes the operations of unconscious processes, the automatic, implicit, and seemingly natural (ego syntonic) character of those processes becomes evident. By definition, one cannot exercise *choice* if the mental processes in operation are outside awareness. This is why freeing the mind (or soul) is so essential to all of us for the attainment of mature thought. I believe Reiner points us in the direction of recognizing the need for acquiring mature conscience, a birthing of the mind, and the capacity to think in order to realize our full and true potential. I do not, however, want the reader to have the impression that I would think the attainment of such goals to be contingent necessarily upon undergoing psychoanalysis. I don't believe that to be true. As Reiner points out, such maturational achievements have a lot to do with the character of the emotional environment in which we are raised. Furthermore, "mature conscience" attainment is not a "have or have not," dichotomous duality; rather, it is better seen to lie along a gradient spectrum, determined in all of us, no doubt, by the infinitely complex factors that contribute to our individual emotional and intellectual development.

THE GOSPEL

The word "gospel" is literally, "good news." In a nutshell, the gospel of Jesus Christ is the good news that man can know himself forgiven of his guilt, his sin, and enter into a vital, life-giving relationship with God who fully accepts him, not by any self-generated efforts toward purification of himself, but only by receiving the grace of God, and appropriating the gift of God inherent in the sacrificial, substitutionary death of Jesus Christ. Theologians from different traditions would likely quibble with aspects of this perhaps too simplistic definition, but it encapsulates the essence of my understanding. I have stated it very simply in order to set the stage for my efforts to probe some of the intersections between the foregoing, on conscience and

12. Ibid., 132. Emphasis hers.

the superego, and the gospel. From the beginning, God had decreed that the consequence of disobedience to his will, i.e. sin, is death.[13]

When Freud, in the above quote, says that the ego ideal, as substitute for the longing for the father, as such, serves as the ground for all religions, I think he had a valid point. So much of religion, insofar as it functions in the role of determining the rules by which mankind is to live, a kind of codification of life, and seeks to control by induction of guilt for infractions of the codes, it does valourize the law of the father. Jesus proclaimed an end to the (Old Testament) Law and the prophets, not by destroying them, but by fulfilling them;[14] in effect, he pronounced the end of religion.[15] Paul had to work hard to drive this point home.[16] According to Paul, the persistent adherence to and implementation of the law was a perversion of the gospel.[17] While Christianity is often referred to as a religion, Jesus meant it to be otherwise. Nevertheless, the fact is that a lot of what passes under the name of Christianity is religion, especially inasmuch as, when examined carefully, this *religious* Christianity is actually a hybrid of Old Testament law with its ideology, and the New Testament gospel. Jesus proclaimed the end of the Old Covenant and the beginning of the New. He insisted that instead of searching the scriptures to find eternal life, people need to come to him for that, since all the scripture pointed to and testified of him.[18]

The gospel should bring liberation, but many people's experience of church and the gospel as it has been lived in various communities, is oppressive. In these communities of Christians, scriptural injunctions to "be holy, for I am holy,"[19] along with many New Testament exhortations to be pure, or to purify oneself, are assimilated into the innate human tendencies we have already considered: the narcissistic desire for omnipotence, and Freud's longing for the father.[20] When the claims of Christ and the Epistles are interpreted in ways so as to be co-opted into one's psychopathology, then superego severity is strengthened by religious ideology. The high ideals of scriptural teachings are readily adaptable to being incorporated into the ego

13. Genesis 2:17.

14. Matthew 5:17.

15. See Cavey, *The End of Religion*.

16. Romans 10:4; Ephesians 2:15; Galatians (the whole letter).

17. Galatians 1:7.

18. John 5:39.

19. I Peter 1:15.

20. Note: Paul Vitz, in his *Freud's Christian Unconscious*, suggests that Freud's own longings for his own father, who was quite religious, gave rise, unconsciously to reaction formation, such that he attacked religion—he felt shame of and could not idealize his father, and so his attack on religion is suspect as to its authentic motive.

ideal, in forming what amounts to superego ideology; when this occurs, and the idealistic, primitive, severe superego predominates in the mind, conscience remains dwarfed and relatively inactive.

If the claim that morality develops very early in the context of the loving, nurturing matrix of mother and infant[21] has validity, then we might consider the morality or ethic of Jesus. As Carveth stated, if the basis for conscience is birthed in a reciprocal love-for-love mode, then Reiner's claim for conscience to form out of a deliberate conscious developmental achievement may nevertheless still require an unconscious substrate of confidence in one's lovability, even if that is acquired later than infancy, through an analytic relationship, or some transformative social relationship. Jesus urges a still higher morality than love given for love received, that of love for one's enemy, i.e. love given even in the face of hate or mistreatment.[22] He even ends his injunction on love for one's enemy with: "Therefore you shall be perfect, just as your Father in heaven is perfect." Some would say that such an ethical standard is humanly impossible to achieve. This may be true, but Jesus did teach these things to his disciples, with the promise that they would be assisted by him; he did not mean it to apply to those who choose to live apart from him. Further, his teaching on the necessity for abiding in him as branches abide in a vine[23] suggests that the living out of such high ethical or moral standards can only come through a close intimate relationship with him, analogous to that of the mother and infant. His emphasis on love and the practice of love in community encourages and necessitates the elaboration of mature conscience, and therefore should displace superego in the role of moral decision-making. And based upon the closing remark by Jesus on enemy love, perfection is to be found in the practice of love, and that is what, he says, God the Father is like: perfection, inhering in love, even for the enemy. Perfection does not inhere in meticulous adherence to a code. Perhaps communion in the various ways it is practiced by Christians, but always conveying profound intimacy, affords opportunity for connection with Christ in ways analogous to a child with his mother.

I wonder also if attainment of the Jesus morality, i.e. the capacity to respond lovingly to an enemy might be the truly "*highest* of the high mental functions," to parody Kant. Ordinarily, reactions to an enemy will

21. Note: Psychological studies of infants as young as three months of age have demonstrated undeniable evidence of a conscience. The infants consistently choose the puppet that treats the other kindly and refuse the puppet that violates the other. See: *The Nature of Things*, with David Suzuki (CBC Television): Babies—Born to be Good? (Nov. 19, 2016)

22. Matthew 5:38–48.

23. John 15.

be determined by unconscious reflexes: fight, flight, or freeze. To act in response to threatening aggression according to the Jesus ethic demands conscious deliberate choice, and the over-riding of impulses that are ordinarily not only unconscious, but also biologically instinctual. I would suggest that such may only be possible through the kind of steady immersion in close relationship with Jesus (however this may be understood) that serves analogously to Carveth's and Reiner's infant-mother pair.

CHRISTIAN REVOLUTIONARY SUBORDINATION[24]

Many people, it is discovered in the course of clinical psychoanalysis, engage with others according to a pattern that can be described in no other way than subjection or even subjugation. A pattern of self-abnegation in relating to others might be termed masochism. Although Freud saw masochism as the inverse of sadism, and both arising out of disturbed sexuality (whether there is anything *but* disturbed sexuality will be addressed in Chapter 8), a common form of compulsive masochistic self-sacrifice has been referred to as "moral masochism." The moral masochist has typically arrived at this mode of mental life through identification with, commonly, a mother who characteristically portrays herself to her child as suffering and in need of succour.[25] The child experiences a kind of guilt if she (moral masochism is especially common among women) embraces life in a livelier fashion than does her mother, although technically, it would more likely be shame she feels, given our understandings around superego versus conscience. She unconsciously transfers to her relationships with other people the impulse to subjugate her own interests to the interests of the other. Among religious people, including Christians, this unconsciously driven pattern of relating often acquires a form of sanctified community "group-think" approval. It may be seen as reflective of humility, Christ-likeness, godliness, etc. In fact, it is nothing of the kind, insofar as it is not occurring by choice but by compulsion, i.e. unconsciously driven, automatic, enacted out of necessity, and the person feels subject to superego reprimand if they do not subordinate their self.

Lydia has a history of fractured relationships, including a divorce. She is aware, and was aware before entering analysis, that her relationships with men had always gone badly, at least in part because relating to a man meant only relating to him sexually, and the sexuality had to adhere to a script for her, which entailed a subjugation of herself to the man in degrading ways. Of course, masochism is only the flip-side of sadism, and the two

24. "Revolutionary Subordination" is a chapter title in: Yoder, *The Politics of Jesus*.
25. Markson, *Depression*.

always go together, even if it is not obvious. We know already about Lydia's "SS," and, not uncommonly, her sadism that is primarily directed at her own self via the agency of the superego, is externalized onto others. In fact, in some measure she and I have learned, after several episodes of targeting her rageful sadism onto me, that she typically then beats on her own self for jeopardizing her connection to a good object. Masochism, including the moral masochism evident in the case of Carmen, is always accompanied by resentment (because she is never rewarded for her sacrifice as she expects), which, of course, feeds the sadistic side of the equation. Compulsive self-sacrifice is never implemented without resenting it. Carmen has become increasingly aware of the anger she has toward her parents.

The point of these remarks is to illuminate the character of compulsive self-subjugation or masochism as a phenomenon that is not noble or spiritually laudable. When Jesus advocated for loving one's enemies, or going the second mile, or putting the interests of others ahead of oneself, he was speaking of such action arising from a moral agent, as a matter of choice, based upon mature conscience. In keeping with the Jesus ethic, there are many injunctions in the New Testament for Christians to submit, spouses to one another, slaves to masters, subjects to authorities, one person to another. Yoder, whose chapter title, "Revolutionary Subordination," delineates Christian submission as an ethical imperative of Jesus, and is eager to differentiate this submission from stoicism—Charles Taylor asserts that stoicism might be thought of as the hegemony of reason, the acceptance of what is, with minimal allowance to the passions.[26] Yoder reasons that revolutionary subordination is neither slavish obedience to a philosophy of stoical acceptance, nor of slavish obedience to dictatorial authorities (and I would say, including an internal dictatorial superego) but rather the outworking "of a free ethical agent when he voluntarily accedes his subordination in the power of Christ instead of bowing to it fatalistically or resentfully."[27] Such an exercise of agency would be in identification with Christ's refusal to exercise the divine power available to him in order to achieve the greater good.[28] As Yoder sees it, "The voluntary subjection of the church is a witness to the world."[29]

As a cautionary comment regarding chosen subordination, it is possible that subordination can be in the service of revenge. Loving one's enemy could conceivably be a torment to him: "dumping burning coals onto his

26. Taylor, *Sources of the Self.*
27. Yoder, *The Politics of Jesus,* 191.
28. Philippians 2:5–8.
29. Ibid., 190.

head."[30] It is said of Nietzsche that he claimed Christian love constitutes supreme violence. While this could be true, perhaps a function of moral agency is that one constantly assesses one's own motives, even in regard to the exercise of love toward an enemy. True love for the enemy, while demanding effort to minimize the element of a Nietzscian vengeance, can never truly achieve purity, since purity of motive for anything is humanly unattainable. Even so, who would not prefer the "supreme violence" of Christian love over the supreme violence of torturous execution?

PAUL'S ENDORSEMENT OF CONSCIENCE OVER SUPEREGO

In Romans 14, Paul explicates a "law of liberty" and a "law of love." He is advising on how Christians ought to govern themselves as people living within community. He recognizes and values differences of view as to what traditions and practices one esteems worthy of maintaining, but also differentiates what constitutes a moral imperative and what does not. While his focus is on the individual's freedom of conscience before Christ, he also advocates for a willing submission and relinquishment of that freedom if to do otherwise is to cause a "brother" to stumble, i.e. to act against his own standards, whether they be superego- or conscience-determined. The exercise of love would (according to the Jesus ethic) lead to putting the brother's well-being ahead of the gratification of one's own preferences. In verse 22, Paul says, "Do you have faith? Have it to yourself before God. Happy is he *who does not condemn himself* [by the agency of the superego] *in what he approves* [by virtue of conscience]" (Emphasis mine). We moderns have simply devised new terminology and delineated the categories of psychic dimension for this vital distinction which Paul was able to articulate long ago. I don't imagine that he was restricting his message to the matter of what may be eaten (although food choice was in focus), but was expressing a timeless principle, one that would transcend the specifics of the ancient religious concerns with acceptable foods.

TRUE KNOWING

I want to draw the reader's attention to some verses in 1 Corinthians 8:1–3:

> Now concerning things offered to idols: We know that we all have knowledge. Knowledge puffs up, but love edifies. And if anyone

30. Romans 12:20; quoted from Proverbs 25:21, 22.

thinks that he knows anything, he knows nothing yet as he ought to know. But if anyone loves God, this one is known by Him.

If one reads the subsequent verses in that chapter, he will find further support and explication of Paul's Romans 14 argument about the exercise of mature conscience, and voluntary submission. The first three verses, however, as quoted, strike me as having pertinence to our thesis about conscience versus superego, and the relevance to knowing, to knowledge, and thinking. Perhaps Paul is referring to having knowledge about food sacrificed to idols having no particular contaminating relevance for a Christian, since he knew that Jesus had said that it is not what goes into a man that defiles, but what comes from the heart. Paul's concern seems to be that this knowledge, i.e. this personal insight as to one's moral freedom, in the absence of being paired with a mature conscience of love, is ripe for the exercise of arrogant dominance over another—"He does not yet know as he ought to know." If, as per Reiner, we perceive a progression, from a more primitive superego dominated mind (albeit alongside a primordial, as yet undeveloped conscience) toward one organized by a developed and refined conscience, thus birthing, as it were, the mind, then Paul's "as he ought to know" might indeed refer to this birth, psychologically.

"But the man who loves God is known by God." What does this mean, and how does it pertain to the preceding verses? Perhaps since to love God is to be known by God, there is implied a necessary, corresponding humility. Maybe the stage is then set for loving the other, and abandoning the competitive eye-for-eye superego mindset in favor of conscience and its attendant *real* knowledge.

Before closing this chapter I wish to consider an example that psychologist, David Benner cites in rightly advocating for the principle that Christian spirituality "involves a transformation of the self that occurs only when God and self are both deeply known."[31] He tells the story of a well-known pastor who had enjoyed a very successful ministry, but who lacked self-knowledge. His knowledge of God, however, was acknowledged to be wide, and his public deportment was thought to reflect his inner experience. Benner says,

> Suddenly the gap between his inner reality and external appearance was exposed. Things that he did not know or accept about himself welled up within him and shattered the illusion his life had represented. Lust led to sexual involvement with a woman he was counselling, just as greed had earlier led to misuse of

---

31. Benner, *The Gift of Being Yourself,* 22.

church funds. . . . his life . . . was a lie that grew from the soil of self-ignorance.[32]

The man's extensive knowledge of God and of himself, Benner says, lacked a transformational quality because it was intellectual and did not penetrate to a personal, emotionally engaged level. For example, the man believed God to be forgiving, but did not know this as an experiential truth. He believed he struggled with:

> sloth—spiritual laziness. He said he had often asked God to for-give him for not working harder for the kingdom. But confes-sion of such a sin was nothing more than a distraction. It kept his focus (and perhaps he hoped, God's focus) off the deeper things about himself that were so profoundly disordered.[33]

We can see in this example a man who has lived under the dominance of his superego, and has persisted in superego-inflicted self-flagellation, but has done so with the result (and perhaps purpose) of evading guilt. In fact, paradoxically, superego supremacy, as so often occurs, interfered in this man's capacity to engage (and perhaps even to have developed) a function-ing conscience and so he had not been able to experience the guilt that he needed to feel in order to partake of true forgiveness. The man suffered, one could say, from a pathological narcissism which naturally co-exists with a primitive superego that dominates the mind. Superego pathology is all about oneself, whereas conscience considers one's impact on the other.

As Lydia gained familiarity with her inner functions, she increasingly recognized how difficult it had been for her to bear responsibility and feel guilt for her effects on others, because of the dominance of her superego disabling conscience.

There are serious practical implications to these concerns around su-perego versus conscience. How do we, as parents, teach our children? Do we promote more in the way of superego pressures on them with our concerns for how well our children perform, and under-value matters of conscience? Do our schools likewise fail to promote true and mature conscience? In the realm of Christian education, whether at a primary, secondary, or tertiary graduate school level, does a failure to understand and design curricula in accordance with this important superego-conscience distinction lead to Christian leaders whose superego pathology and narcissism are inevitably going to break out in egregious ways eventually on the church?

32. Ibid., 23.
33. Ibid., 25.

Chapter 4

Christianity—Opens Up or Closes Down?

AUTHORITARIAN FUNDAMENTALIST EXPRESSIONS OF Christian faith communities, as with other analogous religious groups, impose some important emotional challenges onto their people, particularly in their childhood years. As I have already suggested earlier, there is a great tendency for religious ideology to become co-opted into the psychopathology of the ardently faithful. Freud argued that all non-psychotic people fall into two main categories of personality structure, hysterical or obsessional; he recognized that there were no pure categories, and so both tend to be combined in any one person, albeit one or the other would tend to predominate. My own impression is that hysterical or obsessional features can variously predominate in a single individual, depending on the prevailing circumstances and stresses experienced at any given time. It may be helpful to remember that both broad descriptions reflect fundamental ways by which an individual has unconsciously established defenses against conflict and its associated anxiety. The person with an obsessional personality may latch onto the teachings of Christianity and pursue them with a dedication and even fanaticism that leads him to alienation from other people who cannot bear his endless attention to detail; his preoccupation with ensuring all is meticulously correct is a manifestation of his stripping it all of emotional tone and hence meaning. Further, he is liable to find the claims of the faith (especially injunctions to be perfect, or holy) ideally suited to his need to attain completeness, to leave no stone unturned, to capture every detail, and to impose his particular biases and emphases onto others i.e. to attain control. He strives for certainty and relates to others as if he has found it, and must convince others of the same. It is very likely that if opportunity arose for a probing of his mind, one would find a strong unconscious impulsion toward omniscience.

While it is well known that strong leaders often display effective leadership out of narcissistic tendencies, what may be less known is that many leaders manifest features of psychopathy. By this, I am referring to their limited capacity for true empathy and interest in the mind of another, possibly accompanied by a limited awareness of and concern for how he might affect others. A capacity for strong leadership often struggles for compatibility with empathy, although a paucity of empathy may reflect what one actually means by "strong leadership." Predominantly obsessional people are liable to suffer from limited empathic capacity. Faith communities and churches are not immune, and unfortunately become heirs to their leaders' psychological pathology.

Of course, other forms of psychopathology can also play out in the leaders of faith communities. Witness the mesmerizing charisma and hysterical drama of Jim Jones and other infamous faith leaders.

Jesus made it clear that he was the Good Shepherd who's privilege it was to protect and even lay down his own life for the preservation of the lives of his flock. In declaring that the "truth shall make you free" and identifying himself as constituting that truth in his own person, such that he could say, "Therefore if the son makes you free, you shall be free indeed,"[1] he gives us reason to embrace life with him as leader with optimism and eager anticipation. And then, so as to make the message even clearer, he contrasts the influence of the thief of sheep with himself: "The thief does not come except to steal, and kill, and to destroy. I have come that they may have life, and that they may have it more abundantly."[2] Consequently, his "sheep" inherit the ease of "going in and out and finding pasture."[3] Poetry beautifully expresses the "mythos" of faith. Jesus contrasts himself and his leadership with those would-be leaders who propound an ideology that is inevitably infused with their own psychopathology and hence steals or seduces people into delusion.

Sadly, for many people within faith communities, the liberty and joyful openness described by Jesus as available to them has, in lived experience, been scarce. One of the reasons for this has been the influence of various forms and/or degrees of what has been called fundamentalism. Karen Armstrong, in her book, *The Battle for God: A History of Fundamentalism*, applies her observations to the sweeping impacts of such movements on the world political stage (as opposed to drilling into the effects of religious fundamentalism on the individual [or the collective] mind). She concludes that,

1. John 8:32 and 36.
2. John 10:10.
3. John 10:9.

Fundamentalism . . . has often lost sight of some of the most sacred values of the confessional faiths. Fundamentalists have turned the *mythos* of their religion into *logos*, either by insisting that their dogmas are scientifically true, or by transforming their complex mythology into a streamlined ideology. They have thus conflated two complementary sources and styles of knowledge which people in the premodern world had usually decided it was wise to keep separate. The fundamentalist shows the truth of this conservative insight. By insisting that the truths of Christianity are factual and scientifically demonstrable, American Protestant fundamentalists have created a caricature of both religion and science. . . . Without the constraints of a "higher," mythical truth [her "mythos"], reason [her "logos"] can on occasion become demonic and commit crimes . . .[4]

Perhaps in reactionary modes to many influences in the post-enlightenment world, Christianity has sought to defend its relevance by abandoning its essence "in the mystery of Christ"[5] in favor of trying to compete in the age of reason. Although Christians need ample reasoning of matters to do with faith, they also need to cling to the "mysterium"; what I mean by this is something to do with the sense of wonder that fuels our passions. Christian spirituality cannot thrive on reason alone. At the core of the Christian message is "Immanuel" (God with us), God uniting with mankind, not by virtue of obedience to a code, but in intimate relationship. Perhaps in uniting with us, I am trying to express that what Christianity has to offer that goes beyond religion is the possibility of a transformational object relationship with the ultimate relational object, God. Instead of closing down one's subjectivity along with the infinitely creative possibilities that may elaborate from the core of oneself (a closing down, as I have described in the obsessional above), relating to and being sufficiently mirrored by the God who embraces endless diversity and possibility in his own being should foster opening up of individual subjectivity.

A similar caution might apply to the hysteric, in whom, according to Delay's Lacanian analysis, which builds on Lacan's axiom, "our desire is the Other's desire," the primary "fantasy aims specifically to be the object of the big Other's desire, an object that is always slipping away and leaving the Other unsatisfied. The hysteric is defiant . . . "[6] And so, the hysteric is unconsciously liable, upon embracing Christian faith to succumb to impulses to excite the desire of God, perhaps in order to be exceptional, never realizing

4. Armstrong, *The Battle for God,* 366, 367. Emphasis hers.

5. Ephesians 3:4.

6. Delay, *God is Unconscious,* 72.

the defiance embedded therein. The tragic Jim Jones character might be an extreme example. By contrast, "The primary fantasy of the obsessive is to imagine she has the type of control the big Other has . . ."[7]

To presume to harness knowledge in the service of certainty concerning things upon which we humans cannot be certain is to, according to Soren Kierkegaard, nullify,

> the God-relationship, . . . to live would become much too easy, but also exceedingly empty . . . Knowledge is the infinite art of equivocation or the infinite equivocation; at its utmost it means precisely to place contrasting possibilities in equilibrium. To be able to do this is to have knowledge, and only he who knows how to communicate contrasting possibilities in equipoise, only he communicates knowledge. To communicate decision in knowledge or knowledge in decision is upside-down . . .[8]

The "crime" of Christian fundamentalism that I want to focus upon is that of communities adopting favorite emphases from scripture upon which they stake their very distinctive existence. They acquire unwarranted certainty about matters that should remain open, equivocal, if you will; they promulgate dogmas that derive from a particular and often peculiar point of view; they fail to appreciate how the Bible was written and for whom it was written and the context in which it was written[9]; because of their need to be right and to be in control of knowledge, they withdraw from debate in the marketplace of ideas, and adopt exclusivity, admitting only those who think the same way they do; they therefore become characterized by and strive for uniformity (albeit in the name of unity); by all of these, they impose foreclosure of self, of subjectivity. They treat their followers and themselves as objects, and not as subjects.

Naomi Klein, Canadian author and activist, quoted on fundamentalism:

> . . . The attributes of every fundamentalist: the desire for purity, a belief in a perfect balance, and every time there are problems identified they are attributed to perversions, distortions within what would otherwise be a perfect system. . . . But I think that anyone who falls in love with [such a] system is dangerous, because the world doesn't comply and then you get angry at the world.[10]

7. Ibid.
8. Kierkegaard, *Works of Love,* 217–18.
9. See Enns, *The Bible Tells Me So.*
10. Klein, 20.

When faith communities become characterized by such features as these, the adults who become fundamentalist parents of children inevitably affect those children. The fundamentalist parent is likely to have come to treat their systematized faith as an ideology from which there must not be any deviation, either by himself, or by his children. The family comes, in effect, to live under an ideologically totalitarian regime. One such parent was once heard to say, in reference to troubles among his adult children and their spouses, "we were just fine until the outsiders [the sons-in-law and daughters-in-law] came in." Clearly the ideal of the purity of the insiders had come to reign in this family. As alluded to above, such families and groups *claim* to espouse community and unity among believers, but, in fact, they foster disunity and division, characterized by all manner of alienation. Take, for example, the daughter-in-law who comes to hear of the above remark; her previously unarticulated, inchoate sense of alienation suddenly comes clear. And maybe this point deserves emphasis: so often such undercurrents of purity-based discriminations among the people affected remain matters of an uneasy *sense*, a feeling of unsafety that is seldom fully recognized for what it is, let lone spoken about. The exclusionary purity mindset is unlikely to be recognized by the perpetrators themselves, and it may only be the fortunate few among the sufferers growing up in such a system who, likely from outside influences giving rise to perspective, can acquire sufficient objectivity to be able to distance from what has been hitherto implicit within their own minds. This is not to say that all persons living within communities characterized by fundamentalist features either suffer or are impaired with respect to their subjective self; many may find themselves comfortably adapted to the norms of the community.

Children of such Christian fundamentalist parents, from very young, will be immersed in the emotional milieu of purity exclusivism. The parents' primary concern for their children may be that they "come to know the Lord" and follow in the "right path," the "narrow road that leads to salvation." A potentially very damaging consequence for the child is that, he may feel that all that is subjective about him has to be filtered, as it were, through the screen of the ideology. His essence, his authentic, emotionally charged idiomatic self may never find the needed mirroring from parents who are themselves subjectively dulled; he does not receive what is required in the interpersonal milieu for elaboration of himself as subject. He may feel himself *visible* (recognized for who he really is) to his parents only insofar as his attributes meet with the approval criteria of the screen. He is likely, then, to accommodate to the environment, since, after all, there is no other context for him (this is his world), in such ways as to develop a "false self."[11] The true, natural self is unlikely to grow under totalitarian ideologies that can only demand conformity, and have to stifle elaboration of an individual, possibly divergent (from the family norm) self. "Soul murder is a crime in which the perpetrator is able to destroy the victim's capacity for feeling joy and love."[12] While soul murder may refer to the results of a particularly devastating abusive form of parental non-recognition, including failure of attunement and adequate responsiveness, the phrase suggests vividly the death that is dealt to a child's vitality by emotional and attitudinal surroundings that demand conformity and are deaf and blind to a child's true needs.

For Christian parents, a fair question may be whether it is possible to "live under the lordship of Christ" without succumbing to sectarian totalizing ideology. In other words, if Christians are called into a life of discipleship to Christ, is it possible for such a life to remain free of ideologies of control, of uniformity and conformity, of violation of idiomatic subjectivity? I will not attempt anything but the briefest of answers. The more I have studied the gospels and the life and words of Jesus, along with the whole of scripture that points ultimately to him, the more I see Jesus embodying a mindset of inclusivity, embrace of diversity, recognition of the unique individuality of the other and love which conveys the highest respect for the inherent value of the other. In his encounter with the Samaritan woman at Jacob's well,[13] Jesus, employing metaphor and culturally specific idioms, identifies a core desire in the woman, that of water that would forever slake her thirst. He does not offer her a systematic ideology or a formula, but a metaphorically accurate response to that for which she sought and felt need; that which might be recognized as truth, personified in himself as the Messiah. In his response to the rich man who sought from him the means of attaining eternal life, previously mentioned in chapter 2, Jesus speaks directly to the core of the man's longings, his desires, and identifies his particular, unique obstructing psychic phenomenon that holds him bound, i.e. his aspiration to be perfect. In his response to the woman caught in adultery,[14] and to the legalists who were intent upon fulfillment of the letter of the law by stoning her, and who wanted to test whether Jesus would situate himself inside or outside of the law, he offered her acceptance, the precise thing she needed, when she herself knew she was condemned. He refused the opportunity to condemn sin and to conform to the legalists represented by the scribes and

11. Winnicott, *The Maturational Process.*

12. Shengold, 121–38.

13. John 4.

14. John 8:1–12.

Pharisees, by telling her, "Neither do I condemn you." His mission was not "to condemn the world, but that the world through Him might be saved."[15] My point here is to demonstrate that Jesus' way was one of invitation to engage with him in ways that allow for the opening up of the self, that foster expansion or growth into the best one can potentially be. His way was not to apply a "one-size-fits-all" ideology that forecloses the elaboration of the self.

Following from this, I think Paul's admonition to would-be disciples is most apt: "Let this mind be in you which was also in Christ Jesus. . . ."[16] I would suggest that the mind of Christ (a mindset of loving openness to the other and oneself) and sectarian totalizing ideology are mutually incompatible.

Mitigating against the tendencies toward violence (whether physical, emotional, or psychological) induced by fundamentalist ideologies, is the appreciation of the narrative character of the pilgrimage into which believers in Christ are called. In describing the hermeneutical strategy of Stanley Hauerwas, Richard Hays says:

> . . . the life of discipleship is necessarily a life "on the road," an unfinished story in which we participate. What the gospel offers is the opportunity to join in a great "common adventure" that gives our lives dignity and meaning. The metaphor of pilgrimage emerges again and again in Hauerwas's work as the most apt description of the church's experience. The story of Israel depicts a journeying people, still awaiting God's fulfillment of his promises, and the church finds itself in the continuation of that journey. This account of Christian existence as life within an unfolding narrative discourages any attempt to formulate a systematic ethic. Our need is not for rules and principles; rather we need *skills* that can be taught us only by those who are more expert in the demanding craft of discipleship.
>
> . . . the church is to be formed by the story of Jesus and by the example of those who have narrated it to us—formed as a "community of character," a people whose life "stands as a political alternative to every nation, witness to the kind of social life possible for those that have been formed by the story of Christ." This alternative is the way of peace, forgiveness, and love of enemies; war and violence must be foreign to the polity of God's people, for "violence derives from the self-deceptive story that we are in control—that we are our own creators—and that only we can bestow meaning on our lives. . . ."[17]

15. John 3:17.

16. Philippians 2:5.

17. Hays, *The Moral Vision of the New Testament*, 258. Emphasis his.

Too many people have been wounded (been victim of a form of violence) by the church's authoritarian literalist interpretations of scripture.

AUTHORITATIVE CLOSURE

In considering the fundamentalist mindset, we can identify some inevitable effects of claims to certainty. So often, alongside certainty, one finds presumptions of simplicity, reflecting a desire to have complex, hidden things prematurely and unwarrantedly clear and unambiguous. What might be the effect of this on others? The impact can constitute forms of trauma if, for the child or an adult whose aspirations to understanding their own mind, the theological claims of their community, the phenomenological world around them, and, perhaps most pertinently, their own disturbing conflictual inner longings, are met with trite cliches, aphorisms, or scriptural quotes which serve only to foreclose all further dialogue. Whether one openly or only tentatively strives to have his questions and confusions heard, and then finds, if not clear answers, at least a dialogue that may help to open further the murkiness, and to thereby feel oneself engaged with a responsive, listening, and maybe even similarly questing other is to experience healthy, generative community. The soul can "sing" when this occurs; there comes a feeling of expansiveness, the thrill of being connected to this important other, gratitude for a sense of belonging, optimism that further openness is available, and even the clear sense that one has been loved. By contrast, when that open quest is met by the other with a scripture quotation that is presumed to amply address the question and whatever nuances may lie beneath it, the aspirant is liable to feel shut down, closed up, and closed out from real, meaningful engagement. Further, there is, potentially, shame generated in the questioner that he would have questions and doubts that are not addressed by what is offered. His internal question of himself might go, "What is faulty about me that I can't be satisfied with an authoritative, simple scriptural answer?" He feels dismissed at best, while at worst, he may feel belittled. Either way, he is not likely to feel loved, understood or opened to his own questioning or to those around him; he may feel resentment and will no doubt close himself up to future encounters. He is likely to close against his *own* inner longings and questions, essentially identifying with the aggressor against himself, i.e. fortifying superego hostility.

Although I do not doubt that answers for many of life's deep and difficult questions can be found in scripture, I think concerns about complex matters that defy simplistic resolutions demand complex, nuanced responses that will most likely leave much remaining open and uncertain, in place of closed finality. To respond with a supposedly authoritative scripture only and to make that the final word, is to, as it were, invoke divine authority and induce in the inquirer abject shutdown. This is traumatic (by definition, a shock that overwhelms the individual's capacities for processing such impact), albeit on a microscopic scale. When parents and communities employ such means, children are exposed to infinite numbers of incremental micro-traumas.[18]

Stephanie

In her late 20's when she first came into therapy, Stephanie had suffered many years with insomnia, for which she was taking medications. She traced the onset of the insomnia to a court case several years earlier, in which her allegations of sexual assault against a man did not yield a verdict of guilt. She had since then been beset by growing anxiety such that in the months prior to her referral for therapy, she felt unable to learn, to apply her professional skills reliably, or to cope with the demands of her life. A suicide attempt had led to the referral.

Stephanie came from a family of Christian parents who, especially when she was young, often loudly argued and fought. She was the youngest child, with two older brothers. She described an unhappy parental marriage situation in which her mother typically denigrated and humiliated her father whose response was to retreat into silence, or, on more than one occasion, to leave the family for a time. She acquired from a very young age a late night habit of listening, on the staircase, for her parents' conflicts with a view, to remedying their faults and achieving restoration of peace and harmony. She describes her early life as cloistered from the world, having to attend not only church, but also the church's school, and hence her entire life was guided by the church's ideology (however much theologically informed). She recalls her childhood queries into matters to do with her body functions, particularly those related to the genitourinary systems, being met with uneasy responses that felt to her to be disconnected, inadequate, and dismissive, whether from her parents or her teachers. Commonly, her efforts to engage her mother in discussion about something vital to her were met with "God-talk," i.e. cliches and aphorisms that were typical of that Christian community and which constituted for her, empty speech. They were bereft of meaning, and lead to foreclosure. Or a verse quoted from scripture would perform the same foreclosing function. There never was any discussion with Stephanie of bodily changes related to sexual maturation, nor of sex, nor of any of the related feelings. In fact, the overall climate of the family and of

---

18. See Alice Miller's *The Drama of the Gifted Child* and others written by Alice Miller.

the church was one of denial of the existence of sexuality and matters of the body, concerns which were so much a part of her reality, and about which she sought understanding in both home and school.

In the context of the therapeutic consulting room, Stephanie reported feeling a comfortable, non-judgemental zone of safety that she had never before experienced. Notwithstanding the relational dysfunctionality in her family, we can see something of the totalitarian nature of the Christian ideology that dominated the minds of Stephanie's parents and the church community of which they were part. The comfort she derived from her sessions in her analyst's office came not only from non-judgment, but also from careful attention to the details of her thoughts and emotions as they were articulated. She was seldom, if ever, given answers by her analyst, but was sustained by the sense that she had a definite and reliable place in the mind of the other that afforded her opportunity to experience and explore having a mind herself. The content of her mind was duly attended to with respect, such that she began to feel herself understood, and not automatically screened out (dismissed) by an ideological filter as she had been with her parents, with whom she still cannot attain a place of understanding occupancy in their minds. If she tries to have her (more empathic) father appreciate that she still is deeply affected by the sexual assault (trauma may be temporally old, but can remain alive as if in the present in the mind and body of the victim), she typically receives a response like, "Do as *I* did, and just leave it at the foot of the cross."

Stephanie has suffered from the alienation that derives from ideological fundamentalism. Her particular response to this has been to form a peculiar, paradoxically binding attachment to her parents, from which she has not been able to free herself. I believe that this is because she has yet to overcome an alienation that was forged within her own self, such that she was never able to establish a sufficiently stable core identity; her primary identity inheres in being the one to remedy her parents' malaise. At the time of the sexual violation, she froze, was unable to protect herself, or in any way to call out for help, which was close by. In effect, her alienation from her own self led to a neglect of herself, replicating thereby, her parents' longstanding neglect of her psychological and emotional self. She has never had a boyfriend, or felt loved as a person from any man that she has been with, the modes of which have been sexually playful engagement in which she is exploited as a willing play thing. She recognizes that she has always sought love in these interactions, but has inevitably substituted the temporarily intoxicating pleasure of being the object of desire. In so doing, she feels herself devalued, and yet has felt unable to do otherwise. What is in the unconscious demands endless repetition. Having unconsciously positioned herself as the magical salve of her parents, she can only repeat the pattern with potential love-objects, who are induced themselves to unconsciously replace the parents in disregarding her subjectivity and treat her as a thing.

When her response of disappointment to the judge's decision at her court case was analyzed, it became apparent that in her mind, someone had to be found guilty, and since the assailant was not, because of the lack of sufficient evidence, she has, via the agency of her punitive superego, deemed herself guilty. Parental neglect of the child's subjectivity is incorporated into the child's superego, rendering it hostile to the child's wellbeing; it will find fault where there is none.

In summary, insofar as fundamentalism adheres to literalist presumptions to know that which cannot actually be known with the clarity and certainty claimed, the hidden, profound nature of God is turned into a caricature. Furthermore, the complexity of people is avoided and they are presumed simple, understood as only conscious straightforward beings; the truth of people is missed by virtue of the rush to make immediate sense, to have tidy stories; these desires "must be suspended, so that God [and the individual mind] is given space and time to bring a profound process to consummation"[19]. In concluding her analysis of Joseph's and Jacob's stories, Gottlieb Zornberg recognizes that explicit, deliberate speech about God and what he is about disavows the hiddenness of God, blocks channels of language, including I would say, one's dialogue with one's own unconscious, and, thereby, paradoxically, closes down true insight, or the truth.

VEERING PAST NORMAL

In exploring the various ways in which psychoanalysis can help us see how Christianity may open up or close down the dynamism of the mind, I want to lean on the ideas of Christopher Bollas on "normotic illness" in *The Shadow of the Object: Psychoanalysis of the Unthought Known*. He refers to

> . . . a particular drive to be normal, one that is typified by the numbing and eventual erasure of subjectivity in favor of a self that is conceived as a material object among other man-made products in the object world.
> . . . A normotic person is someone who is abnormally normal. He is too stable, secure, comfortable and socially extrovert. He is fundamentally disinterested in subjective life and he is inclined to reflect on the thingness of objects, on their material reality, or on "data" that relates to material phenomena.

19. Zornberg, *The Murmuring Deep*, 340.

. . . [The disinterest in the subjective element is] whether it exists in himself or in the other. The introspective capacity has rarely been used. Such a person appears genuinely naive if asked to comment on issues that require either looking into oneself or the other in any depth.

. . . By the subjective element, I mean the internal play of affects and ideas that generates and authorizes our private imaginations, creatively informs our work and gives continuing resource to our interpersonal relations.[20]

While Bollas does not attempt to define what the normal is to which the normotic feels driven, if we think about this trend toward normal in the context of Christians trying to live their lives in obedience to God, we might consider the plentiful injunctions in the New Testament to pattern one's life after those of Christ,[21] and Paul.[22] The term "imitate" means to take as a model, to try to follow the manner, style, etc. of, or to pretend to be, or to impersonate or mimic, or duplicate.[23] Paul is explicit: "Imitate me, just as I also imitate Christ" and "Therefore be imitators of God, as dear children."[24] His intent is that followers of Christ learn to imitate Christ, or Paul as a surrogate "father" in place of Christ, and who was, in effect, their spiritual father; his concern is that they conform to the distinctive character of Jesus the way a child comes to manifest the character and stylistic manner of his father/parent. The risk is that, especially since the model to be imitated is not materially present, is invisible and therefore only knowable through the written word (albeit knowing is understood to come also through communion (or the eucharist) and through discipling with the community of believers), insofar as there is a tendency toward the fundamentalist style of certain, clear, unambiguous knowing, when this is coupled with the drive to be normal, the conditions are ripe for Bollas's "normosis." The wish to be normal is powerful in people. Adolescents loathe to be found markedly different from their peers. I am asked all the time by patients how they can become "normal."

Stephanie suffers from the pressure to be normal that was exerted upon her by her normotic parents and Christian community; it could be said that the cry of her heart was one of desperately wanting to acquire a

20. Bollas, *The Shadow of the Object,* 135–37.

21. Luke 6:40 "Everyone who is perfectly trained will be like his teacher"; John 13:14–15 "For I have given you an example, that you should do as I have done to You"; Romans 8:29, "For whom He foreknew, He also predestined to be conformed to the image of His Son. . . ."

22. 1 Corinthians 4:15–16 ". . . for in Christ, I have begotten you in the gospel. Therefore I urge you, imitate me."

23. *The Collins Concise Dictionary,* 562.

24. 1 Corinthians 11:1 and Ephesians 5:1.

subjectivity (or perhaps to discover the as yet buried subjectivity that had been neglected for the sake of "normal"). If Christian parents have, themselves, a drive to be abnormally normal that has been inculcated by their experience of their particular close community that upholds a plastic Jesus who is to be imitated in accordance with scripted directives, then their capacity to "see" not only their own unique selves, but also the idiomatic self of their child becomes severely limited to that which aligns with the requirements of the template. Bollas says,

> At the most fundamental level the normotic was only partly seen by the mother and the father, mirrored by parents whose reflective ability was dulled, yielding only the glimmer of an outline of self to a child.
>
> . . . I am not arguing that normotic adults inevitably produce normotic children.
>
> . . . Perhaps the difference between normotic children and those who emerge into health (or neurosis [psychoanalysts understand normality to consist in the ordinary state of neurosis, i.e. none of us is free from troubling conflict or interactional patterns]) is that some children find a way to be mirrored even if the parents are not providing this. By finding their reflections elsewhere they internalize a mirroring function and utilize intrasubjective dialogues as alternatives to interpersonal play. They develop an introspective capacity, and life for them will be meaningful even if incomplete.
>
> . . . It may be . . . that the child's disposition to be emptied of self reflects his own death drive, an activity that can only be successful, in my view, if the parents wish it to be. Parent and child organize a foreclosure of the human mentality. They find a certain intimacy in shutting down life together, and in mastering existence with the unconscious skill of a military operation. Because the normotic person fails to symbolize in language his subjective states of mind, it is difficult to point to the violence in this person's being, yet it is there, not in his utterances, but in his way of shutting life out.[25]

It is a diabolical paradox to consider that the very gospel that proclaims the offer of life as a fountain of living water could be distorted into an ideology that can so deform minds that it becomes the means of death. Could it be that widespread impressions of this kind of deadening "Christianity," serve to repel people from it? Of course, as with most mental phenomena, normosis, too is not a matter of an either/or occurrence, but rather one

25. Bollas, *Shadow of the Object,* 142–43.

of degree of capacity to feel and know one's own desire, imaginations, and creativity. The more one has succumbed to pressures to accommodate, to whatever script for normal, the less likely one is to find a sense of possessing a rich subjectivity. Christian parents may be more susceptible than others to fear of the core drives of aggression and sexuality that strive for expression in their child. They may then attempt to curtail the possibilities of such expression by carefully programming all aspects of the child's life, according to the script that occupies their minds. They will not risk:"The child's creative invention of life is not encouraged."[26]

Bollas, in describing the case of Tom, identifies the sense of isolation Tom experienced following a suicide attempt, an isolation reinforced by the family leadership pattern of his father:

> . . . for his father led the family with cliches about how strong people put things behind them. As the interview progressed, we were all moved by the utter failure of Tom's family to *think* about what they had all been through.[27]

A particularly common tendency I have observed among Christians, as per the experience of Stephanie, above, is to employ cliches or what is often referred to as "God-talk" which may include quotes of scripture in place of *thinking*. This pattern constitutes a form of avoidance of the hard work of dealing with potentially distressing mental products. The recipient of thought-destruction often has not learned to be able to think and is in need of another who can think along with him. The psychoanalytic clinical encounter aims at precisely that.

> When the thinking capacity of the parts of the personality in conversation with one another proves inadequate to the task of thinking one's troubling experience, the minds of two separate people are required for thinking one's previously unthinkable thoughts.[28]

This quote comes after the author, Ogden, notes the essential role of the (m)other in inscribing into the mind of the child the capacity to tolerate one's own affectively charged thoughts so as to be able to think. Quoting Bion:

> As a realistic activity [i.e. an actual interaction involving two people] it [the infant's contribution to the projective identification] shows itself as behavior reasonably calculated to arouse in

26. Ibid., 145.
27. Ibid, 149. Emphasis his.
28. Ogden, *Bion's Four Principles,* 21.

the mother feelings of which the infant wishes to be rid. If the infant feels that it is dying [i.e., feels as if he is losing his rudimentary sense of self as a consequence of his inability to cope with his disturbing emotional experience] it can arouse fears that it is dying in the mother. A well-balanced mother can accept these and respond therapeutically; that is to say in a manner that makes the infant feel that it is receiving its frightened personality [no longer dissolving or fragmenting] back again but in a form that it can tolerate—the fears are manageable by the infant personality.[29]

Although in this work, Ogden and Bion are pointing to the faults that can impair thinking such that the person opts for *magical* thinking in contrast to *reality-based* thinking, Bollas' normotic succumbs to the same faulty processes, but in the opposite direction, i.e. too normal, or too much "reality." When Christians embrace forms of simplistic theology as their sole reality in the ways outlined in this work, the reality they attempt to force into their children may serve as a nucleus for magical thinking; i.e. the ideals and principles of Christian theology can only facilitate personality growth if they are integrated with a capacity to truly think about one's own subjectivity and that of others. And this presumes that the ideals and principles of Christian theology have not themselves been "thingified," i.e. rendered rigid, oppressive dogma that stifle, rather than foster growth of the mind.

29. Ibid., 20.

Chapter 5

Religion or Relationship

QUALIFYING RELIGION

MANY CHRISTIANS WILL CLAIM that Christianity is not a religion, and is therefore distinct from other world religions. The basis for their claim is that to truly be Christian is to enter into a relationship with Christ as a living, sentient being that is liberated from the hallmarks that typically characterize religion. They would view the organizational trappings, the constructed patterns of engaging in worship and the accumulated traditions with their rules for conduct as constituting religion. One might begin to conceptualize a religious Christianity as distinct from a religionless Christianity, sometimes referred to as Christian spirituality.

One clear meaning of the term religion is the reference to a system of belief involving an invisible and supernatural being. The Collins Concise Dictionary:

1. belief in, worship of, or obedience to a supernatural power or powers considered to be divine or to have control of human destiny.

2. any form or institutionalized expression of such belief: the Christian religion.

3. the attitude and feeling of one who believes in a transcendent controlling power or powers.

4. Chiefly R.C. Church. the way of life entered upon by monks and nuns: to enter religion.

5. something of overwhelming importance to a person: football is his religion.

Another common meaning inherent in the word religion is, as per item 4, the adherence to a way of life, a system of beliefs, perhaps an ideology, and to a code of conduct that is embedded in that system. As per item 5, a person's stated religion may not align with that which takes pre-eminent place in the ways in which he invests his attitudes, feelings and values in actuality. And, of course, as per item 2, it is plain that many who would refer to themselves as Christians (or Muslims or Jews, etc.) may, out of customary usage, societal norms, and circumstances of birth, view their Christianity as little more than form, a matter of identification with an institution. The followers of Jesus in the New Testament were those of his disciples who walked closely with him for roughly three years, or those who came to believe in him as the Son of God through some form of transforming contact with him, or those who came to believe in him in such a way as to form a relationship with him through the oral or written accounts of others. According to the Book of Acts, Saul, who became Paul, had the unique experience of a dramatic transforming encounter with Jesus that changed everything for him and for the world.[1] When I speak of Christians in this chapter, I will be referring to the group identified by Jesus in speaking to Thomas, who insisted he could not believe in the resurrected Christ without seeing and touching for himself; Jesus said, "Blessed are those who have not seen and yet have believed."[2]

Dietrich Bonhoeffer, while imprisoned in Nazi Germany, struggled with efforts to articulate his growing appreciation of Christianity as religionless. Upon declaring that God uniquely presents himself in the world and offers his help to us in Christ as weak, powerless and suffering, he says:

> This is the decisive difference between Christianity and all religions. Man's religiosity makes him look in his distress to the power of God as a *Deux ex machina*. The Bible however directs him to the powerlessness and suffering of God; only a suffering God can help.[3]

He goes on further to emphasize that to be a Christian one must fully embrace and live life in the world:

> He must live a "Worldly" life and so participate in the suffering of God. He *may* live a worldly life as one emancipated from all false religions and obligations. To be a Christian does not mean to be

1. See Acts 9.
2. John 20:29.
3. Bonhoeffer, *Letters and Papers,* 122. Emphasis his.

religious in a particular way, to cultivate some particular form of
asceticism (as a sinner, a penitent or a saint), but to be a man. It
is not some religious act which makes a Christian what he is, but
participation in the suffering of God in the life of the world.[4]

He later wrote of having thought for a long time that he, "could acquire
faith by trying to live a holy life. . . ."[5] Accordingly, he expressed some concern
about the dangers of his earlier work, written during that time, *The Cost of
Discipleship*, a book I read as a young man, and felt deeply influenced by.

In this chapter, I will attempt to explore some aspects of the believing
Christian's experience of relationship with Jesus, employing some elements
of psychoanalytic theories in order to hopefully shed light on how a religionless faith might look. I referred above to the dangers inherent in the
injunctions to imitate, and to the possibility of viewing Jesus in a plastic, i.e.
stamped out, molded, predictable, and definable form. This latter would, in
effect, serve as an image, adherence to which and worship of which might
qualify as idolatry—no different from that highlighted in Psalm 135:15–18:

> The idols of the nations are silver and gold, The work of men's
> hands. They have mouths, but they cannot speak; Eyes they
> have, but they do not see; They have ears, but they do not hear;
> Nor is there any breath in their mouths. Those who make them
> are like them; So is everyone who trusts in them.

Taking scripture's overall view, one gets the strong impression that
drifting toward idolatry is an inherent tendency in mankind. Sincere Christians are no less liable than others to this fallacy, and insofar as they dimin-
ish the living reality of Jesus Christ into a shrunken predictable, tamed and
lifeless mould, they, according to Psalm 135, similarly deaden themselves.

ALIVE RELATIONALITY

So, if I take as premises items 1 and 3 from the Collins definitions above as
applicable to Christianity, albeit with the caveat that "control" be replaced by
"influence," such that God has influence, but does not control so as to rule
out a significant measure of human free will and autonomy, then Christianity qualifies as a religion. If, at the same time, Christianity is fundamentally
a relationship, then we are inferring something more dynamic, mutually
influencing and reciprocal than a simple sense of top-down control from a
distant deity.

4. Ibid., 123. Emphasis his.
5. Ibid., 125.

Regardless of the particular psychoanalytic model of mind development that one considers, the nurture portion of the aphoristic "nature vs. nurture" complex is considered powerfully determinative of adult mental and relational life. Recall Harlow's famous experiments with monkeys which inevitably drew close to the comforting cloth surrogates, in preference to the wire ones, even though the latter dispensed milk. And recall the tragic findings that orphaned human infants deprived of warm human interaction end up dying. And so, psychoanalysis, regardless of the model, recognizes the early nurturant relationship as crucial: the subject, whether treating the other as the object upon which the instincts focus their aim (Freud), or whether internalizing impressions of the other(s) to create an internal populated world (Klein), or whether generating implicit knowledge of relational function (Kohut, Stolorow, and others), or whether inscribing untranslatable enigmatic messages from the (m)other into the (sexual) unconscious (Laplanche), from the beginning of life, forms his mental constructs from his engagement with others. One author, writing about the essential interactional elements in development, put it thus: "Paradoxically, the only way to become oneself is through participating in shared intentional directions with others."[6] The social, emotional, psychological environment in which one develops is powerfully determinant of the personality and character of the adult. Hence, clinical psychoanalytic work explores, among other emergent elements, the details of mnemic, or forgotten memory traces of relational experience, long ago relegated to the unconscious, as they emerge in the consulting room. Generally most important are the emergence of unconscious relational configurations repeating themselves in the relationship that exists between the analytic patient and his psychoanalyst, the phenomenon called transference.

Transference, although universal to all human interpersonal interactions, is uniquely attended to in a psychoanalytic work, as the matrix within which transformation can really take root. The reason for this is that what is transferred from the unconscious of the patient onto the person of the analyst are elements of the patient's past experience of significant others, along with the associated raw emotions, in ways that can be recognized and worked with in detail by the trained analyst. These perceptions, ideas, fantasies, and emotions emanating from the mind of the patient are then explored as mutually shared experience by two people who are present in the same room, and who have contracted to engage in the analytic enterprise of the patient's psyche. Of course there is and needs to be asymmetry between the two, with the analyst

6. Nahum, *The Something More*, 715.

preserving abstinence[7] and neutrality,[8] lest the engagement devolve into a socially typical relationship of mutually gratifying or, alternatively, conflictual experiences. The analyst, too, has his own transferences (called countertransferences) that need to be recognized, managed, and deployed skillfully in the service of the analysis. He is prepared for the taxing demand for conscious and deliberate self-awareness of his own transferences by his own analysis, which is a required integral part of his training.

Let me, then, apply some of these principles to the relationship between a person and Jesus. Is a Christian's ostensibly "real" relationship with God more than an expression of residual infantile fantasied longing for the perfect father or mother? Is it more than a projection of his own needs onto an invisible perfect "magic object," the exercise of which is directed toward compensation for his own imperfections and deficiencies? How might a relationship with God, in the person of Jesus Christ, compare with human relationships, of which psychoanalysis has a lot to say?

Christian life begins, as does human physical life, with birth. It was in the context of Jesus' discussion with the ruling pharisee Nicodemus that he uttered these famous words:

> Most assuredly, I say unto you, unless one is *born again*, he cannot see the kingdom of God. . . . That which is born of the flesh is flesh, and that which is born of the Spirit is spirit. . . . The wind blows where it wishes and you hear the sound of it, but cannot tell where it comes from and where it goes. So is everyone who is born of the Spirit.[9]

Nicodemus might have spoken on behalf of all of us: "How can these things be?" Paul refers to the phenomenon of new life in Christ as a mystery,[10] encompassing previously hidden references in Old Testament stories and prophecies, and the breakdown of divisions between Jew and Gentile. What is mysterious is the possibility of new birth even when one is old. The metaphor of progressive growth and development depicted as birth, childhood, adolescence, and adulthood weaves itself throughout the

---

7. Laplanche and Pontalis, *The Language of Psychoanalysis,* 2: Abstinence from gratification of either his own stimulated longings or those of his patient, so that, "The patient finds as few substitutive satisfactions for his symptoms as possible."

8. Ibid., 271: Neutrality with respect to "religious, ethical and social values—that is to say, he must not direct the treatment according to some ideal, and should abstain from counselling the patient; he must be *neutral* too as regards manifestations of transference . . . 'Do not play the patient's game' . . . ."

9. John 3:3, 6, 8. Emphasis mine.

10. Ephesians 1,3; and Colossians 1:27.

New Testament scriptures to convey the maturational experience of new spiritual life analogous to the developmental path of physical life.

If we focus our vision of early mental life development through the lens offered by Jean Laplanche and remind ourselves of the "fundamental anthropological situation," that is, the unavoidable asymmetry between the infant who has, as yet, no unconscious, and the (m)other who has a sexual unconscious and who inevitably conveys messages to her infant which are not only outside her own awareness, but are also significantly untranslatable by the infant, then we can draw some parallels to relating to Jesus. Laplanche called his theory, after Freud, "The General Theory of Seduction," because the mother cannot help but function, with all the ways in which she engages with her infant, as a seducer. What is meant by this is that her touches, her caring caresses, her warmth, her skin, her softness, her breasts, her soothing tones in speech, her scent, her taste, etc., all are infused with her own unconscious sexuality and sensuality, and all of which are very pleasing (exciting) to the infant. Sexuality here is meant to express the existence of desire for the other, arousal from baseline that is not necessarily specifically genital, but is nevertheless directed libidinously toward uniting one to the (m)other. This is sexuality writ large, i.e. beyond, but not excluding, familiar genitally-focused sexuality. In so many ways, the mother presents an exciting mystery to the infant who can only partially decode and inscribe into his own psyche the enigmatic messages emanating from her. Laplanche claims that it is through repression of the untranslatable bits of her transmitted sexual unconscious that the infant forms his own (sexual) unconscious. So, the reader may by now perceive that the "sexual" unconscious has to do with inevitable arousals of desire with the manifold physiological, drive components, and emotional accompaniments that are inherent in all interpersonal engagement and which get laid down in early life in the context of the "fundamental anthropological situation."

If we accept the scriptural claim that Jesus was in fact God incarnate, and if he could not have had an unconscious quite like that of the rest of humanity, then when a person awakens to the stirrings in his soul that direct his attention to God, in the person of Christ he enters a somewhat analogous asymmetrical relationship. Jesus, in the Nicodemus encounter, refers to the soul stirrings that impel a person to seek after Christ as deriving from the activity of the Holy Spirit, the third person of the trinity. The asymmetry structures around the fact that Jesus has all the attributes commonly ascribed to God: power (omnipotence), knowledge (omniscience), holiness (absence of defilement), complete self-sufficiency. Man, on the other hand, has only incomplete, derivative power and knowledge, can only embrace self-deception in reference to his tragic frailties, and is finite and dependent.

Man's transformational coming-to-know engagement with Jesus has to rely on the scriptural accounts of Jesus' life, his words, his relationships with other people, and with his heavenly father. Prayer is recognized as the mode of conversing with God, and although apparently one-sided, perhaps the words of God are "spoken" in ways that go beyond the written words of scripture. "In the beginning was the Word . . . All things were made through Him. . . ."[11] His speech is inscribed in Christ and in creative action and perhaps in creative interaction.

Laplanche's model squarely focuses on the mother as unwitting seducer, in her being an exciting other for the infant/child. I will argue that God, the trinitarian Christian God, analogously serves as seducer of the hearts and minds of man. The following few paragraphs digress briefly to lay the groundwork for what follows.

DESIRE, SEXUALITY, AND SPIRITUALITY

> Hope deferred makes the heart sick, but when *desire* comes, it is a tree of life.[12]

Desire exists, humanly, because of our profound sense of lack. Peter Rollins said:

> . . . we shall use the term *sacred-object* to describe whatever it is we think will fill this lack, whether that be money, health, a relationship, or religious practice.[13]

Romantic, intimate, sexual relationship is perhaps most subject to attributions of "the sacred-object." If orgasmic experience represents the epitome of pleasure and ecstasy, then it makes sense that sexual intimacy is subject to being freighted with intense expectations of magical powers for satisfying our lack. In the later chapter on sexuality, I will acknowledge the impossibility of sex ever actually delivering on what we expect of it, and I will address reasons why. Ti.po.ta.[14] has a You Tube musical video which poignantly illustrates the wonder of playful, sensuous, delightful, sunshiny, romantic relationship, as portrayed in the video portion, juxtaposed with the lyrics which shift to moonlight (only a reflection of sunlight), shadow, longing for the magical other, and frustration thereof. It poetically alludes to the inevitability of

11. John 1:1–3.
12. Proverbs 13:12. Emphasis mine.
13. Rollins, *The Divine Magician*, 13. Emphasis his.
14. https://www.youtube.com/TI.PO.TA.—Moonlight Avenue.

disappointment as a manifestation of the death drive that ultimately shuts down the frustrations of yearnings that can never be fulfilled.

According to the Proverb (referred to above) writer, possibly Solomon, the absence of desire is a sickness. Psychoanalysts know about a kind of sick deadness that can pervade a person's mind/soul when there is no apparent desire alive in that person.

> Cursed is the man who trusts in man And makes flesh his strength, Whose heart departs from the Lord. For he shall be like a shrub in the desert, And shall not see when good comes, But shall inhabit the parched places in the wilderness, In a salt land which is not inhabited. Blessed is the man who trusts in the Lord, And whose hope is the Lord. For he shall be like a tree planted by the waters, Which spreads out its roots by the river.[15]

Jeremiah, writing the "word of the Lord," similarly asserts the dry deadness that descends when hope or trust or desire is perverted. His emphasis is that desire rightly and primarily focussed on the Lord is the source of life.

> They [the children of men] are abundantly satisfied with the fulness of Your house, And you give them drink from the rivers of Your pleasures, For with You is the fountain of life; In Your light we see light.[16] . . . Delight yourself also in the Lord, And He shall give you the desires of your heart.[17]

A picture develops of God himself being the ultimate object of desire and his things, that which is of him, serving as satisfaction of man's cravings for fulness.

> Blessed are those who hunger and thirst for righteousness, For they shall be filled.[18]

> Let us walk properly, as in the day, not in revelry and drunkenness, not in lewdness and lust, not in strife and envy. But put on the Lord Jesus Christ, and make no provision for the flesh, to fulfill its lusts.[19]

Not surprisingly, the New Testament refines the ideal and primary object of desire onto the person of Jesus. Paul, in the last quote, urges Christians

15. Jeremiah 17:5–8.

16. Psalm 36:8, 9.

17. Psalm 37:4.

18. Matthew 5:6.

19. Romans 13:13, 14.

against debasement of desire into the fulfillment of "fleshly lusts." He sets up a commonly used construct in the epistles, of conflict between the flesh and the spirit. More will be said about this in Chapter 8.

The overall message of the Bible is that God is the source of life and that life consists in the experience of desire, specifically and ultimately in desire for life, for God himself as the source of life. And Jesus did not just teach about and offer to give life, he also claimed to *be* life.[20] The term *desire* implies lack, the experience of deficiency and the longing for something more, perhaps for completeness. In that desire derives from a discrepancy between what is and what might be, it consists in a powerful driving or motivating force directed toward filling the lack. Desire also suggests need that demands supply from outside oneself. And so, just as the infant finds in his mother an exciting, satisfying, plentiful, and yet also, at times, frustrating and enigmatic object of desire, so the person who awakens to his need of Jesus Christ finds in him a similarly exciting, satisfying, plentiful, and at times frustrating and enigmatic object of desire.

Sarah Coakley, in introducing her thesis exploring the "question of the trinitarian God," recognizes:

> the necessary and *intrinsic* entanglement of human sexuality and spirituality in such a quest: the questions of right contemplation of God, right speech about God, and right ordering of desire all hang together. They emerge in primary interaction with Scripture, become intensified and contested in early Christian tradition, and are purified in the crucible of prayer. Thus the problem of the Trinity cannot be solved without addressing the very questions that seem least to do with it, questions which press on the contemporary Christian churches with such devastating and often destructive force: questions of sexual justice, questions of the meaning and stability of gender roles, questions of the final theological significance of sexual desire.[21]

Coakley strives to establish a

> trinitarian *ontology of desire*—a vision of God's trinitarian nature as both source and goal of human desires, as God intends them. It indicates how God the "Father," in and through the Spirit, both stirs up, and progressively chastens and purges, the frailer and often misdirected desires of humans, and so forges them by stages of sometimes painful growth, into the likeness of His Son.[22]

20. John 11:25; John 14:6.
21. Coakley, *God, Sexuality and the Self,* 1–2. Emphasis hers.
22. Ibid., 6. Emphasis hers.

She argues that desire begins with God, and that the relationships among the three trinitarian entities comprising God are characterized by desire. For her, sexual desire is "the 'precious clue' woven into our created being reminding us of our rootedness in God."[23] I take this to mean that for her, human sexual desire constitutes a uniquely human signifier of having been created in the image of God, and that sexuality is a vital "clue" to that special status among all of creation. Accordingly, I must quote her further:

> . . . Freud must be—as it were—turned on his head. It is not that physical 'sex' is basic and 'God' ephemeral; rather, it is God who is basic, and 'desire', the precious clue that ever tugs at the heart, reminding the human soul—however dimly—of its created source. Hence . . . *desire is more fundamental than 'sex'*. It is more fundamental, ultimately, because desire is an ontological category belonging to god, and only secondarily to humans as a token of their createdness 'in the image'. But in God, 'desire', of course signifies no *lack*—as it manifestly does in humans. Rather, it connotes that plenitude of longing love that God has for God's own creation and for its full and ecstatic participation in the divine, trinitarian, life.[24]

RELATING TO GOD

We have considered the natural human situation of birth with its asymmetry premised upon the unconscious of the mother and the absence of same in the infant. Further, we have touched upon the all-to-often clichéd idea of re-birth arising from the story of Nicodemus and his encounter with Jesus. We have also considered briefly, the matter of sexuality, in its "large" sense existing within the Godhead, i.e. among the persons of the trinity. I might now suggest how desire, emanating from God as his yearning for reciprocal love for, and received from his own creation, forms the ground of a relationship based upon God as the seducer of mankind. We do not need to posit an unconscious in the mind of God as there is in the mind of the life-giving mother, but we do perceive that man is,

> Moved, captivated by divine messages that escape his full understanding, [and so Adam] lives henceforth with these unconscious transmissions implanted within him. . . . The child receives the impact of the other in all her beauty; he is dazzled

23. Ibid., 309.
24. Ibid., 10. Emphasis hers.

by a light beyond his comprehension. The alienness of the other is registered; its unassimilable, stimulating message is locked within. From now, the child will be haunted, decentered by his own unconscious life. In Freud's words, "The ego is not master in his own house."[25]

In this quote, the author moves smoothly from a consideration of the impact of God's spoken messages to Adam in the Garden of Eden, to the infant child's internalization of the exciting untranslatable messages emanating from the mother in such a way as to see how the "strangeness" of the other implants into the self. To engage as a twenty-first century person with the incarnate God, Jesus Christ, is to engage with the (alien, strange, yet dazzling) Other. Far from the plastic portrayal of certainties regarding the person of a familiar Jesus that the fundamentalists would offer, the Jesus of the Bible is, while comprehensible, also incomprehensible. Regardless of whose first-century eyes one looks at him through, whether his disciples', or the religiously upright pharisees', or his parents', or the Roman authorities', he consistently defies their expectations, their presumptions as to his predictability. His otherness exceeds efforts at taming or containing him within familiar constructs. He is enigmatic and without equal. And particularly since his own desire is so compellingly manifest as love, even for his enemies,[26] there stirs in man a corresponding desire that, unlike God's desire, is rooted in need, vulnerability, lack, finitude, and limitedness.

Just as we need to be wary of formulating a stamped-out caricature of Jesus that embodies our wishes to control, measure, and have certainty, so individual Christian believers need to resist, in becoming faithful, abandoning their own idiomatic unique and particular self in favor of conformity to some artificial standard of acceptability. Jesus' mode of interaction with the many people who encountered him in the gospels was varied and unpredictable. Some who were healed were told to remain silent, some were told to go tell their priest, and some were told to go and tell their townsfolk. His impeccable perception of what was needed by an individual caused Jesus to attune his intervention with him so as to touch that person where he was most vulnerable (recall the rich young man). While the beauty and power of the gospel lies in the invitation to enter relationship with God through Jesus Christ "as one is," i.e. without prior self improvement, it is both exciting and daunting to realize that one will be changed; it would be impossible to experience an authentic encounter with the Other without being altered.

25. Zornberg, *The Murmuring Deep*, xv.
26. John 15:13, coupled with Romans 5:8–10.

The infant born into this world has no choice but to reckon with the (m)other. The person who is enticed by God to partake in spiritual re-birth does have choice: he may refuse to relinquish his self-determined efforts directed toward ensuring his acceptability (to his own superego, to his community, to his parental imagoes), in effect resisting the inevitable transforming influence of the penetration into his mind of the alien (albeit loving, benevolently empathic, and merciful) God, however dazzlingly exciting he may appear to be. Narcissistic pride which serves as cover for shame which in turn covers for intolerable vulnerability can serve as a blockade to the openness demanded for new birth. Such universally experienced emotions can lead to all manner of efforts to master by grasping after control and certainty. Gottlieb Zornberg puts it thus:

> Seduction, of course, contains a traumatic element—the break-in from the outside, which becomes an inner "foreign body" and now breaks out from within [referring to the breaking through the repression barrier of that which is unconscious]. "Laplanche's essence of the human soul," writes Adam Phillips, "is a traumatic but unavoidable . . . receptivity to the other . . . Too open, [it] learns forms of closure." This is the "ineluctable narcissistic closure of the apparatus of the soul," which attempts to master, to translate those seductive messages. Constructing coherent narratives in which the trauma is domesticated is one such form of closure. Psychoanalysis offers an opportunity to reopen the relation to the enigmatic and traumatic order.[27]

I contend that Christian "re-birth," meeting God, also offers the opportunity to re-engage the "enigmatic and traumatic order" inscribed in the unconscious mind/soul by virtue of a kind of second-order birthing seduction encounter, that is, with the Other, God. The latter affords the soul closed off in its constructed "closures" to confront its disturbing long-held guilt, shame, and vulnerability as phenomena that are rendered no longer potent in their capacity to alienate; the point is that the Christian re-birth experience is one of full-on acceptance and reception by the ultimate Other who previously could only be construed as the implacable judge. The sinner is embraced as entirely righteous, despite his alienating unrighteousness: "For He made Him who knew no sin to be sin for us, that we might become the righteousness of God in Him."[28] He can afford to relinquish his domestications of trauma and coherent narratives in favor of encountering the enigma of the untamed God.

27. Zornberg, *The Murmuring Deep*, xvi.

28. 2 Corinthians 5:21.

LIMITATIONS TO PSYCHOANALYSIS AND CHRISTIANITY

While psychoanalysis and Christianity both have their contributions to make toward helpfully addressing the disturbing "foreign body," strangeness of the unconscious elements within the mind, both also have their limits. Psychoanalysis rightly applied cannot and must not over-reach its capacities to open that which has been inaccessible, closed off, and therefore strange. In the course of an optimal analytic treatment, favorable outcomes may be realized, such as enhanced mental and emotional flexibility, less reliance on archaic defensiveness, in place of endless repetition in behavior, more choice, greater affect regulation, substantially increased self-knowledge, and therefore more effective mindfulness, the ability to observe one's own emotions and thoughts, and to think about one's thinking. Such outcomes herald increased likelihood of greater relational richness, improved access to imagination so that creativity and play and even worship may be enhanced. Psychoanalysis inevitably allows the recipient to recognize his subtle, previously concealed magical wishful fantasies and so evokes acceptance of limitations inherent in being human, with inevitable frailties, propensity to aging, and ultimately dying. Although the psychoanalytic enterprise might open awareness as to the possibility of much beyond the limits of self and the self's world, it cannot and must not reach further toward pronouncements or claims to knowledge of that which lies beyond its limited sphere of interest.

Psychoanalysis cannot pretend to resolve the ultimate humiliation that it is specifically adept at uncovering: ". . . that man is not at home in himself, in other words, that he is not master of himself and that finally . . . he has been decentered."[29] Laplanche cites Freud in highlighting the importance of the Copernican revolution and the Darwinian revolution in decentering man's presumptions of both the earth occupying the centre of the universe, and of his own special central status in the animal realm; similarly he claims psychoanalysis has decentered man from his presumption that he is master of himself. Psychoanalysis may disentangle by degrees the ties that bind any one of us to our fantasies, conflicts, and defensive compromises, yet it offers no final or ultimate solution beyond learning to live more comfortably with our internal alienations.

Christianity, on the other hand, while similarly recognizing that man is not master of himself, but is, in fact, enslaved,[30] offers full and final ultimate deliverance notwithstanding that the full realization of which is deferred

29. Laplanche, *Between Seduction and Inspiration,* 130.

30. See Ephesians 2:1–7; John 8:34; Galatians 4:1–7; Romans 6.

until after death. But Christianity similarly must not claim to pronounce or to know the details of knowledge about the mind and its formation and functions that have only come to light through centuries of philosophical, observational, and increasingly rigorous scientific investigation. Christians in the past and even in recent time have done great damage when they have asserted some distorted version of "sola scriptura" to the extent they insist that scripture must be the only authority in matters that have to do with human experience of the mind. When sincere believers claim that the sciences and theories of man are to be disregarded because they have no legitimate authority, they bring disrepute upon the church, exposing it to charges of fanaticism or bigotry. Christianity, however, unlike psychoanalysis, does rightly claim authority to speak to that which lies beyond the bounds of human endeavor and comprehension. It portrays dimensions of existence inaccessible to man's instruments of scientific investigation, or to his pretensions to mastery; it offers truth,[31] perfect love[32] and forgiveness[33] through an eternal relationship of mutual interpenetration[34] with the trinitarian God.

We have already alluded to the difficulties that can be encountered in arriving at self-forgiveness, when we considered the tendency for the superego to persist in its condemnations. All too often, in my experience with patients in analysis, although they may have cried out to God for his forgiveness, and know that God is bound to fulfill his promise to indeed forgive, they continue to live under a heavy weight of condemnation. It is at points such as this that psychoanalysis has much to offer. It has the power to uncover the often unconscious bonds by which the person persists in a heavy, self-imposed condemnation by the agency of the superego, and why it is that it seems so essential to cling to the guilt and shame which might otherwise be relieved through the infinite forgiveness of God. For example, one of the reasons that Carmen struggled so to realize relief from her sense of guilt is that she would feel herself to be a traitor to her identifications with her parents if she were to attain emotional and moral freedom. In the course of her analysis, once she realized that her superego's insistence that this form of "loyalty" to her parents must not be altered was untrue, she was able to truly achieve new freedom. In effect, when a person's superego supplants God in holding the person condemned, such that forgiveness from guilt cannot be realized, it amounts to an unconscious form of idolatry. The person is remaining under the oppressive condemnation of their superego, when all the while, they are forgiven by God.

31. John 14:6.
32. 1 John 2:5.
33. 1 John 1:7–10.
34. John 14: 20; John 15; 9–17 and John 17.

OVERCOMING DIVISION

> For He Himself is our peace, who has made both one, and has broken down the middle wall of separation, having abolished in His flesh the enmity, that is, the law of commandments, contained in ordinances, so as to create in Himself one new man from the two, thus making peace, and that He might reconcile them both to God in one new body through the cross, thereby putting to death the enmity.[35]

Paul is writing explicitly about the end of hostility and division between Jew and Gentile, building the case for both having the same access to God and becoming one believing body or community. If, however, we link the Ephesians quote with another of Paul's when he is clearly addressing his own internal struggles, we might arrive at another conclusion:

> I find then a law, that evil is present within me, the one who wills to do good. For I delight in the law of God according to the inward man. But I see another law in my members, warring against the law of my mind, and bringing me into captivity to the law of sin which is in my members. O wretched man that I am! Who will deliver me from this body of death? I thank God—through Jesus Christ our Lord! So then, with the mind I myself serve the law of God, but with the flesh the law of sin.[36]

We could say of this latter passage that Paul is engaging in self-analysis and discovering the kind of intra-psychic division and conflict with which psychoanalysis concerns itself. He would persist in his wretched state of conflict and bondage were it not for the ultimate hope he has in a deliverer, Jesus Christ. His language of "members" hearkens toward the psychoanalytic mode of recognizing distinct aspects of the mind, or clusters of functions within the mind that exist in conflict with other aspects, structures or functions; e.g. conflict between id and superego, or conflict between ego and both.

And so, for the Apostle Paul, his candid disclosure of on-going struggle to overcome the impulses arising from within him that are against the good suggest that conversion to Christ does not automatically eradicate sin, even though, legislatively speaking, the gospel claims that he was forgiven entirely and that the debt against him had been paid. The question then, of whether Christian faith and the re-birth of which we have spoken substantially alters the unconscious and its conflicts and strange capacity to impinge upon

---

35. Ephesians 2:14–16.
36. Romans 7:21–25.

conscious life begs an answer. Should Christians expect that their mental life will improve? Is there reason to presume that Christians would be less liable to symptoms like depression, anxiety, somatization of conflicts, mood disturbances, and personality disorders? What about psychosis?

I think there is no simple answer to these questions; there may be a theoretical and theological approach, some of which I will offer, which may suggest that improved mental health should be expected. But then, there are more experiential and practical considerations that come into effect that may be understood to influence actual outcomes. Along theological lines, let us consider the matter of the new birth. In the beginning, God formed "man of the dust of the ground, and breathed into his nostrils the breath of life; and man became a living being."[37] The prophet Ezekiel forecast a renewed creation of the "heart" of man: "I will give you a new heart and put a new spirit within you; I will take the heart of stone out of your flesh and give you a heart of flesh. I will put my Spirit within you. . . ."[38] Then, Paul says, "Therefore if anyone is in Christ, he is a new creation; old things have passed away; behold all things have become new."[39] Further, Paul uses language suggestive of growing and maturing in this newly created life,[40] acquiring wisdom, competency, discernment, etc., by virtue of having one's senses exercised, using terms to imply psychological development.

To take up once again the analogy between the newborn's mind development and that of the spiritually newly born, just as the child incorporates into his psyche the "law of the father," i.e. the guiding principles for living within civilization, so Jeremiah, speaking the words of God, said, "I will put my law in their minds, and write it on their hearts . . . no more shall every man teach . . . for they shall know Me."[41] It is as if there comes into being a new mode of inscription of the "law," i.e. of the nature and character of God through the vitalizing encounter with the Other that transforms, perhaps significantly through identification. All relational encounters achieve some measure of inevitable transformation in the mind of each of the participants; aspects of the unconscious are shifted in degrees, perhaps depending on the nature of and intensity of the encounter. Consider the impact of falling in love with a dazzlingly beautiful other versus that of coffee with a casual friend.

In exploring the story of Abraham, Gottlieb Zornberg recognizes that "the imperative of transformation is the driving force . . . to leave one's place

37. Genesis 2:7.
38. Ezekiel 36:26, 27.
39. 2 Corinthians 5:17.
40. Ephesians 4:14, 15; See also Hebrews 5:12–14.
41. Jeremiah 31:33, 34.

. . . ultimately to seek to become other" and that Abraham and Sarah, to embrace "a fertile self-realization" had to "emerge from their enclosure in the present (deathly sterile when outgrown)."[42] She ties together another thread, concerning Adam and Eve, in her development of the theme of the necessity for "an act of radical discontinuity . . . as the essential basis for all continuity: for that act of birth that will engender the body and the soul of a new kind of nation [existence]." Citing the Genesis 2:24 imperative, "Therefore a man shall leave his father and mother and be joined to his wife, and they shall become one flesh," she says, "The sterility of the child's involvement in the 'family romance' has to be left behind, in order that the self may find the Other . . . in order that the new being may be born."[43] The child who remains locked in his oedipal configuration with the parents can never become fruitful and multiply. A radical discontinuity is required in order for there to be new creation.

Relevant to our consideration of religious conversion, so-called new birth, Gottlieb Zornberg further questions the matter of how such transformations occur, including that of Abraham in moving from a culture of idol worship, in response to God's promptings, and into the worship of the true living God. She draws upon William James' analysis of "instantaneous conversions, in *Varieties of Religious Experience*. What lies behind such experiences, in James' analysis, is a long incubation period, in which subconscious elements prepare themselves for a flowering, which is as much of a process as an event".[44] This is highly reminiscent of the gospel's way of describing the sowing of seed, the watering of same, and the growth that eventually leads to the bearing of fruit in the form of full-on faith.

Finally, Gottlieb Zornberg cites the work of Thomas Kuhn, "in *The Structure of Scientific Revolutions*, [he] writes of the process by which scientists come to reject old paradigms—the activity of puzzle solving within the parameters of 'normal science'—and to see reality in terms of new structures: discovering a new form of phenomenon is necessarily a complex event, one which involves recognizing both *that* something is and *what* it is. . . . In science . . . novelty emerges only with difficulty, manifested by resistance, against a background provided by expectation."[45] Applying these ideas to the matter of conversion to Christianity, we do well to be reminded how prone we humans are to be biased, blinded if you like, by the enticing and fascinating objects of our desire, whether in scientific or intel-

42. Zornberg, *The Beginning of Desire*, 78.

43. Ibid., 77.

44. Ibid., 80.

45. Ibid., 81, 82. Emphasis hers.

lectual exploration, or in ordinary lived life. The Bible refers to that which saturates our attention and affections, insofar as they displace God as the biblically rightful occupant of the focus of man's desire, as idols. And idols, of whatever form, including, potentially, the idolatry of religion, are dead; furthermore, as the Psalmist says, "Those who make them are like them; so is everyone who trusts in them."[46]

Paul takes up this theme of the need for radical discontinuity when he insists that coming to life in Christ necessitates a transcending of the "dead[ness] in trespasses and sin"[47] that characterize humanity. Sin and trespass may fundamentally be understood to consist in idolatry, an inevitable primary focus on the material, social, and emotional matters of regular life at the expense of relating to one's creator, the foremost requirement in the economy of God. Obviously, whether natural birth, with its violent expulsion into the world from the enclave of warmth and total provision, or spiritual re-birth, with its radical departures from customary paradigms, attachments are severed and new ones formed.

INTERSUBJECTIVITY, WHOLE OBJECTS AND RELATING TO GOD

During the closing two decades of the twentieth century, innovations in psychoanalytic theory led to departures from classical Freudian theory which emphasized the role of the analyst analogous to that of the surgeon, who must, to be effective in his work, remain coolly detached, and uninvolved in his patient's subjective experience in order to be effective. Freud also employed two other metaphors to express the activity of the analyst: a telephone receiver which is receptive to all that is spoken, without interference, and a mirror such that the patient would see only that which was of himself reflected back from the analyst, and virtually nothing of the analyst himself.[48] The classical approach came to be seen as a "one person" psychology, in that only the subjectivity of the person in analysis was considered to influence and constitute the interpretive content of the work. Out of the development of Kohut's psychology of the self, and building upon the spatial metaphors of Winnicott (transitional object and transitional space), emerged Stolorow and Atwood's claim, against the notion of an "isolated mind," that a more accurate portrayal of the human mind is of a "continual embeddedness of human experience in a constitutive intersubjective

46. Psalm 115:8; see verses 3–7 also.

47. Ephesians 2:1.

48. Freud, *Recommendations*.

context."[49] Accordingly, the clinical psychoanalytic situation was envisaged by them as consisting in an intersubjective matrix in which the subjectivities of both analyst and patient were inextricably co-mingled. There were significant implications of this change in view for technique, for perceptions of reality (from classical ideas of "objective reality" versus "reality" emerging from the co-constructions arising from the intersubjective matrix itself), and for perceptions of deeper unconscious mental products such as primary process. Contemporary psychoanalysts situate themselves along varying points on the continuum between the classical "one person" analytic encounter as envisioned (but not likely actually practiced) by Freud, and the hyper-intersubjectivity that can manifest as mutual analysis in some relational contexts. While such concerns remain controversial in the field of psychoanalysis to the present day, for my purpose, I want to question whether a Christian's relationship with God might be properly construed as a two-person intersubjective field, or whether it is best conveyed by the construct of a one-person encounter.

How many of us are so free from psychopathology that we are capable of true "whole object" relationships? Do we inevitably focus on some part(s) of the other, out of our wish for gratification of desires, to the detriment of the whole? For example, depending on the extent of schizoid (characterized by "come close for I need intimacy, but stay away because I am terrified") features in a person, the aspect of God's character as judge might prevent him from being experienced as a whole object. The markedly schizoid person may not be able to engage with God as anywhere near a whole object, i.e. as immensely loving and generous as well as judging.[50] As Rizzuto claims, one's perception of and relational experience of God will inevitably be formed, at least initially, on the model of one's experience and internal representation of the parent(s). And so one's experience of God is inevitably and appropriately influenced by one's projections onto God of various aspects of the internalized parental representations or imagoes. But is a relationship with God one of stasis, or one of dynamic interplay and growth? Is it conceived as an intersubjective entity in which both subjectivities are dynamically engaged, and influencing each other, or is it conceived more as the subjectivity of the person engaging with an impersonal object, albeit bearing complex features? If God is personal, with personality and emotions, and bearing all the "strangeness" of an other, and having full subjectivity, then surely we conceive of the relationship with him as intersubjective. If so, then what might arise as implications?

---

49. Stolorow and Atwood, *Contexts of Being,* 22.

50. See Rizzuto's discussion of Daniel Miller, *The Birth of the Living God,* 130–48.

One consequence of considerations pertaining to a self that is constituted intersubjectively (if by this might be meant that the essence of one's self is determined by the intersubjective contexts of one's past or that of the moment) that strikes the modern mind is whether there is a bedrock true self, or only some fluid existential being that is constantly constituted by the contemporaneous context. Winnicott gave us the notion of a "true self" in contrast to a "false self," the product of accommodation to the other that was necessitated in order to survive. Bollas gave us the notion of an idiomatic self as distinct from a normotic or adapted self. Slavoj Žižek claims a subjectively felt uniqueness to his personality that is "provided by my fundamental fantasy, by this absolutely particular, non-universalizable formation."[51] (In other portions of this work I write about the formation of fantasy in relation to the development of the unconscious.) While these authors suggest something in the order of a bedrock self toward a knowledge of which a person undergoing psychoanalysis might strive, Žižek complicates the argument with the following:

> Now, what's the problem with fantasy? I think that the key point, usually overlooked, is the way that Lacan articulated the notion of fantasy which is, 'OK, fantasy stages a desire, but whose desire?' My point is: not the subject's desire not their own desire. What we encounter in the very core of the fantasy formation is the relationship to the desire of the Other: to the opacity of the Other's desire. The desire staged in fantasy, in my fantasy, is precisely not my own, not mine, but the desire of the Other. Fantasy is a way for the subject to answer the question of what object they are for the Other, in the eyes of the Other, for the Other's desire. That is to say, what does the Other see in them? What role do they play in the Other's desire.
>   . . . true fantasy is an attempt to resolve the enigma of the Other's desire. That's the desire that is staged in fantasy. It's not simply that I desire something, that I make a fantasy. No.[52]

We can see a lot of Laplanche in these ideas regarding the formation of fantasy in response to the desire of the other, and in the idea that the uniqueness of oneself inheres in the core fundamental fantasy. We seem to be left with two components to one's subjectivity: there being a true bedrock self, of which (unconscious) fantasy is constitutive, but also, the inescapable reality that the unconscious fantasy is formed in consequence of a negotiation of one's role in the complex network of intersubjective forces, themselves reflective of their owners' desire, of one's social environment.

51. Žižek, *Interrogating the Real*, 58.
52. Ibid., 58, 59.

By engaging in a relationship with God as a whole object (person), and not as a part object (e.g. as severe judge), perhaps new birth could consist in the transformation of unconscious fantasy by virtue of the interplay of intersubjective forces between God and myself. And might that intersubjective encounter, as it necessarily entails my responding to the immense and enigmatic desire of the Other, reconfigure my desire, and my fantasy?

Žižek claims that, "The psychoanalytic cure is effectively over when the subject loses this anxiety [the anxiety that one does not exist], as it were, and freely assumes their own non-existence."[53] He calls upon the dense and paradoxical writings of Lacan in ways that I won't pretend to understand, but I might take this notion to mean that since every human lives constantly under the knowledge of his own death, that he has some primordial anxiety about the reality of his own existence. I had personal experience of this existential or nihilistic anxiety during my own young adult crisis. To "freely assume [one's] own non-existence" then, might mean to come to a place of acceptance of one's natural human frailty (sickness, aging, decline) and the transient nature of one's earthly existence. To unite in relationship with the God who is life itself, in whom life is constituted, and who delights in extending that life to his creation is to subsume non-existence in (Godly) existence.

53. Ibid., 57.

Chapter 6

Parameters and Challenges of the Unseen Other[1]

SKEPTICS AND CYNICS WILL dismiss the idea of relating to an unseen God as purely the manifestations of fantasy of utopia arising out of dystopic experience of life. Some, as per Freud and others, will view faith in a messiah as residual infantile longings for the out-grown parent and therefore dismiss religious faith as a mark of immaturity or as a manifestation of obsessional neurosis. For some, faith in the invisible God might be little different from the preoccupation of a small child with their "invisible friend." While unlikely to raise concern so long as the latter can be seen to play the role of a "transitional object,"[2] the phenomenon Winnicott saw as essential for healthy development of the mind and of creativity in young children, the same display of relating to an invisible being in the adult might raise suspicion of sanity. And yet, Winnicott did not confine his perceptions of transitional phenomena to children, but in recognizing points of contact between inner reality and outer reality for any individual human, he further posited:

> an intermediate area of *experiencing*, to which inner reality and external life both contribute. It is an area that is not challenged, because no claim is made on its behalf except that it shall exist as a resting-place for the individual engaged in the

1. Acts 17:23—Paul refers to the Athenian inscription "TO AN UNKNOWN GOD."

2. Winnicott, *Playing and Reality*, 2: Winnicott says, "I have introduced the terms 'transitional objects' and 'transitional phenomena' for designation of the intermediate area of experience, between the thumb and the teddy bear, between the oral erotism and the true object-relationship, between primary creative activity and projection of what has already been introjected, between primary unawareness of indebtedness and the acknowledgement of indebtedness ('Say: "ta"').

perpetual human task of keeping inner and outer reality separate yet interrelated.

It is usual to refer to "reality-testing," and to make a clear
distinction between apperception and perception. I am here stak-
ing a claim for an intermediate state between a baby's inability and
his growing ability to recognize and accept reality. I am therefore
studying the substance of *illusion*, that which is allowed to the
infant, and which in adult life is inherent in art and religion, and
yet becomes the hallmark of madness when an adult puts too
powerful a claim on the credulity of others, forcing them to acknowledge a sharing of illusion that is not their own.[3]

For Winnicott, much adult experience of art, music, religion, and
other realms entails necessary illusion, that which is intermediate between
inner and outer reality, the former accessed by apperception, the latter by
perception. Yet, he cautions against claims for illusion that too forcefully
strain the credulity of others who don't share it. A fine balance between
madness and sanity is suggested.

Marilyn Charles, in writing about the interplay of fictional literature
with life and psychoanalysis, makes a compelling argument for how it is that
when we read good literature, we experience "expressive enactments;"[4] she
is essentially referring to new experiences at an emotive level, deriving from
identifications between reader and author (and possibly via the medium of
the characters created by the author) which lead to reflection and conceptual
shifts in the reader. I perceive the possibility of forming a relationship with
God in similar fashion, through the reading of Scripture primarily, although
God may well disclose himself in perhaps apperceptively and perceptively[5]
recognizable ways in nature, in prayer, and in the interstices between the
experiences of life in its demands and occupations, and in people.

TRANSFERENCE, PROJECTION AND IDENTIFICATION

Identification

In the course of normal expected development, a child is understood to form
his mental structures and personality through unconsciously identifying
with traits found in the people around him, and thereby undergoing some

---

3. Ibid, 3–4. Emphasis his.

4. Charles, *The Stories We Live*, 4.

5. Perception refers to that which is a function of the senses; apperception is a
term referring to that which is psychologically or intuitively sensed.

measure of transformation in himself. Gradually, there is built up through multiplied identifications, and, no doubt, modifications thereof such that one pattern of identification may be modified by the assimilation of some other attribute, to form a personality. Shifts in personality quality and characteristics through the process of identification likely go on throughout life, and are not restricted to childhood. A mature adult may change over time by virtue of the influence of close association with a colleague or his spouse, perhaps by virtue of experience or what is read. It may be unlikely that identification occurs with a "whole object," i.e. with the person in total, but more likely with a particular aspect of the object, i.e. with a "part-object." From a traditional body-based Freudian perspective, "in the main, part-objects are parts of the body, real or phantasied (breast, faeces, penis) and their symbolic equivalents."[6] This view derives from drive/instinct theory that focuses heavily upon the role of the body and its drives, and the objects (targets of the drives) and aims (purposes or satisfactions to be met) of the drives as perceived by Freud; the "symbolic equivalents" of breast, faeces, and penis might refer respectively to a person's capacity to love, give, nurture; to destroy through judgement; to potently and creatively generate anew. Freud outlined three fundamental stages (oral, anal, and genital) of childhood development, that revolved around specific anatomical structures and their central role in the developmental stage of the child. The mouth of the infant connects with the breast of the mother and is the first point of contact with the object; the anus, around eighteen to thirty-six months, is the body sight most involved with struggles for control and power over ownership and release of feaces, and is connected with psychological development of urges to control or hurt or destroy—such is the matter of toilet training; the genitals become a focus of concern for the three to five year old child, in terms of determinations of difference, particularly sex distinctions and measures of superiority, power, and competence. The symbolic equivalency of the penis will be considered in more detail in Chapter 8 on sexuality.

When it comes to the mature person entering into a relationship with God, being "converted," questions concerning identification with God or, more specifically, with Jesus Christ come to the fore. New Testament exhortations to Christians to imitate Jesus are abundant, yet from a psychoanalytic point of view, the term "imitate" seems inadequate. To imitate suggests a conscious, deliberate attempt to mimic, and likely at an observable behavioral level and fails to address deep, thorough-going change. Through long and more or less continual association with God through scripture

---

6. Laplanche and Pontalis, *The Language of Psychoanalysis,* 301: in their definition of "Identification."

reading, prayer and communion both in the formal eucharistic sense and in the informal social sense with God and other believers, one can conceive of significant identifications occurring that are more unconscious assimilations rather than mimicry. The New Testament in particular is packed full of the primary emphasis upon Jesus' "law of love" as the new commandment; the goal laid out is to become like him in manifesting love. Can one love by deliberate mimicry? Perhaps one *can* manifest something like love through intentional acts of the will, in defiance of spontaneous impulses to irritatedly striking out at an other who offends. How much more superior would it be to identify with a magnificent loving other, rather in the way that an infant identifies with the loving bountiful mother, with whom his primary contact is the breast, and thereby forms the ground for an effective conscience? When a person has come to know and to live in a milieu of loving kindness (as per the realm of Christ), he is

> truly in his element; he acts spontaneously and naturally, and "walks in the ways of God [based upon Deuteronomy 13:5]" by acting of his own accord, of his own free will and unforced consciousness [and, I would say, unconsciousness]. . . . It is when man knows himself as world-making that he comes closest to the Father whose creativity asks for the ultimate compliment of imitation.[7]

Gottlieb Zornberg also makes the point that when a man is operating in the world of law, the world of codes and rules for behavior, "in which man acts out of necessity or obedience, . . . [he] in that sense is *not* God-like."[8] The point here is to try to strike at the far deeper sense of "identification with" in contrast to "imitation of." And what is specifically in focus as that with which we are to identify is not only the love that inheres in God and is most manifest in Jesus, but also the creativity that is integral to his being: "All things were made through Him, and without Him nothing was made that was made."[9]

While it is true that God is clearly depicted in scripture as exercising judgement and as being potentially wrathful in his judgement on sin, Christians are specifically urged to not imitate or identify with God in his judgement,[10] leaving the exercise of judgement to God alone.

---

7. Zornberg, *The Beginning of Desire*, 108.

8. Ibid. Emphasis hers.

9. John 1:3.

10. Matthew 7:1–5; Romans 14:3,4 and 13.

Projection

To get the psychoanalytic sense of how the term "projection" is used, I quote Laplanche and Pontalis:

> . . . operation whereby qualities, feelings, wishes or even "objects," which the subject refuses to recognize or rejects in himself, are expelled from the self and located in another person or thing. Projection so understood is a defense of very primitive origin which may be seen at work especially in paranoia, but also in "normal" modes of thought, such as superstition.[11]

A psychological defense serves in an effort to protect the subject from distress, and so, as in projection, to re-locate disagreeable ideas or feelings to the outside of oneself, often to other people, may thereby achieve immediate relief. There are ways however, in which projection is necessary, expected, and healthy. A young child, for optimal development of his capacity to manage his own intense affects, under reasonably suitable conditions of maternal care, needs to be able to project such affects onto his mother in order for her to then be able to take into herself such feelings with the purpose of detoxifying them and returning them to him in a way that he can then make use of and incorporate; this mirroring-type function requires projection. A form of projection is also seen in which ideal, wished-for qualities that cannot be acknowledged in oneself for various reasons, despite their actual existence in the self, are projected into an idealized other. Finally, perhaps because of the impossibility of locating perfections within the self, qualities of absolute perfection may be attributed to, again, another, who, by such projecting (along with splitting) is excessively idealized. As noted before, the mental phenomenon of "splitting" is a necessary capacity for distinguishing one thing from another, or better from worse, etc; when splitting is relied upon excessively, in a defensive self-protective manner, however, it tends to consist in a primitive, extreme separation of phenomena that reality cannot support. And so, when one tends to locate all goodness in the other, the necessary corollary is to locate all badness in oneself. Realistic understanding holds onto a blending of good and bad in all of us. Pathological splitting therefore fosters distortion of both self and other.

From this very brief discussion of the phenomena of projection, it is readily apparent how likely it is that all manner of qualities and personality features are likely to be projected onto God. Christians are not infrequently warned by preachers to be wary of their proclivity to project onto God what they *wish* for God to be like, or, just as probable, what they *fear* God to be

11. Laplanche and Pontalis, *The Language,* 349.

like. Appropriately, they are urged to inform themselves of a more accurate image of God, from their study of scripture. Such an effort is, of course, profitable and necessary, just as it is for the young child to grapple with the reality of his mother having interests and engagements with others beyond the child alone, i.e. that she is not only what the child presumes her to be through his projections. Perhaps, however, we can playfully imagine God, as a living relational being, receiving man's projections in the manner of a competent parent, who employs her child's projections in the further growth of the child's psyche. No doubt the invisibility and infinite richness and diverse complexity of the character of God affords especially fertile opportunity for projecting. Lest, however, we think of the Judaeo-Christian God as nothing more than a bundle of projections, we remember that Jesus was an historical figure. Furthermore the pre-Christian era of God worship was based on the many recorded experiences of the Jewish peoples' interactions with God who they perceived actively and actually intervened in their affairs. Finally, projection, apart from being a defense, is also a normal and unavoidable component of interpersonal interaction, vitally enabling empathy.

Transference

Transference, as mentioned previously, is a phenomenon that, although ubiquitous in all relationships to infinitely varied degrees, is the sine qua non of psychoanalysis. The analytic situation, characterized by the request for the analysand (patient) to freely associate, in conjunction with the carefully listening analyst who employs *evenly hovering attention* (meaning avoidance of the assignment of value to particular utterances over others), and sitting out of sight, affords opportunity for the analysand to regress toward the asymmetric "fundamental anthropological situation" and thereby loosen the repression of the previously repressed. Rizzuto puts it like this:

> . . . a relaxation of defensive maneuvers made possible by the presence of a respectful, reliable, and understanding object will permit the reestablishment of undisturbed memorial processes. When this happens, the disturbing aspects of oneself and the objects of the past return to awareness; many of them, however, return not as memories but as reenactments of the entanglement of oneself with certain aspects of the object of the present, the analyst. We call that process transference. The process permits retroactive reality testing. By that I mean the opportunity to reexperience past emotional entanglements with objects and reexamine them

by teasing out the component elements of fact, fantasy, wish, fear,
and the resulting interpretation of what they meant.[12]

Psychoanalysis is unique in its fostering and using of transference, with
its reexperiencing of important past configurations of relational complexes
and untranslated bits of messages from the adult world. What is then analyzed are the emotions, beliefs, fears, and wishes that are part of that transference, enabled by the fact that they are occurring *with* the analyst and so
the consulting room becomes, in effect, the laboratory of, as Rizzuto claims,
reality testing, and potential transformation through such interchange.

It will be obvious that transference involves projection. Inevitably,
Christians transfer onto God their past emotionally entangling experiences
with their parents and important others. Concerning a closely related phenomenon, Winnicott[13] remarks on the mirroring role of the mother, such
that the child looks into the face of the mother and will, optimally, see there
something of himself, reflected back, a sure indication to the child that he
has been seen, known, recognized and approved. The child acquires thereby
a solid sense of existing. If the mother is depressed or preoccupied with
matters other than the primary place of her young child, she is liable to not
be capable of reliably and predictably serving as a mirror to her child. That
child may grow up with insecurity as to his existence, or he may feel insub-
stantial. One such patient described feeling herself to go about unseen, like
as if she was a phantom, a vapor. She lacked an essential vitality and felt an
inescapable deadness. For someone whose mother has suffered inability to
mirror competently, the insecurities of a tenuous sense of existence and the
lingering need to be adequately mirrored will undoubtedly affect his experience of God. He will inevitably and unconsciously transfer onto God, the
early subjective experience of hollowness or insubstantiality encountered
upon looking into the face of his (unresponsive and therefore psychologically dead) mother. I might note here the risk for a child stemming from
having a devout Christian parent whose primary preoccupation is with
God and the concern to please God, so much so that the normal "primary
maternal preoccupation"[14] is corrupted in such a way as to interfere with
the mother's capacity to *see* her child for who he is, as opposed to a project
to be rendered suitable for the kingdom of God (See Stephanie, Chapter 4).

Although one relates to God who is portrayed as replete in all re-
spects, and infinite in his capacities for responding to individuals and their

12. Rizzuto, *The Birth of the Living God*, 80.

13. Winnicott, *Playing and Reality*, Chapter 9.

14. A phrase from Winnicott to mark the usual attitude of a healthy mother to her
foetus and newborn child.

emotional complexities, the absence of an actual face that bears the expressions of an emotional mirror, and a voice that is immediate in the customary human sense, go together to render the absolute necessity for projection and transference in order for there to be a relationship. This does not mean that the projections and transferences need necessarily persist unaltered, static; I believe them to exist in constant dynamic fluctuation, as in any intimate relationship. I've already referred to the shifts in one's experience of God that can and should derive from familiarity with scripture and from prayer. Two other forms of corrective, perhaps akin to the detailed examination of transferences and projections that are integral to psychoanalysis, are the "Jesus hermeneutic" and the (Christian) "community hermeneutic." The former recognizes that all scripture ultimately points to Jesus as the focus and that scripture's interpretation is to be achieved through the lens that is the person of Jesus. The community hermeneutic acknowledges the existence of Jesus living spiritually within not just individual Christians, manifestly expressed in the in-dwelling of his Holy Spirit,[15] but in the body of believers who function together to inspire, challenge, correct, encourage, and teach one another.[16]

USING AND DESTROYING THE OBJECT

Winnicott[17] elaborates his sense of the necessary developmental transformative experience of any infant through its acts or fantasies of destroying the object; he may achieve this by expressing rage at his mother. When he sees that his mother withstands his attack, he realizes she has a real, external existence, and is not just a cluster of his own projections. In order for the destruction of the object to be effective in achieving the developmental hurdle of a separate existence for both self and object, the object needs to survive the destructive attack. A simple everyday enactment of this phenomenon is the nursing infant eventually biting down on the nipple of the breast that is feeding him so that the mother is hurt. Her reaction of non-retaliation contributes to herself and her breast acquiring independent external existence for the infant; i.e. the infant is on the way to a capacity for "me-not me" differentiation. Winnicott also recognized this phenomenon occurring in psychoanalysis when the aggressive hostile transferences of the patient onto the analyst are met with non-retaliation from the analyst. He noted that interpretation of such events is neither necessary nor helpful, since the experience of "destroying" the analyst and having him survive as a benign,

---

15. See John 16:5–15; John 15:1–8; Ephesians 1:13.

16. Ephesians 4:7–16.

17. Winnicott, *Playing,* Chapter 6.

non-retaliating object is what is in itself transformative. He claimed that such experience is what enables the shift from relating to an object on the basis of, primarily, projections, to usage (which emphatically does not imply exploitation) of the object in ways that promote structuring of the mind for the subject, the establishment of external reality and persons as distinct, separate beings with their own minds.

Lydia was introduced in Chapter 3. Having multiple features of early, primitive, pre-verbal types of mental function evident, particularly in her relationships with people, including her narcissistic and competitive mother who always needed to defeat Lydia, her relations have always been marred by hostility. Exquisitely sensitive, thin-skinned, she would characteristically react to any perceived slight with hurt, followed immediately by hostile aggression. In the first years of analysis, many events in the course of four-times weekly sessions afforded opportunity for such reactions; particularly distressing were my absences for vacations. And so there were many occurrences of vocally angry hostility expressed toward me, even to the extent of slamming the door upon exiting my office before a session had ended, and then leaving a terse phone message that she would not be returning. She is still in analysis with me, and so, clearly, she did not follow through on the threat, but nevertheless, each time, caused me to feel the heat of her wrath and to anxiously worry whether she, in fact might not return. Or, upon a return from my vacation she might remain angrily silent for several sessions on end. On one notable occasion, she attempted suicide, again causing me to feel the pain of doubt regarding my analytic and therapeutic efficacy, and a measure of guilt as to my role in it.

There came a point in the second year of analysis when I sensed that she needed to know whether or not I was affected by her hostilities and aggressive acts, or whether my tolerance and "survival" meant that I was unfeeling and disconnected from her. I decided to engage in a measure of uncharacteristic self-disclosure in telling her that I did feel hurt, angered, disturbed, by her explosions. This led to considerable relief in her, to know that my many non-retaliations were not because of what she had projected onto me as a kind of hard impermeability, a feature of her own fantasied self as omnipotent and indestructible (the split-off opposite, in fantasy, of her actual subjective experience of being so shamefully incapable and weak), but were a manifestation of what might be understood as analytic "love." This latter is the out-working of the analyst's deep commitment to his analysand's essential being as a suffering fellow human who therefore has infinite value and is deserving of utmost respect, including in the midst of the powerful transference struggles that analytic work entails. She had been able to "use" or "destroy" me profitably.

Lydia is now able to reflect upon those early-years experiences with delight and gratitude as to the transformations that have occurred and which continue. I am no longer a bundle of projections to her; I have become a real, external object. Accordingly, her own relationships outside of analysis have begun to take on a different cast.

Destroying God

In her analysis of Abraham's journey through the "Akedah" (Hebraic term for "the Binding of Isaac, signifying Abraham's readiness to sacrifice his son at God's command.")[18] Gottlieb Zornberg, in referring to Winnicott's thesis about destruction of the object in order to use it, says,

> . . . where the object survives, where the infant can express aggression in ultimate trust, a new balance of connection and independence is set up. Love becomes possible. . . . Fear and destructiveness are the shadows that [Abraham] must battle, if he is to achieve a new rigour of love. If Abraham can live through the reality of his fear of God as totally Other, then his love will become not simply a "bundle of projections" but the love of a real Presence.[19]

Of course Christians see in the account of Abraham's willingness to destroy his precious son, the son of promise-fulfillment, the means by which God's promised heritage would come to be, a prefigurement of God's own sacrificed son. Both Abraham and Isaac had to survive this monumental event and did so in ways such that their relationship with the God who required it was transformed. While Christian believers engage in their relationship with God by means of projections, transferences, and identifications, their experience of God is transformed from being nothing more than a bundle of projections, their own and others', to awareness of God's independent objective existence, with a separate mind, by virtue of their own historical identificatory and vicarious participation in the crucifixion of God himself. Every time they partake of communion they are reminded of not only their own part in the destruction of God, but also, of God's survival (resurrection) and non-retaliation. God, as object, can now be loved, because he lovingly survived. Man then has the opportunity to transcend his own being to find reality and his own place in it.

18. Zornberg, *The Beginning of Desire*, 422.
19. Ibid., 121.

This theme could be taken up along many different lines, including whether and how this analogy between Winnicott's "use of the object" and Christians' destruction of, symbolic ingestion of (in the eucharist), relationship and co-indwelling[20] with Christ withstands critical appraisal and might work out in practice. One also might consider Freud's ideas around the horde mentality of destroying the Father out of sexual motivations, i.e. access to the females.[21] Efforts to elaborate these themes here would take me beyond both my purpose and my comprehension at this time, but may be worthy of further investigation by any who see merit in doing so.

20. John 17:20–23.
21. See Freud, *Totem and Taboo* and *Moses and Monotheism.*

Chapter 7

Light into Dark Places

SUFFERING AND NEGATIVE CAPABILITY

Embedded within the teachings of the New Testament is the expectation that followers of Christ will, as he did, suffer. While present and future rewards are also integral to the teachings regarding faith in Jesus, Christians are indeed urged to embrace suffering as integral to their new commitment, rather as a mark of their identity: "And he who does not take his cross and follow after me is not worthy of me. He who finds his life will lose it, and he who loses his life for My sake will find it."[1] The kingdom of God, as it is referred to in the New Testament, stands alone and against all sovereignties, political entities and ideologies that determine various forms of praxis for individuals and populations of peoples. The Apostle Paul, in writing his letter to the Colossian Christians first emphasizes the preeminence of Christ in all things, and then, after building the case for reconciliation in and sacrificial service for Christ, goes on to posit the inadequacies and deceptions of philosophy, legalism, and carnality (what might be referred to as life lived out of basic urges). Walsh and Keesmaat analyze the book of Colossians to recognize that to live Christianly is to live contrary to the values of "empire," i.e. counter-culturally, and to therefore inevitably face suffering by virtue of one's non-conformity to things like rampant materialism, meeting violence with violence, the ethics of revenge, or blind adherence to prevailing empirical ideology.

---

1. Matthew 10:38, 39.

> But Nympha [the authors' fictional resident of Colossae] meets in Paul's gospel a Jesus who invites her into a covenantal relationship of wholeness, setting her free from the oppressive absolutes of the [Roman] empire. She is set free *into* a subversive praxis of secession from the empire and a communal ethic of full-life restoration in Christ. The truth she encounters in the communities that have been spawned by this gospel is no fascist repression but a radical liberation.
>
> So we say . . . come into the embrace of the Other who rules, but from a cross, who is sovereign but wears a crown of thorns.[2]

It could be said of Jesus that he was characterized by a radical distancing of himself from those features of humanity so common to us all, that is, our manic defenses.[3] These defenses are called "manic" because they are defenses that have the quality of grandeur, are designed to make us feel good about ourselves and, in effect, to deny the intolerable realities of our own failings and weaknesses. An everyday example is the man who purchases a hot sports car in order to feel more powerful in himself, to disguise humiliating weakness (castration anxiety), whether conscious and acknowledged, or not. Many of the aspirations for certainty, or the kinds of presumptuous knowing that were referred to previously as omnipotent defenses would also fall into this category. I think it safe to assert that none of us is free of such basic needs, however subtly they may manifest.

"Negative capability" is a quality so named by Keats:

> "At once it struck me, what quality went to form a Man of Achievement, especially in literature, and which Shakespeare possessed so enormously—I mean Negative Capability, that is when man is capable of being in uncertainties. Mysteries, doubts, without any irritable reaching after fact and reason."
>
> This description can be compared to a definition of conflict:
>
> "An emotional state characterized by indecision, restlessness, uncertainty and tension resulting from incompatible inner needs and drives of comparable intensity."[4]

Ferro, in elaborating the necessity for analysts to reach for negative capability as it was invoked by Bion as essential in psychoanalysis for protection against excluding our patient while we risk a kind of intimate coupling with our theories and our pet "mytho-symbologies"[5] (e.g. Oedipus Com-

---

2. Walsh and Keesmaat, *Colossians Remixed,* 232–33. Emphasis theirs.

3. See Philippians 2:5–8.

4. Keats' Kingdom website 2004–2015: www.keatsian.co.uk.

5. Laplanche, *Between Seduction.*

plex, castration complex, primal scene, etc.), says, "It is basically the only way in which we can be truly in touch with the patient—and here I must stress the concept of unison—rather than with our theories. . . ."[6] An effective analyst, therefore, would need to divest himself of his need for certainty and therefore his presumptions to know the mind of his patient, and be prepared to tolerate ambiguity, regardless of how disorienting that can be.

So it is for a Christian; he cannot know with unequivocal certainty that what it is to which he commits himself in faith is valid, however much sincere ardent believers may claim. Belief in God is always and has always been a matter of faith.[7] But to live as a sincere believer who can embrace negative capability in a world that largely eschews a life of faith is to suffer relinquishment of adherence to the tenets of the imperial rule of the commodity/consumerist worldview; or, in some instances, national identity or familial identity. All such liaisons for the Christian must be subordinated to the identification with Christ that demands primary place. Reliance on manic type defenses has to go.

Job, who manifested the epitome of suffering, also displayed immense patience in the face of his "friends" manic presumptions to know the reasons that lay behind his horrendous misfortunes. Job was distinguished by negative capability; he acknowledged he could not know why and challenged his friends to relinquish their claims to know. Abraham, who although tolerant of ambiguity and uncertainty as to where it was that God would lead him, and how it was that his offspring would populate the world when he was required to sacrifice his son, became impatient with not knowing and took matters into his own hands, birthing Ishmael with his wife's handmaid. The Psalms, full of urgings to wait patiently for (or before) the Lord, emphasize the humility required to do so. It seems to inhere in humans to strive to overcome their limits and frailties with manic omnipotence rather than muster the courage to humbly wait, tolerating not knowing.

AUTONOMY RECONSIDERED

I have pointed out that both Christianity and psychoanalysis see mankind as not able to actually realize the autonomy he imagines he has. Nevertheless, if one of the chief aims of man is to rid himself of shackles and attain freedom, then from what tyranny is it that he needs to be freed? Christianity claims that

6. Ferro, *Mind Works,* 204.

7. Hebrews 11:1, "Now faith is the substance of things hoped for, the confidence of things not seen."

man, in his natural state is enslaved to sin,[8] which may in turn translate into bondage to one's own insatiable appetites[9] (including the quest to be like God, or a god to oneself), or idolatry.[10] Psychoanalysis asserts that the repressed unconscious acts as a stranger haunting one from within such that it has a deterministic influence over what one does, how one thinks, loves, works, etc. In fact, while psychoanalysts might recognize normal from abnormal or neurotic modes of mental functioning, it also inevitably concludes that at best, the most normal among us will only be so to the extent that, " . . . free-dom and flexibility to learn and to change through experience and to adjust to changing external circumstances"[11] (i.e. flexibility) predominates as the mode of function in any given sphere. Wurmser quotes Kubie (1954) to highlight distinctions between normal mental process and neurotic:

> Thus the essence of normality is flexibility, in contrast to the freezing of behavior into acts of unalterability that character-izes every manifestation of the neurotic process, whether in impulses, purposes, acts, thoughts or feelings. Whether or not a behavioral event is free to change depends not upon the quality of the act itself, but upon the nature of the constellation of forces that has produced it. No moment of behavior can be looked upon as neurotic unless the processes that have set it in motion predetermine its automatic repetition irrespective of the situa-tion, the utility, or the consequences of the act.[12]

Wurmser clarifies that, "whenever the unconscious system predomi-nates, the resulting action must be repeated over and over, because its goals are largely unconscious symbols and unconscious symbolic goals can never be attained." Kubie:

> Since the predominant forces are unconscious, they will not be responsive to . . . logical argument—neither to the logic of events nor to any appeals to mind or heart.

In attempting to clarify the "essence of the neurotic process," Wurm-ser seeks to describe further qualities that enable him to encompass more than mild, but also what he perceives as the more severe forms of neuroses, severely regressive patients that are often labelled as borderline or deeply narcissistic. I will again quote him:

8. John 8:34.

9. Ephesians 2:1–3.

10. Rev 9:20; 1 John 5:21; Ezekiel 36:25.

11. Wurmser, *The Power of the Inner Judge,* 304.

12. Ibid., 304.

The second condition [for the neurotic process] consists in the *polarization of the opposites,* the dichotomization of the judgements of good and bad, of pure and impure, of the sacred and demonic, or God and Devil—the extreme quality of love and hate, of trust and distrust.

Closely connected with that is a third criterion: the experience of *absoluteness and globality* of a value, an ideal, a commitment, a principle, the claim of totality for affective or cognitive comprehension . . . of self and world and the equal totality and absoluteness of the denial and exclusion of that which does not seem to fit to this absolutely held principle. . . . Put in different words: there is an *overvaluation,* an overestimation of self or others; it is a transgression of the limits, a dissolution of the boundaries, in value, truth, and action.[13]

I have quoted these portions at length because I believe that the features of neurotic mental processes (and they affect us all) as outlined are critical to the understanding of my further efforts to explore the impact of Christian faith on matters like freedom, autonomy, mental health, and the questions of Christian orthodoxy. For example, one might consider, upon reflection on the above, how likely and easy it is for Christian doctrines to be incorporated into one's unconscious mental life insidiously and potentially destructively, yet without the subject being capable of recognizing this fact. Christian doctrines regarding the good, the bad, the pure, the impure, God, or Satan, are easily assimilated into already established narcissistic and neurotic pathology; an example of this was mentioned in the parents of Stephanie.

FORMULAE AND FETISHES

When Christian authors, even those who are trained in psychology, write about how believers can overcome their life struggles to become better, more effective or more content people, if they fail to account adequately for the unconscious and its binding influences, tend to rely upon invocations of the power of God, or the role of the Holy Spirit, to effect change. When I read such things, I am left with discomfort as to how this happens, whether there is a real transformation of the unconscious by one's relationship with God, the scriptures, other Christians, prayer, and the activity of the Holy Spirit, or whether there is an assumption at work that may, in effect, be reliant upon magic. An example:

---

13. Ibid., 305. Emphasis his.

We're told we must obey God but that we must do it in His strength. Every effort [perhaps both conscious and unconscious] to live in the power of the flesh will inevitably fail. Above the waterline (i.e. responsible efforts to obey in actions, thoughts, and feelings [roughly equivalent to conscious intentions]), we do what we should, including immersing ourselves in God's Word, praying, and serving others. As we do these things, God's power eventually overwhelms all those problems below the waterline (i.e. motives, urges, memories, attitudes [roughly equivalent to the unconscious]) and we are enabled to live in consistent victory.

When we fail above the waterline, then more effort is called for—perhaps spending more time in the Word or in prayer or enlisting in our church's witnessing campaign. Obedience to Christian duty and bathing our mind and soul in God's truth keep us from quenching or grieving the Holy Spirit.[14]

Having considered the concept of manic defenses, my discomfort revolves around Crabb's recommendations for what may seem to amount to little more than efforts directed toward fortifying the manic defenses against the complex, powerful stranger unconscious. While such fortifications may be beneficial and sufficient for many, for others, such recommendations can be damaging insofar as an underlying implicit assumption may be that a person who comes to belief should be truly and actually, in their subjective experience of their own neurotic patterns, transformed. This assumption would effectively translate to the expectation that Christian conversion leads (automatically?) to a transformed unconscious. Or that a person, by sincere determined conscious effort to follow the above recommendations should be able to overcome their particular (unconsciously determined) psychopathology. To the extent that such a message is promoted within the Christian community, there is potential for serious damage to those who do not find it experientially so; damage in the form of alienation, perceptions of inadequacy, doubts as to the legitimacy or sufficiency of the quality or quantity of their faith. And since when can unconscious neurotic processes be modified by the strengthening of manic defenses?

One major advantage to being a Christian in coping with neurosis is the fundamental reconciliation that he has come to, i.e. acceptance of how deeply and fundamentally flawed and in need of restoration he is. Humility of this order offers the progressive possibility of relinquishing manic-type defenses as they become conscious and no longer necessary. The person may arrive at awareness by a cumulative familiarity with and submission to the Judaeo-Christian scriptures that have a powerfully penetrating quality.

14. Crabb, *Inside Out*, 49.

They have the capacity to enlighten and to convince and to convict; in fact, they are unapologetic in their claim to such impact.[15] So, while relating to God and his community in the manner evinced above may well bring about even significant unconscious transformations (perhaps akin to the transformations of unconscious processes that derive specifically from the *relationship* between the analysand and the analyst, and less from the insight acquired from rendering the unconscious conscious[16]) the application of those principles in formulaic fashion can be detrimental. Christian "formulae" can acquire the character of a fetish[17]: "false icon, that, like fetishes, only *substitute* for belief . . . [not actually] icons of belief" (Emphasis mine). Kaplan makes a distinction between,

> . . . an infant's security blanket, the so-called transitional object, and an adult's sexual fetish. Both are tangible, inanimate objects that have been endowed with magical properties that ease the strain of relating to the world of reality. In contrast to the transitional object that serves as a bridge between the comfortably familiar and the unfamiliar, the sexual fetish arrests growth and prevents any further exploration of reality. By serving as a cushion and a haven, the transitional object enables the little human adventurer to test the new realities of his expanding world. The security blanket can be given up when its developmental purpose has been served. The sexual fetish is hard, unyielding, ritualized, unbending. It is a prop that can never be given up because the territory of female sexuality is an eternally unknowable and dangerous environment.[18]

Commodity fetishes, products of the money-trade economy, to which Kaplan sees women to have a particular susceptibility, she claims are:

> . . . everywhere in the social order. They are reminders of our alienation from nature and from our personal selfhood. And yet they represent a way of escape from our anxieties, our plights, the terrible depression and madness that might overtake our souls. Without illusions of some sort we would all succumb to despair. . . . The commodity fetish is an object of belief, but in

15. Hebrews 4:12; Psalm 139:23, 24.

16. In any psychoanalytic treatment, regardless of the theoretical orientation which guides it, implicit, subtle and difficult-to-measure relational elements are thought to effect change, by virtue of the attitude and disposition of the analyst toward the patient: acceptance, non-judgement, respect for inherent human value and dignity regardless of personal opposition, etc.

17. More on this in Chapter 8: Sexuality.

18. Kaplan, *Female Perversions,* 316.

it there is an absence of belief, a fending off only of despair and violence.

> . . . What are our icons of belief? A genuine icon is meant to enable groups and communities to convene, and because the group shares ideals and illusions there is a tacit agreement not to put to test the truth or reality of these fictions. They are illusions that comfort us and bring us together into shared realms of experiencing. But these days our social icons and uniforms and flags and crosses and art collections are functioning like fetishes. Instead of bringing us together, they insidiously undermine our possibilities for communion or human relatedness. The fetishized icon separates one person from another and functions instead as though it were a law unto itself. It becomes a dogma that demands submission and obedience.[19]

Christian doctrines that function as genuine icons of faith must always be protected from deterioration into fetishized icons with their damaging consequences.

Another disturbing trend toward fetishization of a Christian principle is seen as occurring through a slippage from a key, life-enhancing concept of unity to a deadening movement among members toward uniformity. Paul teaches in Ephesians 4 on the importance of unity within the church as the body of Christ. In developing this theme, Johnson, in writing about Christian soul care says:

> The goal of Christian and pastoral soul care then is thoroughly interpersonal. It entails a communal unity in faith, through the personal, sweet knowledge of Jesus, such that we all grow into his likeness, everyone moving, little by little, into his image, helped by each other's love.
> Paul was thinking developmentally and encouraging the Ephesians to grow in unity by *becoming increasingly alike* . . .[20]

Is this what unity means? It can be disheartening for any person to perceive that because of their association with or membership in any organization, whether religious or otherwise, that they are therefore "branded," defined, as if the branding now encaptures all there is about that person. An Evangelical Christian is presumed to think and hold values that have become stereotypically associated with the "Evangelical brand." While it is true that Paul urges the Ephesian Christians to strive for unity, his further teachings regarding the matrix for that unity, i.e. in Christ, and the

19. Ibid., 315–18.
20. Johnson, *Foundations for Soul Care,* 42. Emphasis mine.

metaphor of body parts having differences of function suggest, rather than likeness to one another, diversity. The scriptural emphasis seems to be on unity achieved through diversity, but the contemporary trend toward a kind of plastic uniformity within some segments of Christianity is dehumanizing and, I would contend, disrespectful of God himself who is infinitely diverse (witness the created universe). Unity as an ideal, as an icon, risks descent into the fetish of uniformity.

ESCAPING THE CLAUSTRUM (OR, WHAT IS IT WITH MOTHER?)

Claustrum is the latin word for cloister, enclosed space. Our term, claustrophobia derives from it, the fear of closed spaces. Receiving various emphases from differing theoretical schools in psychoanalysis, the notion of necessity for separating from or disentangling from the enclosing mother of one's origin is recognized as a necessary developmental challenge perhaps never fully achieved. Of course we all begin within a very tight, enclosed space and then enter the world via a traverse through an even tighter enclosure, the vaginal birth canal, expulsion from which into open space nevertheless leaves us still and for an inordinately long time, completely dependent on her who gave rise to us. That utter and complete dependence renders the mother in possession of what amounts to virtually absolute power over the infant. Each infant then must, in the course of time, and with varying success and highly variable complications and subjective struggles, depending so much upon the personality and capabilities of the mother, and also, the temperament and genetic endowment of the child, negotiate the journey to independent adulthood. Mahler[21] is credited with emphasizing the particular necessities, and their associated problematics, of separating emotionally and psychologically from the mother and differentiating oneself from her. She saw the mother-newborn pair as constituting a kind of symbiotic matrix from which the separation and individuation challenges could be exceedingly difficult.[22]

Modern recognitions of "helicopter" mothers, or overly involved mothers, and the excessively protected child who can never be allowed to venture into the world to discover for himself, but for whom all experience of the world must be structured, programmed, and sanitized of risk

21. Mahler, *Symbiosis and Individuation.*

22. Note: The notion of mother and child forming a symbiotic "soup" has largely been discredited by subsequent infant observation which has demonstrated the object relation between distinct individuals inhering from the outset.

indicate the kinds of difficulties that children may encounter in extricating themselves from some mothers' suffocating enclosure. Jacques Lacan[23] introduced us to the idea of "le nom du pere," recognizing that the father, in some sense that may relate to the Judaeo-Christian notions of the Father, and to the Freudian emphasis on the father in *Totem and Taboo*, embodies the law, roughly the rules that regulate society and prohibit excessive indulgence. The father, whether actual or symbolic (the symbolic role of the father in instances of absence of the actual father may be fulfilled by society, church, etc.), is situated at the third point of the oedipal triangle and by virtue of his claim on the mother, instantiates a kind of "cut," a limitation to the mother's innate impulse to own, envelop, control, protect, and determine the elaboration of her child.

Every therapist sees people who struggle to get emotionally free from powerful influences lingering from their mother. Sam was a twenty-four year old university student who was fraught with the symptom of anxiety, overlaid on his personality marked by strong obsessive-compulsive tendencies. Central to his complaints were his on-going torments at the phone calls coming several times daily from his mother who lived in a city one hundred kilometres away, always requiring of him to give account of his whereabouts and his well-being, both physical and emotional. His father, whose place in Sam's mind seemed markedly diminished relative to that of his mother, was apparently impotent in his role of influencing the mother to divert her excessive and ruinous attentions away from her son. Needless to say, Sam exhibited many of the personality qualities characterizing his mother, and felt unable to disentangle himself from her because of guilt at the prospect of hurting her, fear of her collapse should he deprive her of his self as an organizing nucleus around which she was structured. Sam had not been able to get from his father what he needed, in large part because the father was likewise a controlled pet of the mother.

Dorothy Dinnerstein, in examining the matter of autonomy between men and women, asserts that both, albeit with unequal outcomes, are inevitably bound by an original dependency on the mother, such that having generally been raised in the care of a female caregiver/mother, they subjectively experience her as the original, first tyrant.[24]

> *Female will is embedded in female power, which is under present conditions the earliest and profoundest prototype of absolute power. . . . But what makes female intentionality formidable is something more than the mother's power to give and withhold*

23. Lacan, Seminar: "Psychoses."

24. 1976, *The Mermaid and the Minotaur*, Chapter 8.

> while we are passive. It *is also the mother's power to foster or forbid,*
> *to humble or respect, our first steps toward autonomous activity.*[25]

While Dinnerstein's purpose is to understand the differences in negotiating this original tyranny of the all-powerful and potentially encompassing mother between men and women, in terms of their power advantages and disadvantages in the grand enterprises of creating human reality and in making history, she observes man as the agent in these activities while woman functions as a concerned spectator who maintains life while man extends life's range through his activities.[26] I wish to consider the impact of this original "tyranny" on the quest for personal autonomy in conjunction with the quest for faith in an all-powerful God. She claims that in the face of "our most stubborn childhood wish—the wish to be free and at the same time to be taken care of—Patriarchy remains a refuge that we are afraid to dismantle."[27]

But first, let me remark as an aside on another critical problem. Richard Hays sees a biblical corrective to one egregious form of human reaction, possibly arising in response to maternal power, in Elisabeth Schussler Fiorenza's *A Feminist Critical Hermeneutic of Liberation:*

> . . . women's bodies are battered, raped, sterilized, mutilated,
> prostituted, and used to male ends . . . As in the past so still today
> men fight their wars on the battlefields of our bodies, making us
> the targets of their physical or spiritual violence. Therefore the
> ekklesia of women must reclaim women's bodies as the "image
> and body of Christ."[28]

She highlights the inherent contradiction between the eucharist's "this is my body" and the misuse of the human female body that Dinnerstein infers may arise not only from the unconscious seeding of resentment in the male mind, but also as likely in that of the female, by virtue of the the all-powerful mother of birth and early life. Hays asserts that in the communion in the body of Christ and through equal participation as members of the body of Christ, women are equal to men. As such, are women any more or less liable than men to seek refuge in patriarchy?

Critics of religion as a form of adult perpetuation of the "bliss" of childhood, like Freud and Dawkins,[29] claim that the patriarchal refuge that Judaeo-Christianity offers (or might it be the matriarchal elements of God

25. Ibid., 161–67. Emphasis hers.

26. Ibid., 212.

27. Ibid., 189.

28. Hays, *The Moral Vision*, 273.

29. Dawkins, *The God Delusion.*

as nurturer/care-giver?) is a contrivance of man to deal with his dilemma of wishing to be free while also taken care of. I'm not convinced of the notion that to become a Christian is to opt for the comforting care of a maternal God. While it is true that God does offer his continuity and reliability as an immanent personal presence, and is often portrayed as nurturer, it is also a "fearful thing to fall into the hands of the living God,"[30] albeit the context of that statement suggests that this is so if one has not availed himself of the freedom from judgement offered by God in Jesus Christ. Yet, as I have indicated earlier, to align oneself with Christ is to accept a mantle of suffering.

Segments of Christianity may interpret that being a Christian is to become identified with a stereotype, and to be entirely predictable. I have asserted the claim that to engage with Christ as a disciple/follower may be to truly realize one's own idiomatic self. In other words, Christianity, truly lived, may afford the believer opportunity for the realization of personal inner potential that can only be tapped by encounter with the evocative enigmatic Great Other. Far from being called into a "rose garden," the anticipated suffering inherent in Christian faith, as daunting as it may be, may also serve as the ground from which personal creative potential may spring.

Drawing from Simone de Beauvoir's *The Second Sex*, Dinnerstein asserts, "The person who succumbs to the temptation to forgo liberty and become a *thing* is lost, ruined."[31] She refers to each person having a moral obligation to strive for the liberty from one's common, stereotyped role and character that come to us from our up-bringing as female-raised children and achieve transcendence. Perhaps our "sexual arrangements" have been key in keeping women immune from the risks and exertions of history-making and men from overcoming the,

> nothingness void [that is] left by suppression of the essential part of the self that is a sane human creature [that] would counterbalance, and be reconciled with, what she calls transcendence: the part that lives in the present, in the body, in the steady, stable, living flow between persons and between each person and the non-human surround.[32]

I understand these authors to be striving to comprehend the thing-ness (the dehumanization) that may mark human beings who do not in some manner struggle to transcend the common roles to which our biology and our sexual arrangements in terms of rigid gender-role may consign them. From the biblical perspective, humans are locked into their "thing"

30. Hebrews 10:31.
31. Dinnerstein, *The Mermaid,* 212. Emphasis mine.
32. Ibid., 213.

state by more than the deterministic influences of traditional or otherwise parental arrangements; they are captive to the matters that occupy their minds, their money, and their energies, matters which function, in effect, as idols or fetishes. So often, such things have the import they do because they are expected to confer upon us some form of magical experience (power, pleasure, status, etc.) Martin Buber recognized the risk of becoming (or remaining?) an "it" in place of an "I" or "Thou."[33]

The non-human surround includes the one God who Christianity claims not only created humanity but confers upon it a kind of full humanness when it engages with him in a living flow relationship. The prophet Micah, speaks on behalf of the Lord, who expresses his disdain for ritual, for offerings of any sort, even so far as to decline one's firstborn in exchange for his soul:

> Shall I give my firstborn for my transgression, the fruit of my body for the sin of my soul? He has shown you, O man, what is good; And what does the Lord require of you But to do justly, To love mercy, And *to walk humbly with your God?*[34]

These are the expressions of a personal, living relationship which infiltrates all other relationships with justice and mercy. My question then, is this: if humans inevitably have to struggle for liberty from the ubiquitous entrapments of their biology, their unconscious, their social arrangements, their fetishes and idols, and from their sin, is true human autonomy anything more than an illusion? Is it possible that the best approximation to freedom is the choice that will lead to least dehumanization, least self-deception, and maximal opportunity for the idiomatic self to realize potential in the context of the highest possible interrelationships?

Paul writes of Christ having abolished "enmity, that is, the law of commandments . . . so as to create in Himself one new man . . . that he might reconcile . . . putting to death the enmity."[35] We saw earlier the role of the legalistic superego in dominating the minds of people, and thereby keeping them bound, oppressed. The peace that Paul claims Christ brings through his very self may go beyond unifying Jew and Gentile, and beyond the enmity between the individual and his creator, to shifting the enmity that exists within the psyche, between the (stranger) unconscious and the conscious self and between the ego and the superego. And yet, lest we focus overly on the individualistic benefits of being a "new creature" ("If anyone is in Christ, he is a new creation; old things have passed away; behold, all things have become

33. Buber, *I and Thou.*
34. Micah 6:8. Emphasis mine.
35. Ephesians 2:15, 16.

new")[36] a more accurate perspective is that from the bible itself, which refers to believers, collectively, as "the body of Christ." Yoder says,

> It has seemed self-evident that we were being promised here, overlapping with the language of a new birth (John 3:5f), a metaphysical or ontological transformation of the individual person. . . . The accent [of a more recent, smooth translation of 2 Cor. 5:17 to "if anyone is in Christ, new is creation," or "there is a whole new world"] lies not on transforming the ontology of the person (to say nothing of transforming his psychology or neurological equipment) but on transforming the perspective of one who has accepted Christ as his context.[37]

The transformation emphasis is on overcoming solipsism and its inclinations toward a mentality of division of the "us-versus-them" kind and on promoting community that finds its contextual existence in Christ as a new context for being, a social reality. The ethic of Christ revolves around love, essential for the blossoming of robust conscience, and hence, effective in transforming minds and social policies away from their over-reliance on superego, i.e. legalistic determinations.

DESTINY VERSUS AUTONOMY

Bollas asserts that the articulation of the self *is* the fulfillment of one's destiny. This implies that the progressive articulation of what has been at some level known, but never actually thought (his "unthought known") into words, i.e. symbolized, is to achieve the fulfillment of one's destiny. Lacan might say that, given that the unconscious is in his view, essentially structured as a language, that the re-claiming or perhaps establishing of links between signifiers renders coherence and discovery. Laplanche speaks about the person needing to resume the work of translating the untranslated fragments, the repressed unconscious bits of untranslatable message delivered unwittingly and unconsciously to him in early life by his mother, by virtue of her own sexual unconscious and the absence of one yet to be developed in him. He insists that the only legitimate hermeneut is the person himself, that the psychoanalyst can only offer assistance by means of his own self with his own enigmatic sexual unconscious, in ways that re-activate the unconscious repressed bits. Summers says,

---

36. 2 Corinthians 5:17.

37. Yoder, *The Politics of Jesus,* 226 and 228.

> When important potential components of the self remain unre-
> alized, the path of life is not one's destiny, but fate, an imposition
> from without. This aspect of unconscious mental phenomena
> consists not of finished entities, such as thoughts or wishes,
> but of potential, the not-yet-realized aspects of the psyche. We
> might say that the unconscious as potential consists of unreal-
> ized destiny.[38]

In some manner or other, they agree on the necessity of self-articula-
tion to uncover essential aspects of oneself, in order to acquire some sense
of one's own destiny.

Given the character of Christ to whom a Christian relates, and given
the penetration and illumination of the self (mind) that scripture claims to
accomplish, then perhaps there is, when a person enters into a Jesus relationship, a facilitation of the articulation one requires to realize potential. This
may assume that one can and does avoid the tendencies (maybe temptation?)
to simply acquiesce and conform to a Christian tradition or brand or convincing personality, and rather engages in the personal search for God, much in
the way Malcom Muggeridge perceived six notable historical characters to
have done (St. Augustine, Blaise Pascal, William Blake, Soren Kierkegaard,
Leo Tolstoy, and Dietrich Bonhoeffer).[39] Destiny may then be understood to
consist in the realization of one's particular self in conjunction with and as a
reflection of the infinitely creative mind of God himself. The above-named
psychoanalytic authors, building on and re-interpreting the work of Freud, do
not see humans as necessarily unalterably trapped by the psychic determin-
ism that inheres in having an unconscious, as if it were rigidly fixed. Rather,
they infer, if not explicitly claim that the existence of the unconscious along
with the prospect of access to it can represent the unlimited expansion of new
possibility and enlarged freedom of choice. Atlas is explicit in distinguishing
destiny as an active enterprise, in contrast to fate:

> For Soloveitchik (2000), fate refers to a level of human existence
> in which the human being is a passive object acted upon by ex-
> ternal forces beyond the individual's control, whereas destiny
> refers to a realm in which the person is an active subject imbu-
> ing life with meaning and significance.[40]

38. Summers, *Self Creation*, 31.

39. Muggeridge, *A Third Testament*.

40. Atlas, *The Enigma of Desire*, 148.

Muggeridge and his cadre of six "third testaments" would support such a claim, albeit based upon their individual deep experience of the quest for God and truth.

Jesus assured his followers that upon his departure the Holy Spirit would come to them and the Spirit's functions would be to convict, guide into all truth, and take of what is Christ's and declare it unto them.[41] Paul took up this theme to teach that the "Spirit helps in our weaknesses . . . makes intercession for us with groanings which cannot be uttered . . . [and who] searches all things, yes, the deep things of God."[42] A fuller reading of those passages reveals hints at the presence of the unconscious in man and the possibility of God influencing the unconscious through the agency of the Holy Spirit. I believe we all have our unconscious (however conceived) altered by the loving, consistent interest of a close and benevolent other. Perhaps, as Nahum was quoted earlier to say, if becoming oneself, or fulfilling one's destiny or realizing one's potential can only occur through "shared intentional directions with others," then the scriptures would certainly concur that doing so with God through his Holy Spirit impels one toward one's destiny in an ultimate way.

Regarding the question that arises in reference to autonomy versus joining with another or others to find one's self, Kegan says " . . . [There are] two great human yearnings . . . one . . . the yearning to be included, to be part of, joined with . . . the other . . . the yearning to be independent or autonomous, to experience one's distinctness . . . is that they seem to be in conflict, and it is, in fact, their relation—this tension—that is of more interest."[43] As complex and as multiply determined as any intention and motivation is in the human being, it need not stretch our credulity to acknowledge Kegan's fundamental dialectical tension within us. Perhaps it is a generative tension that need not be that of the schizoid: come close for I want and need you near, but stay away because I am terrified. Terrified of merging and thereby losing my distinctness? Terrified of disappearing, of being overwhelmed by your presence? Both yearnings, if in dynamic tension may be essential for health.

41. John 16:5–15.

42. Romans 8:26 and 1 Corinthians 2:10.

43. Kegan, *The Evolving Self,* 256.

Chapter 8

Sexuality, Desire, Theology and the Church

SEX AND THE EARLY CHURCH

Historically, the church's stance with respect to human sexuality has been one of tension, fraught with suspicion, fear, blame, avoidance, and moralizing. Perhaps such disturbance derives from the inherent *excess* that characterizes sexuality; excess in the form of intensity of affect, the power of what seems to be an irresistible drive, the implied loosening of all control in response to or in hope of ecstasy. Embedded in the heart of Freud's theories lies the matter of civilization's concern with exerting restraint over the expression of sexual drive intensity.[1] Much of his theories of neuroses revolve around the conflict between drives and drive derivatives and the "civilization" of the individual mind through the agency of the superego. Michael Foucault, in exploring various cultures' efforts to tame the drives, deduces that western Christianity has relied heavily upon the codification of rules and regulations by which to control sexuality.[2]

Peter Brown, in his fascinating study of sexuality in the early Christian church, points out that Paul's teachings and mission had left the early church with an identity problem, since he (Paul) specifically "resisted any attempt to encourage pagans [who became believers] to adopt the clear badges of a separate identity provided to those who converted to Judaism."[3] Circumcision, dietary laws, and other distinctive features of Jewish religious life were

---

1. See: Freud, *Civilization and Its Discontents.*
2. Foucault, *The History of Sexuality.*
3. Brown, *The Body and Society,* 59.

now considered by Paul to be irrelevant to Christian faith, and so the early Christians might have felt visibly indistinguishable from the surrounding culture. Brown claims that it was pagan converts who were impressed with the strict religious requirements of Judaism who put pressure on Paul to adopt religious distinctives for Christians, possibly influencing Paul's emphasis upon sexual practices among them. Paul did impose strict moral standards on believers and by the time Justin was converted, in the early second century, "as his *Apology* made plain, strict codes of sexual discipline were made to bear much of the weight of providing the Christian Church with a distinctive code of behavior."[4] Progressively, and in conjunction with scripture references like Revelation 14:3–5, the purity of the church as the bride of Christ came increasingly to be thought attainable through human efforts toward chaste virginity, of both males and females. Sexuality came to be seen as an important false god, the renunciation of which could enable believers to avoid defilement and attain purity. By the second century, according to Brown, Christian attitudes toward sexuality were congealing, in part, in reaction to pagan ideas:

> Because it was closely associated with the urge to overcome death through the begetting of children, sexual intercourse had always carried with it a tinge of sadness. For many ancient Greeks and Romans, their very need to sleep with women so as to obtain offspring was, in itself, a somber reminder of transience and the grave. But the new way of thinking that emerged in Christian circles . . . shifted the gravity of thought on the nature of human frailty from death to sexuality. For sexual desire was no longer presented as a benign remedy for death. Some Christian thinkers presented it as the first cause of death. Others, less drastic, saw it as the first, most blatant manifestation of Adam and Eve's loss of the immortality conferred on them by the possession of God's Spirit. For all, sexuality edged itself into the centre of attention, as privileged symptom of humanity's fall into bondage. Consequently, the renunciation of sexual intercourse came to be linked on a deep symbolic level with the reestablishment of a lost human freedom, with a regaining of the Spirit of God, and so, with man's ability to undo the power of death.[5]

The reader will recognize the appearance again, in these citations, of the human impulse to attain purity, a component of the primordial human striving toward omnipotence. From a theological viewpoint, such striving is seen as idolatry, since the gospel makes plain that humankind is incapable

4. Ibid., 60.
5. Ibid., 86.

of self-purification, and that efforts to do so suggest that the achievement of Christ on the cross to be of no point, i.e. null and void.[6] From a psychoanalytic perspective, aspirations toward purity reflect residual narcissistic infantile beliefs and superego-imposed demands that are impossible to meet and so lead only to immense suffering consequent to the inevitable internal conflict that ensues. Conflict between, on the one hand, unconscious self-(superego)-imposed expectations and demands to be pure and to function as infallible God, and, on the other hand, the reality of who one actually is as an impulse-driven, flawed and limited human is the cause of much mental anguish. Aspects of psychoanalytic treatment entail movement toward relinquishing such inordinate, unconsciously dominating demands in exchange for acceptance of oneself as humanly blemished, yet nevertheless, or perhaps even because of those very flaws, lovable.

Asceticism has an innate appeal to humans regardless of religious influence, because of the power of primary narcissism to impel towards self-perfection and the imagined possibility, albeit largely unconscious, of becoming one's own ideal god (after the model of Satan). Brown asserts that Christianity came to be "associated with rigorous sexual discipline, and marked by fear of women. . . ."[7] But he also recognized that the,

> highly restrictive codes [that] were applied with zest in the Christian Churches . . . were the creation of moral forces that had never been limited to Christianity. Pagans and Jews also liked to see their womenfolk reduced to order in the same manner.[8]

The "moral" codes adopted were in no way solely or even primarily developed from the Judaeo-Christian scriptures. These were codes devised to generate and constitute a religious system, 'religious' here meaning that which is contrived by mankind to reach toward God. Brown quotes E. Leach (*Genesis as Myth*) to illustrate the religious motivation to generate bridges to God:

> The central "problem" of religion is . . . to reestablish some kind of bridge between God and Man. . . . "Mediation" (in this sense) . . . is always achieved by introducing a third category which is "abnormal" in terms of ordinary "rational" categories. . . . The middle ground is abnormal, non-natural, holy. It is typically the focus of all taboos and ritual observances.[9]

6. Colossians 2:21–23.

7. Brown, *The Body*, 206.

8. Ibid., 207.

9. Ibid., 186.

And so, Brown's tracing of the trends in thought toward the body and sexuality in early Christianity clearly demonstrates that what was at stake were modes of thought that have far more to do with the psychology of narcissism, as well as the reaction-formations to the narcissistic injuries associated with the body as inclined toward powerful drives, illness, aging, and death than they have to do with what a Christological theology teaches; the body came to be seen by one group of influential early Christian ascetics, the Manichaeans, as disgusting, dirty, low. Strivings for purity in the sexual realm acquired special status and became central to many of the early expressions of Christianity. Yet, according to Brown, the clergy and apologists bolstered the adoption of the strict codes by also presenting to their congregants an inaccurate stereotype of the surrounding pagan world as one where "sexual disorder luxuriated."[10] It seems that the Apostle Paul's admonitions against and renunciations of "things [which] indeed have an appearance of wisdom in self-imposed religion, false humility and neglect of the body, but are of no value against the indulgence of the flesh"[11] may have been seriously overlooked. Taking the view of the Apostle Paul concerning ascetic human efforts directed toward the attainment of purity, we can see the contrast between Pauline theology and early trends within the Church. I have gone so far, above, as to suggest that the early church characterization of sexuality, insofar as it was to serve the aims of self-generated achievement of purity, constituted idolatry. By idolatry, here, I mean an attitude of mind, whether conscious and intentional or unconscious, that effectively displaces God and his provision (in Christ) as the sole means of personal reclamation from ruin, and inserts oneself and one's self-propelled efforts as sufficient for salvation.

Elsewhere, I have asserted that contemporary Christianity has tended toward a similarly fetish type of notion around sexuality, insofar as it has presumed the attainability of a purified sexuality constituted by the sexual union between Christian marriage partners.[12] By implication then, according to this notion, and if not by outright declaration, all other expressions of sexuality must be deemed impure. I will invoke arguments to support the assertion of unavoidable and inherent perversity (or, sin) in all modes of sexual expression; in so-doing, the fetishistic character of the Christian stance will become clear (the reader may wish to refer to the aforementioned features of 'fetish' in the previous chapter). At the base of my argument will be, of course, the existence of the unconscious, the influence of which, as Jonathan Lear writes,

10. Ibid., 208.

11. Colossians 2:20–23.

12. Fowler, *Shame, Silence, and Concealment as Death-Knell to Growth.* Paper presented at the Annual Conference of the Christian Association for Psychological Studies (CAPS), April 2014, Atlanta.

> The cost of keeping something out of consciousness, Freud says, is that one *acts* it out unconsciously. Repetition is the return of the unconscious, in unconscious form.[13]

SEX AND THE BIBLE

Adam and Eve and Augustine,

> Now the serpent was more crafty than any of the wild animals the Lord God had made. He said to the woman, "Did God really say, 'You must not eat from any tree in the garden?'"
> The woman said to the serpent, "We may eat fruit from the trees in the garden, but God did say, 'You must not eat from the tree that is in the middle of the garden, and you must not touch it, or you will die.'"
> "You will not certainly die," the serpent said to the woman. "For God knows that when you eat of it your eyes will be opened, and you will be like God, knowing good and evil."
> When the woman saw that the fruit of the tree was good for food and pleasing to the eye, and also desirable for gaining wisdom, she took some and ate it. She also gave some to her husband, who was with her, and he ate it. Then the eyes of both of them were opened, and they realized they were naked; so they sewed fig leaves together and made coverings for themselves.
> . . . the Lord God called to the man, "Where are you?"
> He answered, "I heard you in the garden, and I was afraid because I was naked; so I hid."[14]

This wonderfully poetic account of first beginnings was woven into a construction of St. Augustine's theology, a theory that served to account for his own psychological and moral struggles with his unsettling and restless sexuality. His writings have had enormous influence on many subsequent Christian generations' understandings about the place of sexuality in Christianity.[15] Augustine of Hippo wrote his *Confessions* in 396 AD, his *City of God* in 413, and his *On Marriage and Concupiscence* in 419 AD. He was influenced by and reacted to much of the asceticism and ferment around sexuality in early Christianity to that point. According to Brown, Augustine was the first theoretician of the human mind and sexuality to recognize the

13. Lear, *Open Minded,* 65. Emphasis his.

14. Genesis 3:1–10.

15. Foucault, *The Use of Pleasure,* 253–54; Lear, *Open Minded;* Holloway, *Leaving Alexandria,* 75.

unconscious influence of sexuality: "Sexuality was effectively taken from its physiological context [i.e. as a biological/medical phenomenon only] and made to mirror an abiding, unhealed fissure in the soul."[16] Furthermore, in contrast to other voices which claimed that the Apostle Paul's writings regarding *the flesh* referred literally and only to the body's drives for sexual or sadistic gratifications, Brown asserts that Augustine was clear in appropriately insisting that the Letters of Paul regarding *the flesh* referred to "all that led the self to prefer its own will to that of God."[17]

At this point I would like to emphasize the important influence of this confusion around Paul's dichotomy between the flesh and the spirit.[18] Clearly, many of the ancient early Christian writers focused Paul's concerns onto *the flesh* as referring literally to the matters of the body and its drives that seemed to interfere with the workings of the Spirit of God. Modern Christian voices also have tended to perpetuate the simplistic and prejudiced attribution of matters of *the flesh* to that which issues obviously from the body and its biologically-based drives, to the neglect of that which issues from the will, or the mind, but which asserts itself against God. We can credit Augustine for turning the discourse regarding the flesh toward Paul's original emphasis, a biblical emphasis which I have already demonstrated accords with the psychoanalytic perceptions of the unconscious. Further to Augustine's credit is his recognition of sexuality's central role in the fissured state of the human mind. While authors such as Foucault, Lear and Holloway have tended to target Augustine as responsible for Christianity's inordinate discomfort with sexuality, Brown recognizes more complexity in Augustine's writings. He perceived Augustine to assert that Adam's fall led to the soul (or mind?) losing its capacity to consciously harness all its faculties into service, love and praise of God. Concupiscence came into being, and was understood as,

> a dark drive to control, to appropriate, and to turn to one's private ends, all the good things that had been created by God to be accepted with gratitude and shared with others. It lay at the root of the inescapable misery that afflicted mankind. Sexual desire was no more tainted with this tragic, faceless concupiscence than was any other form of human activity.[19]

While it would seem that Brown concludes that Augustine assigned to sexuality not a causational status (for the fall) but more a victim status, among other similarly victimized forms of human activity, to the effects of

16. Brown, *The Body*, 418.
17. Ibid.
18. See for example Romans 8.
19. Brown, *The Body*, 418.

the fall, he nevertheless proceeds to criticize Augustine for unduly look-ing ". . . down that single, narrow, and profound shaft [of sexuality] to the very origins of human frailty,"[20] and thereby drastically limiting vision of the complexity of the impact of the fall of Adam. And so, while Augustine may have outlined a nuanced, complex conceptualization of the distorting impact of the fall on the mind and will of mankind, he ended up over-emphasizing the existence of sexual desire (concupiscence) as signalling a fateful turn of the will from God to one's self.

He influenced generations of Christians to believe there is inherent sinfulness in sexuality, i.e. that concupiscence (strong desire) resulted from the fall, that sexual desire came into being as a result of sinful disobedience. Presumably, then, he must have conceived of procreation being accom-plished without concupiscence (which he apparently vilified as self-centred desire that disrupts an otherwise singular unified focus on God), but with a form of desire for the other that, while exciting the bodies in readiness for intercourse, was bereft of any self-willed quest for gratification. This latter is, of course, a matter of conjecture, but defies comprehension. The compro-mise outcome of Augustine's emphasis (along with other influences) was the Catholic church's doctrine that sexual desire is sinful unless it is in the service of procreation within the context of marriage; accordingly, sexual desire for reasons of satisfaction of cravings for pleasure, or for consolida-tion of intimate relationship, but devoid of procreative intent or possibility even within marriage suffered from sanction.

Rather than the Adam and Eve story serving to portray sexuality as ground for sinfulness, I see it as portraying sexuality as the victim of trau-matic psychological processes. Eve, and then Adam, succumbed to the per-suasive, seductive temptations of Satan, who appears in the material form of a serpent, and manifests his specifically satanic quality of deceiver,[21] but does not tempt them with specifically sexual possibilities. He does tempt them with appeal to their senses, those of taste, appetite for food, and sight. But perhaps most compelling of all, and uniquely a human temptation, was that of the acquisition of knowledge, wisdom. He appealed to the human epistemological drive, although in particularly pernicious form, insofar as the knowledge on offer was a knowledge that apparently was to be only God's—the knowledge of good and evil. The trauma involved here is that of immediate awareness of the judgement of God for their defiant disobe-dience, and their aspiration to be like God. Promptly, they experience the subjective searing sensation of guilt and shame, and so, strangely, find a

20. Ibid., 422.

21. John 8:44 ". . . for he is a liar, and the father [of lies]" and Revelation 12:9.

way of covering their nakedness, as if their nakedness was a proxy for their willful disobedience. Augustine may have presumed that the knowledge of good and evil, since it led immediately to shame regarding their bodies, coupled with the fact of having indulged their sensualities of taste and sight, meant that the sexual body is a cause for shame.

Trauma is defined as that form of experience which, because of its alien nature and intensity, overwhelms the available ego capacities to deal with the powerful affects that flood the person. In the absence of adequate capacity, there can be no symbolization into usable cognitive and verbalizable constructs; the impact therefore, is typically understood to remain registered as memory traces within the body. Werner Bohleber, citing Freud's *Inhibitions, Symptoms and Anxieties* (1926d), says:

> Freud describes the ego as being absolutely helpless in view of an unbearable excitation in the traumatic situation. The ego, which normally develops an anxiety signal when in danger, is now flooded by automatic anxiety. A traumatic situation can occur due to excessive internal instinctual demands as well as external, real experiences. However, Freud never precisely defined the relationship between the external event and the internal processes. What was decisive was the "too much," the excess stimulation and a paralyzed ego, which was not able to discharge the accumulation of excitation or to bind it mentally.[22]

Adam and Eve, unable to mentally organize what had happened in their realization of having disobeyed, yet knowing themselves to now be subject to death (whatever that might have meant to them, since presumably death would at that point in the creation story not be known) subsumed the trauma into their bodies, and enacted their shame and guilt, by concealing. Did they conceal the entire body, or only as it has always been presumed, the especially excitable bits, those which possess the particular capacity to respond with such pleasurable sensations, the genitals? Phil Mollon describes well the connection between trauma, particularly shameful events, and sexuality:

> Sexuality, it is argued here, is the paradigmatic object of shame and repression, tending to incorporate all else that is repressed and in opposition to the quasi-linguistic structure of culture. Human beings may tend to long for experience that is unmediated by the linguistic—and this is the promise and terror of sexuality.
>   . . . Because sexuality is the fundamental object of repression, it tends to incorporate whatever else is repressed—so that a

22. Bohleber, *Destructiveness, Intersubjectivity and Trauma*, 79.

person's most shameful and unexpressed needs and narcissistic injuries tend to become sexualized.[23]

In place of Adam and Eve's prompt act of shameful self-concealment serving to infer that sexual desire is therefore sinful, I find it far more coherent to argue that, in keeping with the nature of sexuality and how it functions as a lightning rod for non-sexual disturbing human experience, their innocent nakedness became victim to the affects of shame and guilt, and was not the cause of shame and guilt.

Metaphor: Sexual Union, Marriage and Harlotry

I will remind the reader of the ideas previously mentioned, from Sarah Coakley, of desire and ecstasy having a vital place in the interrelationality of the triune Godhead. Jesus repeatedly speaks in ways that convey a cherishing of the Father, along with a cherishing of the Son by the Father. Furthermore, Jesus tells his followers that he will not leave them "orphans, I will come to you,"[24] meaning both that he would send the Holy Spirit to "abide with them" and that he would return eventually himself, or receive them to be with him in future. In chapter 14 of John, when Jesus is preparing his followers for his death and departure, in verse 20, he poignantly says, "Because I live, you will live also. At that day you will know that I am in My Father, and you in Me, and I in you."[25] He speaks of union between himself and the father, among the trinity, and a union into which his followers are invited. For many people the experience of worship and perhaps especially in the context of participating in the sacrament of communion, is accompanied by an ecstasy of varying intensity. Coakley, in company with Freud and Laplanche, among others, would perceive this ecstasy to consist in a derivative of sexuality, which for her, begins in God.

Richard Dawkins, in his attempts to discredit religion as having no place in a mature adult mind, likens religion to falling in love. He asserts that,

> . . . the symptoms of of an individual infected by religion [he then quotes an earlier article written by himself], "may be startlingly reminiscent of those more ordinarily associated with sexual love. This is an extremely potent force in the brain, and it is not surprising that some viruses have evolved to exploit it" ('viruses' here is a metaphor for religions: my article was called

23. Mollon, *The Inherent Shame of Sexuality*, 23–24.

24. John 14:18.

25. See also John 17:20–26.

'Viruses of the Mind'). St Teresa of Avila's famously orgasmic vision is too notorious to need quoting again.[26]

Contrary to Dawkins, who concludes that 'religious falling in love' signals the invalidity of faith, I would argue that, while ecstatic falling in love with God in no way constitutes the sum of Christian experience, it does point to an essential element that, in fact, is integral to any satisfying relationship; accordingly, there are typically pleasurable components that have affective counterparts felt in the body. These may not be felt as genitally sexual, arousing experiences, but nevertheless can be understood to reflect the "large" view of sexuality in its pervasive aspect in human inter-relationship, of positive, warm, uniting of one to an other. Given our embodied existence, our affects or emotions can only be mediated through sensations in our bodies, whether alterations in the tension of our muscles, or the stimulation of the small muscles that cause hair to stand up, or churning of the intestine, or release of gastric acid, or the increase in heart rate and respiratory rate, or the stimulation of the muscles that lead to the feeling of throat constriction, or the stimulation of complex neurological and cardiovascular elements that give rise to tumescence of the genitals, and their secretions.

We might remind ourselves that the Judaeo-Christian scriptures begin with the declaration that man and woman are both created in the image of God. Since God's intention seemed to be that having thus created the man and woman as he did,[27] these two would then do what came naturally to them, i.e. copulate and populate the earth with their progeny. I see no reason to assume that sexual desire came into being as a result of the fall, but every reason to believe that it is fundamental to the nature of God, and hence an integral part of mankind's bearing of God's image.

Both Old and New Testament scriptures employ the metaphor of God and his people relating as lovers, as husband and wife respectively, with the full implications of sexual union employed to portray in a full sense, deeper spiritual union. Furthermore, spiritual apostasy and betrayal, typified by the people of Israel going after other gods and idols, is regarded as adultery in Ezekiel's frank language that is clearly sexual.[28] God's people are consistently portrayed collectively as the female in a dance of courtship that is to consummate in marriage.[29] All of this supports a positive view of sexuality as

26. Dawkins, *The God Delusion,* 186.

27. Note: I am quite content with the likelihood that God's mode of creation may have occurred over eons of time, and through the slow progression of evolutionary processes.

28. See for example, Ezekiel 16.

29. See Revelation 19:7: "for the marriage of the Lamb [Jesus] has come, and His wife [the church] has made herself ready."

integral to and given to mankind by God, not only for procreation, but also for satisfaction, and relational consolidation.

Phallus and Circumcision

One of the cited forms of harlotry played by Israel was with "male images—[you] made for yourself male images and played the harlot with them."[30] There is the suggestion here that the only "phallus" with which Israel was to engage was God himself. If we consider the fact that God required of the people of Israel, not many, but a single outward mark of signification of their allegiance to him, circumcision of all the males,[31] then we must examine the importance to God of meanings invested in the male human penis. In diverse cultural lore, in psychoanalysis, and, I believe, in the Judaeo-Christian scriptures, the concept of phallus conveys far more than the anatomical organ called the penis. The erect penis, as symbol, stands for that which is phallic: power (or potency), generativity, excitement, pleasure, efficacy, and desire. It conveys arousal from passivity or quiescence and responsiveness to the other, i.e. woman, in all her essence (not only bodily). Lacan's use of the term phallus, while complex, suggests the element of excitement, the order of energy that initiates and stimulates in the coupling between lovers, such that either man or woman might be seen to possess the phallus,[32] i.e. to have the energy to initiate or entice and excite.

For God, circumcision served as a concrete, physical display of a critical deep reality for his people. It was to convey that his people were deeply connected by covenant to him, and that their power was not sourced from within their own beings and nor was it to be deployed for their own ends. Their power and creativity were to be seen by them and all the peoples around them as a subsidiary power, derivative of God's power and subject to God. Ezekiel's portrayal of Jerusalem's harlotry lamented her manufacture of "male images" as substitutes for God, and having done so with the very bridal gifts of jewellery that God had given her for adornments. She (Jerusalem) was vilified for having discarded the real, the true for a false image of that which was to only signify. Perhaps one could say that the Judaeo-Christian God staked his claim on being the one and only true God, and that values attributed to and inherent in the phallus, whether ascribed to the penis or to an image, belonged primarily and originally to him.

30. Ezekiel 16:17.
31. Genesis 17:10, 11.
32. Miller, *Lacanian Psychotherapy*.

While in the Old Testament, for the Israelites, circumcision carried within it the vital meanings of commitment and subjection to God, i.e. a metaphor for spiritual and relational realities, for the Apostle Paul, the term circumcision is applied to Christians in such a way as to convey the same metaphoric truth, commitment to and co-existence with Christ, it is stripped of its literal connection to the body: "In Him you were also circumcised with the circumcision made without hands, by putting off the body of the sins of the flesh, by the circumcision of Christ, buried with Him in baptism, in which you also were raised with Him through faith in the working of God, who raised Him from the dead."[33] The idea of commitment to, and subjection under God, and cleansing from godless self-determination is a theme throughout Scripture that is carried by the circumcision motif.

DESIRE, SIN, AND PERVERSION

Although God is often described as self-sufficient, he nevertheless manifests his desire. His desire is for relationship, and specifically, for the female (his people Israel or the Christian church) who excites and pleases him. His passion for her beauty and his compassion for her vulnerability, poignantly expressed in Ezekiel 16:5–14, underline the deep importance sexuality has for understanding not only ourselves as humans, but also God. Human sexuality serves as a shadow of ultimate God-human union, and without the erect penis, the phallus, as the means of connecting what are separate, there is no union and no creation of that which is new. As male excitement in response to the female is manifest so visibly in the fullness of erection, so female excitement in response to the male is manifest in display (as suggested in Ezekiel 16): adornment with jewellery and fine clothes which innovatively cover or reveal the body, colour highlighting and contrasting with make-up, all of which converge in the excitement of exhibition. Obviously, all and any of the foregoing characterizations of male and female excitement are ripe for perversion (distortion) and exploitation. Consider the exploitation of sexuality in our culture for commercial purposes, thereby exposing that which is central to our human essence to potential commodification and debasement. As for pornography, while it can be too simplistically easy for Christians to vilify and moralistically reject all pornography, perhaps a deeper look into motivations for both those who produce erotic images and those who consume them might render greater understanding and less harsh automatic judgement. I suspect for many, Christians and non-Christians, the creation of erotic imagery and for others, the viewing of

33. Colossians 2:11, 12.

erotic imagery enables the discharge of impulses that might otherwise lead to more egregious and relationally destructive behaviors.

If I can allow for a possible concession to forms of (soft) pornography as a kind of lesser evil, in the service of human innate impulses, nevertheless, insofar as the dignity of what I have claimed to be a more or less divine core essence of humanity is degraded in pornography, then erotically stimulating visual depictions of female or male bodies, or of sexual acts may constitute various forms of perversion. Of course, if all humans are infiltrated with fantasies that constitute polymorphous perversity, as I will argue, then pornography will inevitably manifest such perversity in its almost infinite variety. Returning to Ezekiel 16, the remainder of the chapter depicts Jerusalem's perversion of God's intimate co-(mm)-union with her.

Human beings are ineluctably embodied. As such, our experience of the human "other" is as an embodied (including sexual) other. A fundamental of Freud's thesis is that psychic development is rooted in the body: "The ego is first and foremost a bodily ego; it is not merely a surface entity, but is itself the projection of a surface."[34] Our bodies serve as touch-stones of recognition, of both ourselves and the other. Our identity, however it may be conceived, is necessarily intimately entwined with our body. It is claimed that Jean Paul Sartre said, "Having a body means we exist for the other." Consider the influence on one's perception of oneself, even (for some of my patients in analysis) one's assurance of actually existing (when, for some, this is a matter of doubt), of the experience of being truly recognized by an other, and further, the sense of oneself as desirable (or as repulsive), based upon the gaze of the other. Our experience of ourself and of the other is mediated through our bodies.

Desire, we have recognized, implies lack, need, the want of something beyond that which one has. As previously noted, desire may, in effect, fuel life. Silf says (*Wise Choices*), "Desire is energy, the energy of creativity, the energy of life itself."[35] While sexuality is so infused with desire, the desire of one for the other, and the desire to be desired, perhaps such desire can only realize, at best, temporary satiation. It is constantly reawakening, seeking, yet again, satisfaction. And is even the best sexual experience ever truly able to gratify the cravings that impel it for longer than a moment, or a few days? Galit Atlas says:

> It is a deep form of longing that sexuality brings us in touch with. That longing presupposes a sense of early loss with yearning and

34. Freud, *The Ego and the Id*, 26.
35. As quoted in: Martin, *The Jesuit Guide to (Almost) Everything*.

hope of refinding. But what is it that we have lost and search to refind?

> ... Klein (1963) ... writes about a ubiquitous human yearning for an "unattainable perfect internal state" (p. 300) related to the inability to even know ourselvess and each other, to even fully know everything (Bion's O).

> ... The zone we are dealing with [the unattainable perfect, magical state] is unrepresentable, unsignifiable, that which is entirely outside of language . . . This is where the inaccessible piece of the unrepresentable mother [as per Laplanche] becomes the basis for our longing.[36]

Given the depths of content embedded within human sexual desire, it inevitably has about it the features of a chimera, an illusion or delusion, a fantasy of final and full satisfaction, that, of course, it can never deliver. In one of the songs of Leonard Cohen's last, late-life album, "You Want it Darker," he sings with a poignancy of relief that the beast has finally died. The compelling urgency of sexual desire leads to all manner of reliance on sex for secondary emotional purposes. Atlas writes:

> We know that people seek sexual experience for many different emotional reasons . . . : as an attempt to discharge their inner objects and self with excitement and realness and aliveness; to express their aggression and hostility; to hide or expose their vulnerability; to bolster the collapsing or fragmenting self; to heal trauma through the repetition of arousal; to achieve recognition and affirmation through the body; and more.[37]

God desires to be the object of man's desire and promises a measure of satisfaction that transcends all others: "For He satisfies the longing soul, And fills the hungry soul with goodness."[38] James Martin says,

> The deep longings of our hearts are our holy desires. Not only desires for . . . healing . . . but also for change, for growth, for a fuller life. And our deepest desires, which lead us to become who we are, are God's desires for us. . . . And ultimately our deepest desire, planted within us, is our desire for God.[39]

Might desire invested in the spiritual search for God be relatively free of the fantasies and perversions which I will explore as inevitable in human

36. Atlas, *The Enigma of Desire*, 26–27.

37. Ibid., 19.

38. Psalm 107:9; See also John 4:13, 14.

39. Martin, *Jesuit Guide*, 61, 63.

sexuality? Or might the search for God similarly suffer from our human corruptions? Might it be that God, as holy (i.e. without blemish, sin, a repressed sexual unconscious) and whose intentions for humanity are clearly directed at humanity's good, can be worshipped (desired) with a measure of satisfaction that is not corrupted by his own competing interests for gratification in the way human-to-human interactions inevitably are? Perhaps the tone struck by Augustine was accurate, insofar as sexual desire and its satisfaction might be seen as a comparatively poor cousin to the satisfaction of desire one might experience in worship of God.

Freud[40] perceived that sexuality exists and is formed in ways essential to its adult expression during early childhood; he was emphatic that sexuality does not make its first appearance at puberty as is commonly thought. Furthermore, he claimed the existence of the Oedipus Complex, in which the child first experiences sexual desire for his parent of the opposite sex, along with powerful guilt and shame for not only those illicit impulses, but also for the associated impulse to do away with the same-sex parent, so that he can triumph and have as his own, the desired parental object; the child then must repress the ideas and fantasies associated with his sexuality that form around this nucleus. As a result, distortions of endless variety and complexity come into being in the mind from the instantiation and fusion of fantasies, the tendency of other traumas to intrude into sexuality and the conflicting emotions that accompany each and all of these. These distortions, or perversions, which cannot be avoided, came to be understood by Freud as universal and unavoidable for all humans, and so he asserted that human sexuality is inevitably polymorphously perverse. Robert Stoller claims that perversions arise in the fantasy life of the child in consequence of childhood trauma; the fantasy is constructed so as to convert victimhood into triumph, to replace pain with pleasure, and that this necessarily entails hostility toward the object of sexual desire, accompanied by sufficient risk such that excitement is maximized (all ingredients of perversion).[41] To quote Phil Mollon again:

> Another intriguing feature of sexuality is the way in which it strangely incorporates the deepest wounds to the self in the desires and fantasies that it generates in its name. . . . It seems to me that what sexuality does is to take all that is banished from the realm of language—all what in childhood could not be spoken of, the areas of experience that are rendered dumb and invalid, and weave these into fantasy and desire. Sexuality is akin to

40. Freud, *Three Essays on Sexuality.*
41. Stoller, *Perversion, The Erotic Form of Hatred.*

Freud's "navel" of the dream (1900:525)—it is the hole in the symbolic, tantalizing, seductive, gathering all that is banished and repudiated from the symbolic self. . . . The symbolic order means separation from the fantasy of union with the mother. By contrast, sex offers the promise of union with another's body— thus inherently placing itself outside of the symbolic discourse. Sex is thus maximally appealing and at the same time full of dread, in its signification of death and loss of the symbolic self.[42]

If death is embedded in the "beyond the symbolic" of immersion of one-self into a sexual (true sensually saturated ecstasy) experience, then maybe we can make sense of the fact that we are told that Christ is the Word made flesh,[43] yet according to the record, he had no experience of human genital sexuality. Perhaps to do so would have meant partaking in a premature, al-ternative non-symbolic "death" that may somehow have nullified or at least altered the death that was to come for him. Could the Word not abandon the symbolic? Did he choose to not do so? If he was fully human and "tempted in all things, yet without sin,"[44] can we assume that he also longed for that fleshly union with the body of a woman, but refrained from enactment?

Luke 7:36–50 gives us an account of what was likely Jesus' most sensu-ous encounter with a woman that the records give us. In contrast to the Pharisee, Simon, in whose house Jesus was a guest, and who failed to wash the feet of Jesus, a woman entered off the street, a known "sinner," likely a known prostitute, and washed Jesus' feet with her tears, wiped them with her hair, and then anointed his feet with expensive perfume and kisses. I am imagining this woman to have been very beautiful. I am also imagining this to have been a highly sensuous experience for Jesus. However much this may have been so, he allowed this poignant moment to stand and received this woman's gift, mercifully forgave her sins (contrition was likely her pri-mary motivation buried in her act of worship), and used the encounter to teach on forgiveness. He did not exploit this woman's sensuality for his own gratification of desire, except for a holy desire for God to be glorified. (As an aside, I think of this encounter as analogous to a psychoanalyst's appropriate non-self-gratifying response to an analysand's erotic transference).

Given the perverse character of all sexuality as I have been arguing, and if Christ, being God, was free of such distortions, then would physical expressions of sexual desire have had no claim on him? Was his sexuality of a transcendent order that found its satisfactions in both relations among the

---

42. Mollon, *The Inherent Shame*, 32.

43. John 1:1–14.

44. Hebrews 4:15.

trinitarian Godhead, and in his profound love of humankind to the point of sacrificial death? Or might his death itself possibly have achieved something akin to the sexual signified loss of the symbolic self Mollon describes as a component of the ecstasy (and in Jesus' case agony)? These are speculative questions that might deserve further investigation.

On these matters, I believe the theories of Jean Laplanche add more helpful understanding. He rehabilitated Freud's abandoned seduction theory as cause for neurotic conflict, by recognizing that although the evidence for widespread actual seduction by perverse and negligent parents was absent (as did Freud, who therefore scrapped the idea), there was evidence for a universal seduction of the infant. The infant is intimately connected to his mother who has a sexual unconscious, while he does not as yet himself possess an unconscious, and so is uniquely open, vulnerable to all manner of influences from her. To reiterate some of the features of Laplanche's claims, I will enumerate them:[45]

1. "From birth, infants are dependent on adults in an attachment relationship which centres on communication"; the communication is two-way, but for the infant, it is instinctual, based upon the self-preservative instincts; for the adult it is not instinctual, and is only partially conscious, and otherwise unconscious.

2. "Of course all attachment communication entails activity—biological, bodily activity—and associated sensations." The activity and sensations plus verbal communications eventually, by a maturing stage of development, are represented mentally by precise perception and logical thinking, secondary process thinking.

3. "However, the adult in this pair has a sexual unconscious, while the infant does not. This asymmetry is what Laplanche calls the Fundamental Anthropological Situation."

4. "The adult's sexual unconscious compromises the attachment communications, adding an enigmatic dimension—enigmatic both to the child and to the adult." The adult's unconscious was similarly formed by the influence of enigmatic messages from her mother. It is the positive affectively-toned care of the mother for the infant, with its components of pleasure, excitement, sensuality, as well as the affects of resentment, anxiety, possibly envy and hate (the so-called death-drive aspects of the sexual drive) that render her messages to the infant enigmatic.

45. Adapted from: Jonathan House, 2013, *Intro to Laplanche in Less Than a Page.*

5. "The child seeks to make sense of the adult's communications, in Laplanche's terms, to translate them—including the enigmatic elements. This is the General Theory of Seduction. In other words, the child is stimulated (seduced, inspired) to make meaning out of the adult's communications including the enigmatic meanings which parasitize the adult's conscious message and which are generally outside of the adult's conscious and pre-conscious awareness."

6. "At every stage of development, the child's translation of the adult's communication can never fully succeed, especially for the enigmatic aspects. This partial failure leaves untranslated bits—residues which are designified signifiers. These residues constitute the unconscious. This process of partially failed translation is primal repression. Laplanche calls this the Translational Model of Repression."

7. "Humans are a meaning making species. The untranslated bits, the primally repressed, remain a constant source of stimulation to translation, translation which can never succeed, once and for all. These untranslated bits are also the object of meaning making and thus Laplanche calls them the source/object of the drive."

In the effort to make meaning of what one experiences in the course of life, especially early life, inevitably, the repressed untranslated bits become attached to and influence the content and affective tone of cognitions that form into fantasy. The fantasies may take on any manner of idiosyncratic distinctness. If we recall Mollon's recognition of the unique quality of sexuality such that it draws into itself the traumatic, the banished and the invalid, then we can realize the potential for sexuality to acquire unavoidable perversity, and, given the absolutely unique configuration and complexity of the formation of the drive in any one individual, we can also acknowledge the potentially endlessly polymorphous character of that perversity. Since Laplanche asserts that the biologically instinctual component of human sexual life only comes into play at puberty, it does so superimposed onto the already formed sexual drive developed in childhood, as outlined above.

Sex, Transgressive Necessity, and Love

Adding to the elements of early unconscious sexual development outlined thus far, I will add perspectives from an object relations viewpoint. In the course of growing one's mind, inexorably we all internalize elements of our parents, such that we end up with some "good" (i.e. supportive, benevolent, affirming, interested—in a word, loving) internal objects and some "bad" (disaffirming, prohibiting, persecuting, judgemental—not necessarily hostile or morally bad) internal objects, all contributing to the complex psychic milieu of the unconscious mind. Further, we experience in the course of the oedipal journey, various exciting and often disturbing affects, such as mysterious attractions, jealousies, envies, and pains of rejection (or transgressive seductions involving confusing inclusion by the parents, to whom it all seems innocent) at being the unwelcome outsider to our parents' romantic and secret passionate intimacies. And it is not only that we internalize such affective experiences and strive to make sense of them by utilizing and bringing into conjunction with them whatever fantasy material might be recruited and presented to our child mind from an infinite variety of sources (like family lore, fairy tale stories, television narratives, imagination, etc.), but we also conflate these with the repressed untranslated enigmatic messages already populating the forming unconscious. Also, by long intimate association with the unconscious of our parents, unavoidably, the oedipal configurations and complexities from each parent's own childhood experience of their parents compound further our unconscious map for relational being. And, finally, we also form as a distillate from much of this process, our superego, which, as we have discovered, is typically prohibitive and inhibiting of our freedoms to express ourselves and enact our desires and impulses.

Stein elegantly depicts the reasons why passion or romance characteristically and notoriously fade from long-lasting relationships, to be replaced by the mundane preoccupations of everyday life. In answer to the question "Can love last?" she says:

> Love *can* last, we all know it. After all, there are love relations that last for decades, even as long as a lifetime. Love can deepen and grow; feelings of connectedness, devotion and cherishment can accompany people through long spans of time and grow with them. If resentment does not accumulate too hopelessly, if inner bad objects are not enacted too strongly, and if narcissistic vulnerabilities do not transmute into devaluatory processes stripping relations of benevolence and injecting them with vengefulness, love can last and grow. Admittedly, many if not most couples witness their good feelings wearing thin and leaving the stage for bad, sometimes increasingly bad, experiences and shabby feelings. The trust and generosity accompanying the early stages of a couple's love often fade through increasing cycles of disappointment, hurt and alienation. Still, there are many people whose loving bonding defies time and hardship and even deepens with them.
>
> However, a long-standing love often thrives at the cost of passionate desire. Plato the Greek and Augustine the Christian,

each embracing the assumption that love tends to grow with time whereas desire is inclined to wither, recommended that we allow desire to run its course until the day when desire and its troubles come to an end to be replaced by a love that is no longer erotic but based in trust and companionship.[46]

Akin to Stein's distinction between erotic and companionship love, the argument is often made that romantic, passionate erotic love, as manifested in passionate sex, "falling in love" or "love affairs," is different from the love so often portrayed by Christians in the term agape which conveys companionship, respect, care, interest and concern for the other and his or her well-being. Although this distinction is useful to illustrate the point of what happens in actual relationships, I want to caution against losing the idea that *all* inter-human connectedness is infused with desire (or libido), however attenuated might be the overt manifestations of it.

Stein develops her argument further by noting that for most of us, with age, and duration of a relationship, sex, constituting experience so different from our ordinary preoccupations and states of mind, becomes relegated increasingly to the periphery as something for which we no longer have or are willing to devote the time and energy. But, she goes on to assert that passion, which is closely related to suffering and the overcoming of obstacles contrasts with that which tends to prevail in our lives, the secular and mundane, or profane. Passion, by contrast is seen as sacred, i.e., in her usage, as set apart, other-worldly, manifest in sexual and religious experience, often implying ecstasy; sexual passion is "otherness." This otherness acquires its quality of intense erotic excitement from the experience that it:

> *always implies a hurdle* (death in Jesus the Saviour, societal norms in Romeo and Juliet, marriage laws in adultery, internal oedipal prohibitions in marriage) *and its overcoming, a desire not met, a suffering and being tantalized.* Passion therefore always carries *connotations of a conflicted or forbidden desire . . .* Against the desire within a couple, there is, I suggest, a counterpoint and inhibitory force—the superego—an extended sense of taboo, prohibition, censorship, fear and love, the Law, internalized forces of socialization and culture, training and adaptation. . . . The oedipal longings and excited curiosity, the need to defy parental barriers and prohibitions and satisfy the desire to know [think here of the primary couple's (Adam and Eve) desire to know], and to have the mysterious relations between them, stimulate sexual passion in each partner in the couple.

46. Stein, *Unforgetting and Excess,* 763–64. Emphasis hers.

> The powerful attraction to what is behind the scenes (or under the clothes), the fascination with what is enigmatic, allusive, enticing, but not quite within reach, produces a desire to cross boundaries, to lift the veil over the enigma.[47]

Inevitably, then, sexual activity with another is necessarily transgressive, of standard social boundaries and *must* be transgressive in order for it to have the erotic intensity that defines it. Couples who so sanitize their sexual relationship of all "naughty" playfulness risk the excitement prematurely dying.

When we think of perversions, even within psychoanalysis, we are inclined to conjure that which is clearly or obviously outside the range of acceptably "normal," the extreme: The person who hires prostitutes for the purpose of engaging them in bizarre sexual fantasies, or a Russell Williams whose perversion entailed breaking into the homes of, stealing and dressing in the underwear of, raping, and ultimately murdering his female victims,[48] or, more mildly, the analysand who has to have his female sexual partner's feet dressed in sheer nylon stockings in order to climax. My own view is that the transgression of internal object and superego prohibitions and inhibitions in either the mind of oneself or one's partner or both (through the unconscious forces that collude to bring two particular people to be attracted to one another), inheres inescapably in all sexual expression, and that perversion is therefore universal and not restricted to the particularly obvious or egregious expressions of it that invite the label "perversion" as a designation of pathology or criminology. This is the only conclusion I can draw from the observations and theoretical constructs of Freud, Stoller, Laplanche, Stein, and many others. Further, my own clinical work supports this conclusion and so does the view of Scripture regarding the ubiquity of sin. If sin penetrates to all aspects of the human mind, then how can sexuality be other than distorted?

What does the Scripture say about love? Jesus, in Matthew 12:28–31, in response to a question from one of the scribes, "Which is the first commandment of all?":

> The first of all the commandments is: '*Hear, O Israel, the Lord our God, the Lord, is one. And you shall love the Lord your God with all your heart, with all your soul, with all your mind, and with all your strength*'. This is the first commandment. And the second, like it, is this: '*You shall love your neighbor as yourself*'. There is no other commandment greater than these.

47. Ibid., 771. Emphasis hers.

48. Canadian ex-Colonel in the Canadian Armed forces, arrested and stripped of his status and convicted, in 2010.

When asked about the first commandment, Jesus responded with two, because they cannot, for a Christian, be separated. Loving God and neighbor form a unity.

Kierkegaard asserted, "that Christianity has thrust erotic love and friendship from the throne, the love rooted in mood and inclination, preferential love, in order to establish spiritual love in its [primary] place, love to one's neighbor, a love which in all earnestness and truth is inwardly more tender in the union of two persons than erotic love is and more faithful in the sincerity of close relationship than the most famous friendship."[49] He viewed erotic love and friendship as belonging to paganism, insofar as they are poetically upheld in such high esteem by that world. As the biblical story of the good Samaritan teaches, our neighbor is everyone, regardless of race, religion, political conviction, or social status, and everyone of us is one's neighbor. He elaborated his position regarding the lesser status of erotic love and friendship by convincingly claiming that erotic love and friendship essentially consist in loving oneself; insofar as these two loves arise spontaneously, on the basis of natural inclination and affection, they, in contrast to Christian love of one's neighbor, are selfish. They cohere by the gratification of either sensuous desire (which Kierkegaard urges Christianity to value and uphold—"Christianity is far from unreasonably wishing to turn the sensuous against a man by teaching him extravagance [i.e. rejecting sexual love as of the body and against the spirit] . . . of spirituality"[50])—or natural affection, respectively and not exclusively. To clarify his points of distinction and the ranking of loves further, he says,

> In erotic love and friendship the two love one another in virtue of differences [e.g. when the differing sexual proclivities or personality features of two lovers complement each other such that an orgasmic union is forged] or in virtue of likenesses that are grounded in differences (. . . from other men). In this way the two can selfishly become one self. Neither one of them has yet the spiritual qualifications of a *self*; [which to Kierkegaard means a Christian self whose "love is self-renunciation's love and therefore trusts in this *shall* of the commandment to love one's neighbor as oneself"];[51] neither has yet learned to love himself Christianly. In erotic love the I is qualified as body-psyche-spirit, the beloved qualified as body-psyche-spirit. In friendship the I is qualified as psyche-spirit and the friend is qualified as psyche-spirit. Only in love to one's neighbor is the

49. Kierkegaard, *Works of Love*, 58.
50. Ibid., 65.
51. Ibid.

self, which loves, spiritually qualified simply as spirit and his
neighbor as purely spirit.[52]

Neither Kierkegaard nor Stein, with their differing emphases, would
claim that neighbor-love (which Kierkegaard claims to belong to Christianity alone) and desire manifest supremely in erotic love cannot co-exist within
the same persons within the same relationship. Within Christian marriages,
I would guess that the fading of erotic desire for all the reasons that Stein
includes happens as much as in secular unions; this need not mean that
Kierkegaardian friendship and even uniquely Christian neighbor-love cannot simultaneously or sequentially grow between the two long-term lovers;
in fact one might hope that this would be couples' ultimate wish and aim.

Given the complexity of love and of sexual desire, is it any wonder that
people experience in adult life an infinite variety of difficulties with their
sexual experience, difficulties which manifest often in strained relationships, perhaps most particularly with their long-term romantic partner, and
not necessarily as overt specifically sexual frustrations, as common as they
are, but often as conflictual power struggles, marked by disappointment at
unmet expectations, boundary confusions, envies, jealousies, suspicions,
etc. The expressions of love (of whatever type, erotic, friendship, or neigh-
borly) for another, all unavoidably motivated and influenced by the sexual
unconscious, are ineluctably (de)formed, for better or for worse, and, can,
when meticulously analyzed (as in the context of a psychoanalysis) be recognized for the perversities embedded therein. When the Bible refers to sin
that thoroughly saturates all human beings, our comprehension of the reach
of sin into the very fabric of our being is enhanced by recognition of the role
of early life transmission of the prior generation's unconscious upon which
we all, then, must do our best to form meaning, deal with our impurities and
make the best we can out of what we have. Our best will never be pure, never
free from the complex, largely unconscious undergirding of our social, i.e.
sexual being. Even Kierkegaard's Christian spiritual love for one's neighbor
cannot escape influence and contamination from the person's unconscious.

A common recognition among psychologists not exclusively of Christian persuasion is that in addition to sexuality developing through the drawing of traumatic influences into the body and into fantasy-formation, as per
Mollon, sexuality and incest may be turned to out of motivations deriving
from emotional deprivation and lack of fulfillment when the emotional environment of the family is such that its members are left starving for significance and meaning. For example, siblings might engage in incest because of

52. Ibid., 69. Emphasis his.

such unfilled emotional needs.[53] From our look into the roots of the sexual unconscious we can see that there are plenty of opportunities for sexual distortions to inscribe themselves into a developing mind even without there existing any evidence necessarily of overt family or social deprivations or dysfunctions. In other words, apparent (to the outside observer) "normality" in families and their relationships does not in any way assure of absence of psychological conflict or relational strife, affecting sexuality as much as any other aspect of adult experience. In fact, from work done by Peter Fonagy and Mary Target (see previous reference), we understand that if a capacity for emotional regulation, generally, develops from the mirroring of affect from an optimally attuned primary caregiver, nevertheless, particularly,

> sexual feelings are different in this respect because they are systematically ignored and left unmirrored or are only partially so. At the core of this view lies the specific difficulty the mother has in mirroring the infant's sexuality—[e.g. the mother's cleansing hand actions or facial expressions or murmurings of aversion when attending to her baby's genitals, or the tone of voice that changes when instructing her pubescent daughter about menstruation, or a parent's response to his toddler's obvious wish for his erect penis to be admired.] an adaptive failure that structures psychosexuality, indelibly inscribing in the mind the need for an other who makes it possible to experience our sexuality through their elaboration of it.[54]

So, it can be readily seen that existence of universal distortions or perversity in sexuality have little to do with the dysfunctionality of the emotional environment of one's up-bringing, except as to the *degree* of emotional ineptitude in the caregivers, and the degree of severity of dysfunctionality of the social and family environments. Target points out another subtlety affecting the mother's or primary caregiver's role in effectively mirroring her baby's emotional states, and that is the importance of "marking" them. Marking means that the mother conveys to the baby that, "her mirroring responses, in particular to negative emotions, do not indicate how she herself feels, but rather her awareness of her baby's state."[55] Marking is achieved through tone of voice or through facial expression, playful speech, irony, etc. The idea is to enable the child to internalize an accurate representation of his mental state that is neither contaminated by the mother's own personal emotion that could either amplify or dismiss the baby's, nor mis-

53. Balswick and Balswick, *Authentic Human Sexuality.*

54. Lemma, *The Prostitute as Mirror,* 192.

55. Target, *A Developmental Model of Sexual Excitement,* 46.

matched such that confused labelling of internal representations leads to non-symbolization and therefore confusion and inability to regulate. It is a particularly impossible challenge for a mother to mark her infant's sexual states, and therefore regulation of one's sexual affects tends to be unstable.

Having established at least a basic foundation for complex under-standings of sexuality in human experience, including a tracing of some of the historical influences on western Christian attitudes to sex, I will now il-lustrate some points with case material, and then turn my attention to some of the ways in which intersections between sexuality and Christianity may be illumined by psychoanalysis.

Lydia

To refresh the reader's memory, Lydia had grown up with a deeply narcis-sistic mother who had always needed to compete with and triumph over Lydia, who described her mother as always smarter, prettier, and better at everything. Her mother was a frustrating, harsh, and often hostile, but nev-ertheless exciting object to Lydia as a young girl. Mirroring and marking functions were truly flawed in this mother-infant pair. As a consequence, Lydia had difficulty achieving a capacity to regulate her emotional states, and so exhibited one of the features that led to her being psychiatrically diagnosed with borderline personality disorder: intense and rapidly altering affect states, especially manifest as anger. She describes her step-father as showing little interest in her, except when he once tried to persuade her, as a teenager, to join him in sun-bathing naked. She has a distinct memory, from about age five, of being persuaded by a visiting adult man, to come into the bathroom with him, whereupon he exposed himself and had her touch his penis.

Lydia's adult romantic relationships have all been heterosexual, but always marked, as she regrets to say, by very early engagement sexually, and very soon thereafter breaking down from hostility. Her only marriage was brief and manifested the sadomasochistic features of all her relation-ships, as modeled after the relationship with her mother. Not surprisingly, the fantasy to which she reported masturbating throughout much of her adolescent and adult life, as a way of soothing her anxiety so as to be able to sleep at night, consisted in her being subjugated and debased before a hostile standing man, on whom she was performing fellatio. While this pat-tern of fantasy, necessary as it was for her to achieve orgasm, may harbor important elements of early infant development, oral and anal stage residual components, the sadomasochistic aspects of her primary relationship with her mother can be seen to be portrayed in the fantasy.

This illustration of "perversion" highlights the ways in which early childhood traumatic and conflictual experiences can and do become incorporated into the fantasies that underpin adult sexuality. In Lydia's case, hostility is tamed within the fantasy, by sexualizing it, and turning it largely against herself. Unfortunately, it has also meant that mutually tender, affectionate and respectful relating has not been possible for her. During the course of her analysis, and despite the matter receiving little direct attention, the need for masturbation in order to sleep disappeared after about the first year, signalling a reduction in her anxiety; perhaps in time, the consistency, respectful warmth and open explorations in her relationship with her analyst will lead also to improved extra-analytic relationships.

Amanda

Amanda, also previously introduced, has a strong faith in God, and a strong desire to honor God with her sexuality, but suffers deep conflict over important aspects. Although there are many sources contributing to her disturbed sense of herself as contaminated and suffering a frustratingly non-existent sexual relationship with her husband of many years, I will highlight two key early-life features. Her parents both grew up in poor families which held to a strict Catholic faith; when their late teenage relationship led to the unwed pregnancy with Amanda, and forced them to marry, guilt and shame overshadowed their subsequent adult lives, so Amanda believes. Furthermore, psychoanalytic work has revealed that Amanda feels herself likewise contaminated with their guilt and shame, transmitted to her, as if she carried it as well. This latter subjective impression is entangled with and exacerbated by two additional historical facts, one, of having been left by her parents with her grandmothers for most of her first year of life, so that her parents could find jobs at some distance from their home; the second involves Amanda having been repeatedly sexually abused by her uncle, while still a pre-pubescent child, and then fondled by her own father in early adolescence.

As concerns about her own sexual feelings, frustrations, and thoughts came into the analysis, and particularly as they entered the transference, Amanda came to perceive a duality to her experience of desire. She characteristically saw herself as wholesome, maternal in her interests and outlook (despite having no children of her own), and chaste; however, as the analytic work progressed, she disturbingly discovered another manifestation of her erotic desire coming to the fore, of which she had previously only barely been aware, that of herself as an intensely aggressive seductress, "setting the stage, I'm the one in control, luring him in, saying naughty, raw, aggressive things that are not loving, and this isn't me. It's *very* exciting, giving rise to a different kind of [masturbatory] orgasm; it's different from my usual fantasies which are of being soft and caressing. [Acknowledging her embarrassment in talking of this] I know I need to talk about this and that it is very important, but it's conflicted."

Some analytic understandings of the distortions besetting her sexuality include the common need to mitigate against shame inherent in sexuality (arising from the absorbed traumata, as per Mollon, and the inevitable mirroring failures, as per Target) by reaction-formation, a defense in the form of perception of herself as pure and chaste. But the co-existing need to experience her fundamental fantasy of being an exciting, adventuresome, seductive sexual object, fully capable of arousing desire in an other leads to a dichotomous splitting between the wholesome "Madonna" and the degraded seductive "whore" in Amanda's case. As it is also with many other women (and many men's dichotomized perceptions of women), there is little integration between these two polar opposite expressions and subjective experiences of herself. Of course the conventional sanctions from her religious background against sexual pleasure for its own sake or for the sake of relational intimacy played their part in forming her conflict. Finally, the abusive induction into sexual experience before maturity by violating adult males no doubt left her with residual intensified shame at feeling herself actively engaging her sexual appeal in the attraction of a male. In other words, to what extent does the highly exciting and powerful experience of herself as a seductress resonate with and elicit echoes of her confusion as to her role in the childhood abusive encounters?

And so, Amanda, despite striving for purity within her sexuality has found only confusion, conflicting and seemingly unacceptable desires, and profound disappointment.

Graham

This is a man, married for many years, faithful to his wife with whom he has three adult children, and a committed Christian. He came into analysis in middle age, for reasons of a long-standing tendency to depression, first experienced in early adulthood, and a growing concern about the flattening out of passion between himself and his wife, who is also a serious Christian. Focusing on that which is relevant to this discussion, we eventually learned of his inward experience of his sexuality. Having grown up in a conservative

Christian home, where matters to do with sex and those pertaining to the body, and especially the body's specifically sexual parts, were never discussed, he acquired a deep sense of his own sexual interests as unacceptably wicked, and his genitals as disgustingly dirty.

Graham and his wife, who also came out of a devout conservative Christian home, were both virgins at the time of their marriage. Both are well-educated, professional people, whose values and life choices have considerably liberalized from those of both of their parents. During the course of analysis, and in part through recognition and interpretation of pertinent dream material, he came to discover that in order to be potent in intercourse, to achieve pleasure and successful orgasm, he required a fantasy to play out in his mind while in the midst of love-making. The fantasy consisted in his wife playing out a role as a highly exotic, seductive woman, enacting her prowess with a stranger, with whom he then identified. Only slowly did there come into his conscious awareness the consistency and rigidity of this necessary fantasy (even though he could infinitely vary some details). It seemed that his wife's sexual fantasy life might have more or less complemented his own, since they had had an apparently gratifying sexual life for many years. It was only when, in the face of latter middle-age waning of his own sexual capacity and his wife's declining interest in conjunction with menopause, he began to suggest and require of his wife, actual enactments of the previously only imagined role-playing with him, that her resistance to these demands led to conflict in the relationship, and his search for therapy.

We can make inferences about his perceptions about himself: failed early-life mirroring and perhaps also, unconscious transmission of his caregivers' own discomfort or disgust with the genital body. He fantasized the stranger and identified with him because the familiar other, in this case, himself, was actually not a partner who, in his mind, could be excitedly accepted by his wife; he had denigrated and disavowed his sexual self.

Alex

As a thirty-five year old highly anxious and obsessional man, who is also a devout Christian from a family of likewise devout Christian parents, Alex lies on the spectrum of psychological organization that is closer to psychotic disorganization, and, in fact, has suffered from one prior psychotic episode, many years earlier, that involved a lot of paranoid thoughts. As is so commonly the case with highly anxious and/or depressed people, it did not take long to discover in his analytic therapy that he felt oppressed by a highly critical, dictatorial, and perfectionistic internal judge, or superego.

Despite being able to speak freely the patois of "Christian-ese," and knowing much Scripture by memory, he had very little sense of a comfortable
peace and self-acceptance that is promised to a child of God. One of his
recurring paranoid thoughts revolved around whether he would prove to
be homosexual, since, as a pre-pubescent youngster, wrestling with a friend,
he became aware of developing an erection. Throughout his teen and young
adult years, to date, he has not had a serious girl friend, and has never had
any significant measure of intimacy, bodily, or emotionally, with a girl.

One of the matters which fuels his cruel superego, is his repeated
turning to soft porn, consisting only of attractive young women displaying
themselves in progressive degrees of nakedness. There is some indication
evident through his associations that he could wish his own naked body to
be a cause of desire and excitement in an other, instead of his perception of
himself as an undesirable loser. His use of porn for masturbation represents
by identification with and projection into the attractive young women, his
own excitingly erotic fantasy of, himself, being an object of desire. Of course,
given his harsh superego, as well as his besieged conscience that is heavily
informed by the conventional Christian understandings and prohibitions
around pornography and masturbation, his anxieties are amplified by the
fear he suffers; fear of the shame imposed by his superego, and of the guilt
imposed by his conscience, both working in concert against him.

CHRISTIAN STRUGGLES WITH SEXUALITY: AID FROM PSYCHOANALYSIS

Pure Sexuality: A Christian Fetish

As we have already seen, in general, Christianity has historically and continues to the present to be preoccupied with one of two broad notions of sexual
purity: one revolves around abstinence and celibacy and the other around
avoidance of pre-or extra-marital sex of any sort, coupled with a somewhat
reluctantly conceded acceptability of sex within heterosexual marriage,
wherein it is thought "pure." Within the discourse of psychoanalysis, somewhat analogous concerns exist, albeit less so with "purity" versus "impurity"
but more to do with "normality" versus "abnormality."

For example, Donald Moss writes about the struggles within psychoanalysis, in the face of postmodern deconstructions of just about all categories
of what has been thought to be known with a measure of certainty, about
normal versus aberrant sexuality.[56] He recognizes the destabilizing impact of

---

56. Moss, *Sexual Aberrations.*

tampering with concepts of "normal" and "abnormal," while sympathizing with the psychoanalytic imperative toward freedom from judgement of aberrancy with its inherent demand for action directed toward correction, on the whole enterprise of trying "to map sexuality."[57] He anchors his argument by returning to Freud's essay *The Sexual Aberrations,* claiming it

> is line-drawing, regulatory and conservative while also line-breaking, libratory, and radical. The essay gives voice to an on-going collision between two unreasonable and excessive currents. One grounds 'normal' sexuality in a fixed idea of proper aim, proper object [of the drive], . . . [and] proper gender. The other undermines that ground: no fixed aim, object, or gender.
>
> Reason does not possess the power to either reconcile or synthesize these two currents. Yet something like reason is necessary to separate and clarify the two. For this, 'reason' needs an imaginary zero point, a dry spot that functions to divide negative from positive, the properly fixed from the fundamentally unmoored.[58]

Moss struggles with what might constitute the standard needed to distinguish normal (or pure) sexuality from abnormal (or impure). To situate this struggle within my profession historically, I will remind the reader that psychoanalysis began with the understanding that sexuality lay at the core of the complex, conflicted human mind. As my citations of Laplanche have illustrated, he was elaborating on Freud's basic hypothesis that the unconscious is fundamentally a sexual unconscious. I have cited Biblical sources to infer that the Judaeo-Christian model of the mind might also be seen to hold sexuality as a core component.

Lemma and Lynch write,

> Sex has been micromanaged through law and religion because of its subversive, socially destabilizing potential. It was Freud who first bravely placed sex at the heart of psychic development and highlighted its destabilizing power in our psyche and hence the defenses brought into play to manage this.
>
> . . . Freud's original boldness with respect to sexuality has not been upheld with equal vigour by some of the important contemporary psychoanalytic schools that followed in his wake where we observe instead the displacement of sex from centre-stage position to make way for relational considerations. Here the sexual drive is replaced by new conceptualizations of primary love and attachment. This has resulted, as Corbett (2009)

57. Ibid., 180.
58. Ibid., 183.

provocatively put it, in a trend discernible in much contemporary analytic thinking, whereby 'the burlap of desire too quickly becomes the pashmina of mutual recognition.'[59]

There are three further considerations they write about which will illuminate my subsequent efforts to reflect on a Christian preoccupation with purity in sexuality. First, they note a "masochistic structure of desire—the development of a pleasure in waiting," a necessary *work* thereby inherent in desire, which requires that in the time during delay of gratification while anticipating, we have to represent, psychically, our experience. Second,

> . . . at the heart of our sexuality lies otherness. This otherness needs to be integrated into the subjective experience of sexuality. In other words, every desire concentrates on an other, and more specifically the existence of the other confronts us with both our dependence and passivity—positions that mobilize anxiety. The 'elusive, ineffable quality' of the sexual other (Stein, 2008) poses a challenge complicating our very experience of desire and of our wish to be desired.

Third, "Desire does not exist in a vacuum: it is developmentally shaped by the social system within which it is vested."[60] In terms of a contextualization of desire, think of the early infant environment, as per Laplanche, also how experience and concepts of God may be variously represented in differing communities and families, and finally, how desire is met in different societies.

Analogous to Moss's concerns regarding the need for an anchoring point within psychoanalysis for conceptualizing the diversities of sexualities confronted in the day-to-day lives of therapists working with real people, is Christianity's reliance on the anchoring point of "pure sexuality" valid? Put simply, Christianity approves as morally pure and sanctified by the church, heterosexual coupling in the context of marriage. As previously noted, within some faith expressions, notably the Catholic tradition, such sexual coupling is only really approved if there are no efforts to limit procreation, i.e. if the intent is not primarily or solely pleasure. From the Christian viewpoint then all expressions of sexuality that digress from that which is considered moral and pure, i.e. heterosexual marriage, are deemed immoral and impure. Hence, premarital or extramarital sex, masturbation, pornography, gender fluidity, lesbian, gay, bisexual, trans and queer (LGBTQ) are all categories with which most Christian communities have difficulty, since they must be seen as impure. A category that is entirely overlooked and

59. Lemma and Lynch, *Introduction*, 3–4.

60. Ibid., 7.

never even considered is that of the private fantasies of the couple or of the individuals within the couple who are Christianly married that enable their orgasmic sex to work.

Freud begins his *Three Essays on the Theory of Sexuality* with an introduction to "two technical terms":

> Let us call the person from whom sexual attraction proceeds the *sexual object* and the act towards which the instinct tends the *sexual aim*. Scientifically sifted observation, then, shows that numerous deviations occur in respect of both of these—the sexual object and the sexual aim. The relation between these deviations and what is assumed to be normal requires thorough investigation. . . . The concept of instinct is thus one of those lying on the frontier between the mental and the physical. . . . The source of an instinct is a process of excitation occurring in an organ and the immediate aim of the instinct lies in the removal of this organic stimulus.[61]

To situate the specifically Christian perspective on "sexual purity" in Freudian drive terms, optimal sexual expression in Christian marriage would presumably have as its *aim* gratification and discharge of the built up drive urges for pleasure for both partners (and possibly the extension of their pleasurable uniting to the creation of a new being). The *object* of optimal Christian sexual expression would presumably be the whole person of the other, the opposite sex partner. When Christian authors write about sexual relations, typically their explorations go no further than to approvingly note or take for granted the broad arrangement of things as I have just outlined. There would not likely be any consideration of detailed digressions from the generally understood and accepted optimal aim nor similarly from the optimal object. There would not likely be any detailed consideration of the complex psychical factors involved in married couples' sexual idiosyncrasies. Too often, all that one finds is a simplistic acceptance of heterosexual marriage as acceptable, approved, "pure" and sexually moral, with little else said; whether the sexual intimacy of that marriage is dysfunctional or fraught with fantasies that might normally conflict with standard accepted Christian values is never considered.

Is it possible though, given the infinite array of distortions that can and do permeate both aim and object, that sexuality, including that in Christians, is inevitably rife with aberrations from what is so readily assumed to be normal and pure? Might we rightly question whether some of the difficulty Christians have with the more obvious expressions of sexual diversity,

61. Freud, *Three Essays,* 135, 168. Emphasis his.

as manifest for example in the LGBTQ categories, or with extramarital sex, arises from the mindset produced from complacent adoption of the cherished notion that heterosexual marriage confers purity onto sexuality, thus authorizing a kind of cloistered enclave of privileged morality? I would claim that vehement charges by Christians against varied sexual expressions may reflect projections of their own split-off unconscious sexual peculiarities; it is far easier to locate egregious fault "out there" than "in here." Are Christians afforded thereby a smug uncritical satisfaction regarding their own sexuality, such that they can then comfortably (or uncomfortably) judge as unacceptable any other, divergent expressions of sexuality? I would also posit that Christians and the church are literally hamstrung in their ability to think about sexuality in its vast complexity because of this uncritically accepted presumption of attainable purity.

The reader may recall Kaplan's remarks[62] on the deleteriously divisive effects of adopting a fetishistic icon, as I contend the church has done with its idealization of purity within heterosexual marriage. To put it simply, it has left Christians with unduly simplistic and inadequate categories of thought: pure or impure, moral or immoral. It leaves a vacuum of silence, albeit usually suffused with judgement regarding all that cannot easily be categorized into either of these polar alternatives. We have previously noted the paucity of productive thought when one is bound to simplistic dichotomous categories.[63] Insofar as Christian discourse on sexuality is dominated by a bipolar dichotomy of pure/impure (or moral/immoral), thought is hampered by the phenomenon of splitting. We previously saw that splitting, when employed defensively, is a primitive mode of thought that impairs the capacity to adequately consider complex categories of knowledge that cannot be readily assigned to any clear grouping.

The consequences of Christian fetishistic splitting on the matter of sexuality include silence on vast areas of sexual experience that affect Christian and non-Christian alike. It leaves the Christian community oppressed by a hegemony of discourse that is moralizing; by its very structure it inevitably fosters guilt and shame, but very little understanding, compassion or real help for people burdened by their experience of their own sexuality or that of others. And since sexuality is so vital to the core of being human, and since biblically speaking, humans are fashioned in the image of God, the sexuality fetish also skews our perception of God toward one of moralizing watchdog. Let us turn to scriptural sources for understanding why the purity/impurity split arose, and for guidance as to an alternate mode of thinking.

62. See previously, Kaplan, 126.
63. Review Kierkegaard's thoughts on equivocation and knowledge. See 76.

Paul, Jesus, and Conscience

Paul's epistles as well as other New Testament writings[64] advocate for abstinence from "sexual immorality," implying, of course, that there is a "sexual
morality." I have chosen to look specifically at Paul's claims in 1 Cor. 6:12–20
and 1 Thess. 4:3– 7. First, 1 Cor. 6:12–20:

> All things are lawful for me, but all things are not helpful. All
> things are lawful for me, but I will not be brought under the
> power of any. Foods for the stomach and the stomach for foods,
> but God will destroy both it and them. Now the body is not for
> sexual immorality but for the Lord, and the Lord for the body.
>   . . . Do you know that your bodies are members of Christ?
> Shall I then take the members of Christ and make them mem-
> bers of a harlot? Certainly not! Or do you not know that he who
> is joined to a harlot is one body with her? For "the two," He says,
> "shall become one flesh." But he who is joined to the Lord is one
> spirit with Him.
>   Flee sexual immorality. Every sin that a man does is outside
> the body, but he who commits sexual immorality sins against
> his own body. Or do you not know that your body is the temple
> of the Holy Spirit who is in you, whom you have from God, and
> you are not your own? For you were bought at a price; therefore
> glorify God in your body and in your spirit, which are God's.

Let us note that Paul argues against a body-soul dualism, uphold-
ing instead notions of an embodied unity that extends to unification, for
a Christian, with God, or more specifically, with Christ; a kind of body/
soul (spirit)/Christ unity. Next, let us notice Paul saying that the body is
not for sexual immorality, implying, naturally, that it is for sexual morality, or for sexual purity, without specifying clearly what constitutes sexual
immorality or impurity. It is almost as if he assumes that what is implied
by the immorality-morality dualism will be understood. Our explorations
of psychoanalytic concepts around universal and polymorphous perversity
resulting from the infantile development of the sexual drive should cause us
to question what Paul means.

He gives us some clues by referring to the notion of unity with either
Christ or a harlot, using the rubric of "membership." He seems to indicate
that uniting one's body with a harlot in sex serves as a contradiction of one's
unification with Christ. A harlot is an other who is, from the point of view
of the purchaser, solely a sexually exciting object, not one with whom one

64. See, for example, Hebrews 13:4.

expects to have a meaningful relationship. Perhaps this could represent the prototype for sexual gratification separated from broader mutual knowing, trustful relating and commitment, features that characterize the bond between a believer and Christ himself. And since Paul cites Genesis 2:4, that pertains to God's provision of one-flesh unity between a man and a woman as the bond that epitomizes marriage and which symbolizes the committed mutual bond between God and the believer (or the church), then it is implied that joining bodily with a spouse, in contrast to doing so with a harlot, does *not* compromise the unity one has with Christ.

Let us turn to 1 Thess. 4:3–7:

> For this is the will of God, your sanctification: that you should abstain from sexual immorality; that each of you should know how to possess his own vessel in sanctification and honor, not in passion of lust, like the Gentiles who do not know God; that no one should take advantage of and defraud his brother in this matter, because the Lord is the avenger of all such, as we forewarned you and testified. For God did not call us to uncleanness, but in holiness.

In this passage, sexual immorality is again not well defined, but its meaning is apparently presumed to be understood. Perhaps what was meant by "sexual immorality" *was* commonly understood by Paul's readers; perhaps it might reflect a historical and contextual appreciation, known by and to the culture of that time. Perhaps it, as the passage quoted infers, means manifestations of unbridled lust, possibly as was practiced in the context of pagan (Gentile?) ceremonies within some cities wherein "Public ceremonials remained indelibly profane, erotic, and cruel. Nereids [naked stage girls] continued to splash in many cities of the Christian East."[65] What *is* clear, is that what "sexual immorality" meant in the first century is unlikely to mean the same as what the phrase implies today. We contextualize others of Paul's teachings, for example, regarding women's roles in teaching and leading,[66] in matters of head coverings,[67] and Jesus' teaching to wash one another's feet.[68] We must understand that there was a context for Paul's instructions on sex, that may have little similarity to today.

Paul calls for self controlled dignity in keeping with the unity the believer has with Christ. Further, he implies that sexual immorality consists in a form of violation of the other; by corollary, then, sexual morality would

65. Brown, *The Body and Society*, 319.

66. 1 Timothy 2:11–12.

67. 1 Corinthians 11:2–16.

68. John 13:14–15.

consist in respect for, and non-violence to the other. This latter call for morality as non-violation against the other in sex can be troublesome, however, if we recall the inherent need for "transgression" that is deeply embedded in sexual excitement. At the very least, whatever transgressions of normal social boundaries inhere in sex, today's societal legal norm of mutual consent serves as a minimum protection against the exploitation and defrauding of which Paul speaks. As Kierkegaard claimed, erotic love may not be capable of overcoming its inherent selfishness, its aim for self-satisfying pleasure, however much a couple may strive for mutual satisfaction of desire for pleasure. Perhaps by its very nature, erotic love, or lust may render the purity of absence of transgression in the form of use of the other for one's own gratification difficult if not impossible.

Jesus made it quite plain and clear that immorality, or evil, is less a matter of behavior, or observable acts, than it is a matter of the inner thoughts and desires in one's mind. "You have heard that it was said to those of old, 'You shall not commit adultery.' But I say to you that whoever looks at a woman to lust for her has already committed adultery with her in his heart."[69] In effect, he claims that the thought is equivalent to the act, what is called in psychoanalysis "psychic equivalence"; in its psychotic proportions, psychic equivalence can lead to extreme torment, when one believes himself condemned by virtue of his thoughts, as if he were an adulterer or murderer. Given the impossibility of having one's mind purified of such subtle thoughts and desires, and never being able to be sure whether any particular thought or desire qualifies as unacceptable lust or whether it may be no more than aesthetic appreciation of another's beauty and desirability,[70] I believe Jesus asserts this moral principle for the express purpose of displaying the impossibility of self-purification, and the absolute necessity for exercising faith in *him* as the "fulfillment of the law."[71] In other words, because of the unavoidable and ubiquitous pervasion of sin through all of humanity, his statement is more designed to promote a humble acknowledgement of mankind's need of deliverance than it is a statement of a standard to be

---

69. Matthew 5:27, 28.

70. Imagine the consternation that might revolve around a married man's dilemma in noticing with appreciation the beauty of another woman, either her physical attractiveness, or the appeal of her mind and personality. At what point does aesthetic appreciation shade over into lust? Jesus' point is that it is impossible to know. I nevertheless would concede that one does have some choice in the matter of how much one indulges such appreciative thoughts, and whether one permits his thoughts to immerse into frank lust. My dilemma is that the cross-over point is unknowable, from the point of view of Jesus' moral imperative of inwardness.

71. Matthew 5:17.

achieved. It is a matter of grace that one can be saved from the condemnation of impossible demands of a law that only kills.

As we saw earlier in exploring conscience as distinct from superego, Paul also lays emphasis upon the *inner* exercise of faith in matters of moral concern (Romans 14:14–23). "Whatever is not from faith is sin" offers us the opportunity to value all that God has given, including sexuality, but that appreciation and gratitude arises from an orientation of faith. Perhaps this means that how one deports oneself in matters of sexuality must be congruent with the character of one's relationship with God, a relationship that supersedes and informs all others. According to Paul, the details of how this is evinced for any one individual is a matter of conscience, informed by faith. He does, however, emphasize the overriding principle of love for one's neighbor, i.e. flaunting one's freedom of conscience to the hurt of another defies the law of love that has superseded the law of prescription. It underlines the foundation of morality, which is to do no violence to another, or to love one's neighbor as oneself.

To return to the Christian fetish of sexual purity as embodied in heterosexual marriage, and the extent to which the purity/impurity paradigm has dominated Christian discourse and thereby imposed distinct limits on capacities for effective thought, I contend that this discourse has suffered from superego oppressiveness at the expense of conscience. While it is true that encouragement of the development and exercise of individual (and collective) conscience, in contrast to perpetuating superego legalism, could lead to greater expression of variance and acceptance of sexualities within the Christian community, a mature faithful regard for both the "vertical" relationship of fidelity to God, and the "horizontal" relationship of respectful love of the neighbor could serve to preserve that which is good and precious to God. When superego ascends to the place of dominance, displacing conscience, shame pervades to the extent that one strives to expel the shame by strenuous attempts at defending. Manic defenses ensue, in efforts to distance oneself from the stain left by shame. Perhaps the purity rhetoric that has characterized much of evangelical Christian youth ministries reflects such a defensive posture, albeit well-intentioned, as an effort to preserve and protect "sexual purity." It has not, however, been without its severe consequences, in instilling confusion, shame, guilt, and self-loathing in many.[72]

As the principles of moral conscience, as articulated by Paul, along with the love of neighbor as insisted upon by Jesus, are manifest in Christian community, sexual love should find its place as the heart of the community life. Wendell Berry, from his point of view as philosopher-farmer, states:

72. Peterson and Peterson, *Are You Waiting for the One?*

For sexual love is the heart of community life. Sexual love is the force that in our bodily life connects us most intimately to the Creation, to the fertility of the world, to farming and the care of animals. It brings us into the dance that holds the community together and joins it to its place.[73]

Honoring sexuality as a private and yet paradoxically communally cherished entity demands that Christians shake free of their primitive purity perspective in order to shoulder responsibility for better informing young people, for overcoming our own constricting paradigms for how sexuality "should" be, our own and that of (stranger) others, and embrace the difficult challenge of living truly by conscience and not by law, allowing ourselves to grapple with how sexuality actually is. Insofar as the church has tended to fill in the blanks left by Paul's ill-defined "sexual immorality" with codes for conduct, it has been woefully inept at addressing the reality of disorder in human sexuality wherever it appears, outside marriage, inside marriage, and beyond the narrow scope of Christian heterosexuality with its touted clear unambiguous sexual and gender identity.

One author, Margaret Farley, contends that in reference to recent shifts in Catholic and Protestant perceptions of sexuality,

> new understandings of the totality of the person support a radically new concern for sexuality as an expression and a cause of love. The values of sexual intimacy, pleasure, and companionship are lauded as important elements in human and Christian flourishing. This means that, above all, the kind of deep suspicion of sexual desire and sexual pleasure that characterized both Catholic and Protestant traditions for so long has largely disappeared. *That is, the view of sexuality as fundamentally disordered is gone from a great deal of Christian thought.*[74]

While I applaud the sentiments expressed in the first three statements of her paragraph, and although it may be true that a lot of Christian thought has indeed dismissed former views of sexuality as disordered, I think this is a mistake, a denial. I contend that it is only by more fully recognizing, understanding, and incorporating into our Christian discourse, the fundamental disorder in sexuality that psychoanalysis has helped us comprehend, that we can individually and corporately, emotionally, and psychologically prosper. Since the gospel has claimed all along that humans are in every way disordered, but that they are infinitely loved and covered by grace, there is

---

73. Berry, *Sex, Economy, Freedom and Community*, 133.

74. Farley, *Just Love*, 278. Emphasis mine.

no need to adopt a new form of denial, akin, though at the opposite pole of the axis, to the ideology of marital sexual purity.

CHRISTIAN DISTORTIONS OF CHRIST'S DESIRE

Peter: A Paradigm of Desire

Following Jesus' miraculous feeding of over five-thousand people with five loaves and two fish, this happens:

> Immediately Jesus made the disciples get into the boat and go on ahead of him to the other side, while he dismissed the crowd. After he had dismissed them, he went up into the hills by himself to pray. When evening came, he was there alone, but the boat was already a considerable distance from land, buffeted by the waves because the wind was against it. During the fourth watch of the night Jesus went out to them, walking on the lake. When the disciples saw him walking on the lake, they were terrified. "It's a ghost," they said, and cried out in fear. But Jesus immediately said to them: "Take courage! It is I. Don't be afraid." "Lord, if it is you," Peter replied, "tell me to come to you on the water." "Come," he said. Then Peter got down out of the boat and walked on the water to Jesus. But when he saw the wind, he was afraid and, beginning to sink, cried out, "Lord, save me!" Immediately Jesus reached out his hand and caught him. "You of little faith," he said, "why did you doubt?" And when they climbed into the boat, the wind died down. Then those who were in the boat worshipped him, saying, "Truly you are the Son of God" (NIV).[75]

To allow us to get into the mind of Peter, let us consider the first recorded contact of Jesus with those he called on to become disciples. Matthew and Mark simply state that Jesus came across Peter, along with three others, all fishermen, attending to their trade, and said, "Follow me, I will make you fishers of men."[76] All four immediately followed, apparently. Luke gives us a glimpse of Peter's mind when he records an incident early in the disciples' journey with Jesus. After observing Jesus teach the pressing multitudes from the safety of Peter's own boat, Peter heard Jesus urge him to launch out and let down his nets for a catch, and did so despite his misgivings that after having fished all night and caught nothing, it was futile. Upon seeing that the nets were now full to the point of sinking the boat plus a

75. Matthew 14:22–32.
76. Matthew 4:18–20; Mark 1:16–18.

second boat, Peter "fell down at Jesus' knees, saying, 'Depart from me for I am a sinful man, O Lord.'"[77] There is no record of any of the other disciples saying anything, or responding to Jesus the way Peter did. Peter experiences immediate and powerfully affective reactions to what he perceives. His perceptions seem also to leap into ranges of thought that appear to be remote from the immediate incident; i.e. to recognize himself as sinful and only worthy of worship from a place of humility in the face of this dazzling display of Jesus' power suggests he could be very quick to acquire insight. Peter is a man whose intensity of desire is on display. He was a predominantly hysterical personality, full of affect, and dramatic enactments of his desire which quickly focused on Jesus as the Messiah. It was Peter who responded to Jesus' question of the disciples: "But who do you say that I am?" with his reply, "The Christ of God."[78]

Perhaps we could intuit that Peter's enactments and statements of profound comprehension of Jesus' identity and, simultaneously, his own identity relative to Jesus, reflect a heart that is on fire, so to speak, with emotions of love, gratitude, admiration, and even that he was awe-struck by this man he knew to be exceptional. Peter, however, given his humanity (that, fortunately, scripture in no way conceals), displays his ambivalence and shallowness of commitment equally dramatically. When Jesus spoke to the disciples of his impending death and resurrection, Peter proudly insisted that this was not going to happen, as if his own expectations of Jesus had become the agenda in his mind that would supersede Christ's. Jesus' rebuke was sharp: "Get behind me, Satan! You are an offense to me, for you are not mindful of the things of God, but the things of men."[79]

Then, of course, there was Peter's infamous avowal of utter loyalty to Jesus, which was thoroughly obliterated by his thrice denial of affiliation to him. He had even protested Jesus' prediction of his betrayals, by affirming yet again his willingness to die in loyalty to him.[80]

Having reviewed and thereby acquired a sense of Peter's character, I want to return to the walking-on-water episode above. The setting is deep darkness of night and Peter and the others have battled rough water and high winds, unsettling to even experienced boatmen. Furthermore, they had been sent into this predicament by Jesus who was not with them. Naturally, they all experienced terror on seeing a figure walking on the water, an uncanny chill at the possibility of a ghost overtaking them. Upon hearing Jesus' voice

77. Luke 5:8.
78. Luke 9:20.
79. Matthew 16:23.
80. Matthew 26:33–35.

and reassurances, Peter feels an impulse to go outside of his customary reality and, at the same time, test the validity not only of Jesus' claims to Godly
identity but also his own intuitions as to Jesus' claims to infinite power over
the earthly forces that bind humanity. Jesus responds to Peter's request with a
simple "Come." He might have reprimanded Peter for his wish to transcend
his human limitations, thereby highlighting Peter's hubris. Instead, Jesus' invitation was to join him in the wild, perhaps himself testing Peter.

I think this incident, held in conjunction with the other elements we
have seen of Peter's personality reveal the desire in Peter for his passion for
Christ to progress beyond simply that of an internal attitude, into actual
experience. Corresponding to Peter's desire is a desire in Jesus to engage
Peter in a walk into the wild, the sphere of untamed power, magnificence
and transcendence; a sphere occupied and sustained by Christ,[81] the essence
of which Peter had uniquely, among the disciples, glimpsed into. In keeping
with the book of Hebrews, "Let us fix our eyes on Jesus, the author and
perfecter of our faith. . . ."[82] Peter begins to sink at the moment he turns his
attention away from Jesus, but he is upheld. Peter's capacity for participating
in life beyond the tame is contingent upon connection to Jesus.

Extrapolating from this episode in Peter's life, I would contend that
to act upon God's invitation to faith in Jesus is to step out of predictable
safety and to let desire for that which is profoundly and enigmatically Other,
untameable, wild, but good, by faith, move one away from the familiar, to
the new. This is in contrast to what is often portrayed as (by virtue of a
distortion of Christ's desire) an insipid, perhaps even weak act of childish
fantasy-fulfillment and conformity to some pre-established image. And
what is constituted in the new is, like Peter's experience, expansive, unleash-
ing of one's potential, pregnant with creativity and imagination, fueled by
desire redeemed and redirected. C. S. Lewis' Aslan, the lion which allegori-
cally represents God, was not "safe" with whom to come close to, but he was
"good,"[83] and so fear could be transformed, from fear of violence or death,
to a fear that is reverence.

One can have the impression from some of the rhetoric within particularly the evangelical Christian world around conversion and commitment to faith in Jesus, that the experience is directed or governed by a
formula and entails the adoption of a stereotype. If certain steps need to
be followed and criteria fulfilled, then one might wonder if the Jesus being
recommended is not the one of the gospels and the Letters of Paul, but a

81. Colossians 1:17.
82. Hebrews 12:2 (NIV).
83. Lewis, *The Chronicles of Narnia.*

plasticized, commodified unreal Jesus. The psychoanalyst, Jacques Lacan, had a lot to say about what he called the *real*, a term that was current in a particular strand of early twentieth-century philosophy, according to Dylan Evans. In tracing Lacan's complex use of the term real, over time, Evans concluded: "It is 'that which resists symbolization absolutely'" (S1, 66); or, again, the real is "the domain of whatever subsists outside symbolization" (Ec, 388).[84] Symbolization for Lacan had meanings to do with signifiers as component elements of the unconscious which, to Lacan, was understood to be structured like a language. Evans: "It is the [differentiated] symbolic which introduces 'a cut in the real [in itself, undifferentiated]' in the process of signification: 'it is the world of words that creates the world of things . . .'" (E, 65).[85] And "The real is 'the impossible' (S11, 167) because it is impossible to imagine, impossible to integrate into the symbolic order, and impossible to attain in any way . . . lends the real its essentially traumatic quality."[86]

So, for Lacan, the real gives rise to and is the object of anxiety, is unknowable, and unassimilable. In his book, *The Triumph of Religion*, he says, "There is *one* true religion, and that is the Christian religion."[87] He implies that the *real's* enigmatic, anxiety-causing unassimilability can only be addressed by Christianity. Lacan also posits that the true subject of psychoanalysis is the *real*. Perhaps, for our purposes, we can use Lacan's *real* as a lens by which to sharpen our focus on the Jesus who defies being fully known, and who says of himself, "I *am* the way, the truth and the life."[88] He knew that no one could know the Father, except himself, and that for the Father to be known, it could only be through him, Jesus. Jesus claimed that knowing him constituted eternal life. I suspect that Lacan perceived Jesus, though not identical to the *real*, to both represent, as God incarnate, the *real*, and to have power over and be the ultimate answer to the unknowable *real*.

The Jesus of the Bible represents all that humans are not and cannot attain. That makes him eminently attractive, the ultimate object of desire, since only Jesus, he claimed of himself, can fill and address the enormous lack that ignites desire. Furthermore, Jesus repeatedly confounded the expectations of those who encountered him; he was not nor could not be packaged or encompassed by any one characterization, but constantly defied expectations. For example, John the Baptist could not understand why Jesus insisted on being baptized by him.

84. Evans, *Dictionary of Lacanian Psychoanalysis,* 159.

85. Ibid.

86. Ibid., 160.

87. Lacan, *The Triumph of Religion,* 66. Emphasis his.

88. John 14:6. Emphasis mine.

Jeremiah envisioned God as a potter, forming his creatures as clay; "In all creative work there is play between the artist and his material."[89] Just as a psychoanalytic patient wishes to know that his analyst is affected by him, so the believer in relation with God, experiences a desire to know if God is moved or aroused by him. C.S. Lewis asked the question, by way of registering God's impact on people, "Who is this Man who remarks that His mere presence suspends all normal rules?"[90] Relating to one like this similarly stirs all manner of responses.

When Peter took his gaze from Jesus, he "saw" the wind; i.e. that which is not seeable, but which terrifies. Perhaps Peter's act of audacious courage could be prototypical of the act of conversion, the decision to step forward into faith. It consisted in stepping out of the "safety" of the boat (remember that the boat was in peril from the wind), of the familiar into the unsafety of the strange, the Other. James insists that true conversion is a matter of faith in action, not just an idea.[91] The call of God to leave the comfortably familiar to encounter his power as it manifests for the world is captured in journeys of Abraham, Joseph, and Paul.

In contrast to the all-too-familiar stereotype among Christians of the notion that adoption of a life of faith is to enter upon a sanitized or puritanical mode of living, let me take you back to Alexander Schmemann's idea regarding the integration of the secular and the sacred, the sacramentalization of life: "what is denied [by the dichotomization of secularizing] is simply the continuity between "religion" and "life" [with all its dirt and messiness], the very function of *worship as power of transformation, judgement, and change*."[92]Rather than seeking to remove ourselves from our bodies, which are messy, troublesome, and the source of considerable pain, intense urges, and shame, perhaps as embodied beings, we can seek to integrate the flesh with the spirit through the power of worship. If we recognize the inherent sexuality of mutual desire within the trinity, as previously explored in conjunction with the ideas of Sarah Coakley, then might it be possible to not only integrate the flesh with the spirit, but specifically, the sexual body with the Spirit of Christ within the believer? In other words, a poignant and powerful indicator of union with God (i.e. conversion) might consist in integration of the sexual (i.e. the powerfully desiring) self into the Godly, faithful self.

Denial of the dreaded realities of earthly life and death and the various ways in which the *real* impinges on the mind, permeate culture. Consider the

89. Zornberg, *The Beginning of Desire,* 19.

90. Lewis, *God in the Dock,* 405.

91. James 1:22–25.

92. Schmemann, *For the Life of the World,* 133.

practices of dressing up the dead, which constitutes much of modern funeral arrangements. Or consider the perpetration of expectations of beauty and sexual entertainment imposed upon women, which contribute to the commodification of their bodies (contributing to anorexia, anxiety, depression, psychosomatic illness, etc.)[93] thereby denying their infinitely varied personhood. Such forms of individual and societal denial of ugliness, misfortune, disease, sexual, and gender difference, poverty, inevitability of death, deformity, and the like lead to impulses to sanitize, purify, idealize and split, all of which consist in loss of truth, and therefore, of elements of ourselves.

Contrary to one's response of faith in Jesus leading to a kind of homogenization of one's unique personhood into a morass of uniformity, conformity, or depersonalization, I believe the truth lies closer to a dynamic awakening of the elements of the self that feel most truly and idiosyncratically expressive of one's unique being. Perhaps even the fundamental unique fantasy that may lie at the core of one's self that Žižek speaks of can be "sacramentalized" into a transformed element, when understood and integrated into a growing sense of self as a healthy whole person in relationship with God.

93. See: Wolf, *The Beauty Myth.*

Chapter 9

Law, Superego, Life, and Death

> For you [before knowing Christ] were like sheep going astray, but
> have now returned to the Shepherd and Overseer of your souls.[1]

SUPEREGO

EARLIER IN THIS WORK, I wrote of the differentiation, in the course of human
psychological development, of the superego from the larger entity of the
ego, of which the superego functions as a part. It acquires distinct functions
involved in assessing oneself as to one's performance on any of a potentially
infinite number and variety of standards. Although many psychoanalysts,
including Freud, have conflated the functions and activities of superego
and conscience, I argued for recognizing these two functions within the
psyche as separate, distinct from each other in function, character, and origin. Superego originates in large part through identification with aspects of
one's parents (and other figures of authority), especially in early life; aspects
which pertain to the parental activity of guiding, correcting, disciplining,
critiquing, and prohibiting. In other words, the superego results from identification with the aggressor, the one who prohibits, etc. Furthermore, the
superego takes on the role of devising and erecting standards by which it
then measures performance. As such, the superego can be seen to have the
function of an "overseer"; conscience, notwithstanding its important differences, can also be seen to function as an overseer. Previously, it was noted
that very commonly people suffer from the predominance of superego over

1. 1 Peter 2:25.

conscience, but that a goal of maturational growth and emotional (and spiritual) development, whether by psychological treatment or by other life experience, is to enhance the individual's access to and reliance upon conscience such that conscience comes to supersede, in dominance, the place of the superego, as the agency for self- and other-assessment and guidance.

It is evident that the superego is constituted of codes of regulations and prohibitions, operating by the rule of law that essentially follows the pattern of the Old Testament "talion law," eye-for-eye, tooth-for-tooth, and life-for-life. Mental and emotional life governed by this law encourages retaliation (deriving from "talion") as its primary modus operandi. Influenced inadequately by mature conscience which is patterned after the principles of love, forgiveness, the overlooking of faults, etc., the automatisms of the unconscious that are under the sway of the superego lead to impulses and actions for revenge, envy, and the potentially endless obsessional parsing of particulars driven by the insatiable desire for omniscience. It is a life dominated by corrupted and hence "sinful" or "evil" desire, that is, the desire to have perfect and complete knowledge (omniscience); in turn, this desire, as with all human desire, arises as response to the existence and awareness of one's lack. I will say more on this later.

Insofar as the superego finds fault and accuses, and insofar as the more primitive of its tendencies are to exaggerate in its accusations of inadequacy or of worthlessness, or in its demands for attainment of unreachable (perfect) standards of performance, it is a liar.[2] These are the same features that are attributed to the devil, or Satan, in the scriptures. Jesus said, "He [the devil] was a murderer from the beginning, and does not stand in the truth, because there is no truth in him. When he speaks a lie, he speaks from his own resources, for he is a liar and the father of it."[3] John, the writer of Revelation, said, " for the accuser of our brethren, who accused them before our God day and night, has been cast down."[4] Both the book of Job and the prophet Zechariah identify the accuser as Satan.[5] Furthermore, Paul asserts that all people are, before receiving the grace of God in Christ, under the

2. It is exceedingly common in clinical psychoanalytic practice to discover people feeling inadequate and worthless because they are oppressed by a primitive superego that excels in fault-finding, accusations, condemnations and fabrications of ever-loftier standards of performance for the subject whose mind it dominates. It can be seen to lie, if not in the form of outright false accusations, then insofar as its claims are grossly extreme exaggerated perspectives on reality.

3. John 8:44.

4. Revelation 12:10.

5. Job 1:9–11; Zechariah 3:1.

dominating and oppressive influence of Satan, and Peter warns Christians to be aware of the devouring intentions of Satan who is, "like a roaring lion."[6]

While I have highlighted in Chapter 3, Paul's argument for release from internal condemnation by the law of love (Romans 14) and at the head of this chapter, Peter's reminder of return to a better soul overseer (1 Peter 2:25), let me add to these, John's voice:

> For if our heart condemns us, God is greater than our heart and knows all things. Beloved, if our heart does not condemn us, we have confidence toward God. And whatever we ask we receive from Him, because we keep His commandments and do those things that are pleasing in His sight. And this is His commandment: that we should believe on the name of His Son Jesus Christ and love one another, as He gave us commandment.[7]

The clear implication is that we are far better to place our confidence in the love and forgiveness of God than to rely upon our own "heart," our own devices which are so inclined toward endless self-condemnation.

My argument therefore, is that one of the primary ways in which the adversary identified in the Bible as the devil, or Satan, achieves influence over people is via the agency of the superego.[8] I am unwilling to claim that Satan and the superego are one and the same; I am not suggesting that people suffering under the oppression of a primitive superego are occupied by or "possessed" by Satan, albeit very often the sufferers of harsh superego influence complain that they feel uncannily controlled or occupied by something foreign, something "not me," even something "evil." I am also not of the view that people who choose against Christian faith cannot be helped by therapy to achieve considerable liberation from a tyrannical superego. In fact, although through faith, the realization of the benefits of grace can be powerful in its liberating influence from superego dominance, the opposite is too often true, when the tenets of Christianity are perversely incorporated into the already legalistic superego, and are recruited to reinforce its harsh, punitive, and demanding character. This is especially the case when Christianity has muddled the separation of law and grace and typically co-mingled the two in ways that lead believers into either minimal release from internal legalistic pressures, or heightened intensity of such pressures. If the pressure is not intensified from within, then it is from without, from the Christian community when it, erroneously, in contravention of the new law of love,

6. Ephesians 2:1–3; 1 Peter 5:8, 9.

7. 1 John 3:20–23.

8. I was first introduced to this idea by Prof. Donald Carveth, who was citing the writing of Terry Eagleton, whose work I have not succeeded in acquiring.

conveys explicit, or more likely and maybe even more perniciously, *implicit* messages of expectation of purity in thought and behavior.

As a final argument against a wholesale superimposition of superego and Satan, it should be stated that an important goal of psychoanalytic therapy is not to *eliminate* the superego, but to *transform* it to a more benevolent, humane, compassionate, and supportive entity, largely by virtue of the action of a strengthened conscience. One could say that such a transformation entails a patterning after the character of Jesus, who Peter recommends as a prefered "Shepherd . . . of your souls." Such a "benevolent," transformed superego, still remains distinct from conscience, in that its functions are different. A benevolent superego will set standards for the subject's performance that are reasonable, humane, and reachable; furthermore, it will be gentle in its identification of faults and shortcomings, forgiving, supportive, and compassionate, even encouraging in its efforts to help the subject achieve better. The unmodified superego, I conclude, is the primary agency in the mind by which Satan, in his role as the lying accuser, has his impact.

DEATH: INSTINCT AND LAW

Freud defined instinct as, "the psychical representative of an endosomatic, continuously flowing source of stimulation . . . a concept lying on the frontier between the mental and the physical."[9] He made clear that in any science, including the new science of the unconscious, progress had to advance on the basis of unclear concepts, that precise definition of concepts is achieved only progressively. Instinct remains one of those still-debated and imprecise concepts. We have already considered the concept of the life or the sexual instinct, as one that promotes life, union, building up; it is constructive and integrating. Recall also that Laplanche refined Freud's unclear deployment and interchangeability of the terms drive and instinct with respect to the sexual, and noted that not only was the problem one of translation from the German, but also one of epistemological confusion. He clarified that the determinative character of the life/sexual *drive* was fashioned from early childhood experiences of the enigmatic (sexually unconscious) other, and that the (biological) *instinct* portion of this powerful motivator of life only came into its full form with sexual maturity at puberty for humans.

In trying to adequately conceptualize instinct further, Freud concluded that an instinct was characterized by a pressure, that is, a motor factor, or an activity that he believed to be constant, if only in the background. Second, an instinct has an aim which "is in every instance satisfaction, which can only

9. Freud, *Three Essays,* 168.

be obtained by removing the state of stimulation at the source."[10] Third, an instinct has an object, "the thing in regard to which or through which the instinct is able to achieve its aim."[11] The object could change, a condition indicating flexibility, or could remain fixed. Furthermore, the object could be some part of the subject's own body. Fourth, an instinct has its source "in an organ or part of the body and whose stimulus is represented in mental life by an instinct. . . . in mental life we only know them [instincts] by their aims."[12] Of course, Freud had many other things to say about instincts, but eventually he concluded that all instincts revolve around two which are fundamental: life (sexual—Eros) and death (Thanatos). As I have indicated, among psychoanalysts, a lot of skepticism remains around the existence of instincts, or drives, especially the death instinct, as Freud and others enunciated them and built theory of mind around them. Nevertheless, the fact is that all organic life terminates after fairly predictable periods of time (roughly 80+ years for humans), and the organic live matter returns to an inorganic dead state.

Freud came to articulate his belief in the existence of a death instinct that either accounted for or was linked to aggression, destructive impulses, masochism, and sadism, along with the derivatives of these impulses, that in turn may appear only very subtly in the mental life of an individual, such as obsessive-compulsive tendencies. In elaborating his theory of the mind beyond reliance on the Pleasure Principle (i.e. the principle that human drive or motivating force is fundamentally directed toward the maximization of pleasure and the minimization of unpleasure), he had to conclude that not all instinct was accounted for by the quest for pleasure. His paper *Beyond the Pleasure Principle*, was written just after the First World War, in which he lost a nephew, and feared for his own three sons who fought on the front, and witnessed the conflagration of destruction on a mass scale. All this was soon followed by the natural devastation of massive numbers of human lives from the 1918–1919 influenza epidemic in which he lost his pregnant daughter, Sophie.[13] He wrote, "If we are to take it as a truth that knows no exception that everything living dies for *internal* reasons—becomes inorganic once again—then we shall be compelled to say that, *'the aim of all life is death'* and, looking backwards, that *'inanimate things existed before living ones.'*"[14] As may be imagined, Freud saw the life drive and the death drive as in opposition to each other.

10. Freud, *Instincts and Their Vicissitudes*, 122.
11. Ibid.
12. Ibid.
13. Gay, *Freud, A Life For Our Time*.
14. Freud, *Beyond the Pleasure Principle*, 38. Emphasis his.

To draw nearer to the point of this discussion, let me briefly remind the reader once more of an aspect of Laplanche's claims regarding the development of the sexual drive, where his emphasis, while recognizing and retaining Freud's links to the biological, rested more on the importation into the unconscious mind of untranslatable bits of the enigmatic message from the mother, with whom the infant's attachment relationship was critical. The enigmatic, untranslatable fragments of the mother's own unconscious that are inevitably linked to her messages to her child which *are* translatable (i.e. understood by the child), are established in the child's unconscious mind as "strangerness," implying that they represent that which disrupts. Of course, we already have remarked upon the disruptive automatic character of the unconscious that impinges upon conscious life. So it is that Laplanche sees that, "It is within sexuality that the separation between the sexual forces of unbinding (Freud's death drive) and the sexual forces of binding (Freud's Eros) is produced."[15] In essence, according to Laplanche's further re-working of Freud's theories on instincts (or drives), the early child's attachment relationship to his mother (or parents) is the context in which the sexual drive is developed, and the sexual drive itself can be conceived as dividing into forces that bind and those that unbind or destroy. Perhaps our everyday proclivities to care for and empathically regard an other, while the next day express disdain and dismiss (or worse) the same other illustrates Laplanche's point that embedded within our drive (or motivational force) toward each other, there are both binding (loving) and unbinding (hateful) impulses. Or perhaps our passionate erotic desire for intimate contact with our lover (binding), co-existing with our demand from our lover for performance aimed at gratification of our own particular orgasmic fantasy (unbinding) also illustrates the rootedness of both life and death components, respectively, within the sexual drive.[16]

PAUL'S GRAPPLINGS WITH LIFE, DEATH, AND LAW

In trying to convey his perceptions about life and death and faith, Paul, almost in riddles, said, after citing the various hardships and sufferings he and others had endured in their service to Christ,

15. Laplanche, *Between Seduction and Inspiration*, 116.

16. The death drive component in this scenario inheres in the self-gratifying aspect of the experience, potentially (although not necessarily) at the expense of what is comfortable for the partner. Furthermore, the act of sexual intercourse in its various manifestations entails a certain aggressiveness, necessarily so, that inevitably calls upon unconscious repressed fragments that have the capacity to be disruptive or destructive.

always carrying about in the body the dying of the Lord Jesus,
that the life of Jesus also may be manifested in our body. For we
who live are always delivered to death for Jesus' sake, that the life
of Jesus may be manifested in our mortal flesh. So then death is
working in us, but life in you.[17]

Further, and more directly pointed at his own experience of death,
and not so much the death of Christ in him, Paul explored his own personal
experience of sin, the law, and the division within himself in Romans 7,
most of which I will quote:

What shall we say then? Is the law sin? Certainly not! On the
contrary, I would not have known sin except through the law.
For I would not have known covetousness unless the law had
said, "You shall not covet." But sin, taking opportunity by the
commandment, produced in me all manner of evil desire. For
apart from the law sin was dead. I was alive once without the
law, but when the commandment came, sin revived and I died.
And the commandment, which was to bring life, I found to
bring death. For sin, taking occasion by the commandment,
deceived me, and by it killed me. Therefore the law is holy, and
the commandment holy and just and good.

Has then what is good become death to me? Certainly not!
But sin, that it might appear sin, was producing death in me
through what is good, so that sin through the commandment
might become exceedingly sinful. For we know that the law is
spiritual, but I am carnal, sold under sin. For what I am doing, I
do not understand. For what I will to do, that I do not practice;
but what I hate, that I do. If, then, I do what I will not to do, I
agree with the law, that it is good. But now, it is no longer I who
do it, but sin that dwells in me. For I know that in me (that is, in
my flesh) nothing good dwells; for to will is present within me,
but how to perform what is good I do not find. For the good
that I will to do, I do not do; but the evil I will not to do, that I
practice. Now if I do what I will not to do, it is no longer I who
do it, but sin that dwells in me.

I find then a law, that evil is present with me, the one who
wills to do good. For I delight in the law of God according to
the inward man. But I see another law in my members, warring
against the law of my mind, and bringing me into captivity to
the law of sin which is in my members. O wretched man that
I am! Who will deliver me from this body of death? I thank
God—through Jesus Christ our Lord!

17. 2 Corinthians 4:10–12.

So then, with the mind I myself serve the law of God, but with the flesh, the law of sin.[18]

In Romans 3, Paul has clearly insisted on the theology that we are saved by faith, not by works, and that we are no longer under law, but under grace.[19] Grace accessed by faith is the path to life, while sin accessed and evoked by the agency of the law (as explicit in Romans 7) is the path to death. The philosopher, Alain Badiou, puts it thus:

> The subjective path of the flesh, whose real is death, coordinates the pairing of law and works. While the path of the spirit, whose real is life, coordinates that of grace and faith.[20]

In Romans 4:4, Paul asserts that to one who works, his wages are what is due, that this is not a matter of grace, and this is so by the governance of law. The realm of law is that of particularization, performance demanded and measured, distinction of this from that, underscoring difference between self and other, superior and inferior, and it inculcates envy, shame, and evil desire. The realm of grace, by contrast, is one of erasure of difference, and accessible to all, a realm of integration and synthesis or binding together.[21] Badiou says that before grasping the new life of grace,

> the most profound grasp of the connections between desire, law, death and life is necessary. . . . Paul's fundamental thesis is that the law, and only the law, endows desire with an autonomy . . .
>
> The law is what gives life to desire. But in so doing, it constrains the subject so that he wants to follow only the path of death.
>
> What is sin exactly? It is not desire as such, for if it were one would not understand its link to the law and death. *Sin is the life of desire as autonomy, as automatism.* The law is required to unleash the automatic life of desire, the automatism of repetition . . .[22]

I have posited that desire is essential to life, and that, according to the economy of God, desire rightly directed is for God and is pleasing to him. Solomon wrote,

---

18. Romans 7:7–25.

19. See also Romans 5:20,21; and Romans 8:2–4.

20. Badiou, *Saint Paul*, 75.

21. Romans 3:23; Galatians 3:28.

22. Badiou, *Saint Paul*, 79. Emhasis his.

He has made everything beautiful in its time. Also He has put
[desire for and awareness of?] eternity in their hearts . . .[23]

And so, desire in itself cannot be made equivalent to sin. If desire, as
we previously noted, exists within the Godhead, among the members of the
trinity, in the form of ecstatic pleasure in communion with the other, so desire
even in Adam and Eve, before the fall may well have existed in a form analogous to the divine ecstasy of desire for co-union (communion), in the one for
the other, and also in each for uniting with God. Desire becomes sinful when,
originally after the pattern of Satan, as noted previously,[24] it grasps after that
which belongs only to God (strivings for omniscience and omnipotence), and
then subsequently follows that pattern in both conscious and unconscious life,
in infinitely varied ways.[25] As Paul makes clear from the Romans 7 passage,
prohibition, as codified in the law, grants sin its opportunity to produce in us
all manner of evil desire, the automatisms of repetition that Badiou speaks
of and which characterize the repetition compulsions of Freud's unconscious
and of Paul's experience of that which drives him from within.

Julia Kristeva pointed out that the biblical myth of the fall consists
in Eve being tempted by the serpent who, "stood for the opposite of God,
since he tempts Eve to transgress [God's] prohibition."[26] In other words,
God instituted the law at the outset, at the beginning of time, by establishing a prohibition. God the Father, while infinitely loving, is also the giver of
the law; with the abolishing of the Old Covenant (i.e. the rule of law) and
the provision of the New Covenant (i.e. the rule of grace), the law-giving
Father is superseded by the loving energetic (phallic) creator of all things.[27]
Kristeva points out further that in the course of early childhood training,
prohibitions are necessarily entailed: "And it is on the foundation of these
prohibitions that the superego is built."[28] If we conjoin the concepts of law as
given by God, and the instantiation of the law into the unconscious mind of
the person in the form of the superego, we can begin to think more clearly
about the law as both externally and internally forceful.

Turning again, with these thoughts in mind, to Paul's complex exploration of his own subjective experience in the lengthy Romans 7 quotation

23. Ecclesiastes 3:11.

24. See 40 ff.

25. See James 1:14, 15; James 4:1–5; Ephesians 2:3; also Psalm 37:4 for refinement
of desire.

26. Kristeva, *About Chinese Women*, 143.

27. Romans 8:2: "For the law of the Spirit of life in Christ Jesus has made me free
from the law of sin and death."

28. Kristeva, *About Chinese Women*, 151.

above, we see that he speaks not only of the law's role in enabling sin to exploit him, but also of the independent, autonomous character of sin. Furthermore, it is plain that he is talking of an unconscious, automatic process at work, over which he has little control, claiming that sin in him is what violates, and not he himself, or what he refers to as his will, which we infer is that intention in him which is informed by his knowledge of God and good, to do good. I have previously posited not one, but two differing agencies in the mind, the superego and the conscience, which, while derived from different sources, both intend, at least as a part of their function, to serve the purpose of guiding the individual away from transgression. Insofar as Paul laments the automaticity and autonomous character with which sin influences him, I believe he is acknowledging not only the evil character of desire in him that is illicit, but also the presence of the superego accuser, the internal, unconscious enforcer of a legalism that perpetuates the sin. He would be hopelessly bound by and to this "body of death," suffering the effects of the death instinct within him as it manifests itself through these processes of unconscious clinging to prohibitions and desires to breach them, were it not for the deliverance he knows he has in Christ Jesus, through faith in him and his resurrection. He is able to say farther along in Romans: "Christ is the end of the law for righteousness to everyone who believes."[29] His hope is established on the rule of grace and life having displaced the rule of law and death that is universally imposed on all mankind through solidarity with Adam at the fall, by means of solidarity with Christ acquired through faith.[30]

Paul's life is a vivid example of Richard Rohr's thesis that we must transition from the first half of life (not determined by age), which is characterized by strivings to establish our tribal identity, achieve supposed security, learn to manage our powerful passions by kicking against the law, to the second half of life, in which we humbly struggle with our frailties, our failings, and learn to live by a conscience that encourages us to love difference, the "strangerness" in the other and in our own selves.

In summary, for me the concept of a death instinct has meaning in two senses: First, from the point of view of a biologically impelling movement that inevitably ends in death for all biological life as we know it. Second, from the point of view of the unbinding or destroying parts of the (Laplanchian) sexual drive that forms psychologically and developmentally through childhood and is integral to the differentiation of the superego from the larger ego, and which is so much an apparent component of the sin-evil, desire-law system of which Paul speaks.

29. Romans 10:4.

30. Romans 5:12–20.

Psychoanalytic treatment does not explicitly invoke the gospel of Jesus Christ in order to alleviate the regime in the mind of law and death that affects us all, but so-called "analytic love," that is, the love that the analyst manifests for his patient by virtue of the exercise of good psychoanalytic technique has many parallels to the love of Christ as embodied in the gospel. As such, much in the way of psychological and emotional suffering can be alleviated, and actual change in the structure and organization of the personality is often achieved. By these means, the subjectively experienced impacts of the death drive in terms of one's relationship with both himself and others are ameliorated. Nevertheless, obviously, psychoanalysis does not pretend to overstep its bounds to operate within the realm that is ultimately spiritual, or as many would say, religious. Paul's own experience was clearly that of the spiritual, a realization of deliverance from the domain of death to that of life, and although he articulated a frustration with limited release from his on-going awareness of the deadly grip of his unconscious on his life-experience, a powerful portrayal of the death drive active in lived experience, he embraced a solid conviction of hope that he would participate in the resurrection life of Christ. In effect, he evinces the over-coming of the death drive by virtue of the reality of the resurrection of Christ, which in turn, he clearly proclaims is available for all who believe. The patient undergoing analysis, if similarly desirous of a hopeful conviction of ultimate deliverance from the inevitable power of death, would also have to look away from psychoanalysis, to spirituality and faith in God.

Afterword

IN MY INTRODUCTION, I stated that this work arose out of the juxtaposition of my studies and training in psychoanalysis with my long-standing Christian worldview. The latter has been subjected to doubt and investigation for decades, and though has transformed and continues, rather like any dynamic system to do so, it remains intact. The many notes I took on disparate topics while training in psychoanalysis have served as the basis for this work. They, in turn, have been massaged and integrated with my own clinical work along with on-going studies, to form now what I hope consists in a coherent synthesis. Along the way, it has become, as I have discovered, a "psychoanalytic protest theology," a theology that not only reverses our customary human presumptions toward rightness through earned merit, but also takes account of the power of the human unconscious to influence all of life, including spirituality, our hermeneutics, and the organization of religion. I protest against the church's general failure to account for the unconscious and the immense complexity of human beings in its biblical interpretations and their applications to real life. Christianity has therefore tended to portray human experience in falsely simplistic terms. Especially as knowledge in the human sciences of neuropsychology, psychology, sociology, and psychoanalysis has advanced, old paradigms of theology bereft of a conceptual structure sufficient to contend with new complexity have in some instances, left the church crippled in its capacity to speak meaningfully into the lives of contemporary people. New wine demands new wine skins.

Bibliography

Armstrong, Karen. *The Battle For God, A History of Fundamentalism*. New York: Ballantine, 2000.

————. *A History of God: The 4,000 Year Quest of Judaism, Christianity and Islam*. New York: Ballantine, 1993.

Atlas, Galit. *The Enigma of Desire: Sex, Longing, and Belonging in Psychoanalysis*. New York: Routledge, 2016.

Badiou, Alain. *Saint Paul: The Foundation of Universalism*. Stanford, California: Stanford University Press, 2003.

Balswick, Judith K., and Jack O. Balswick. *Authentic Human Sexuality: An Integrated Christian Approach*. Downers Grove, IL: IVP Academic, 1999.

Benner, David. *The Gift of Being Yourself: The Sacred Call to Self-Discovery*. Downers Grove, IL: InterVarsity, 2015.

Berry, Wendell. *Sex, Economy, Freedom & Community*. New York: Pantheon, 1992.

Bohleber, Werner. *Destructiveness, Intersubjectivity, and Trauma: The Identity Crisis of Modern Psychoanalysis*, London: Karnac, 2010.

Bollas, Christopher. *Forces of Destiny: Psychoanalysis and Human Idiom*. Jason Aronson, 1991.

————. *The Shadow of the Object: Psychoanalysis of the Unthought Known*, London: Free Association, 1987.

Bonhoeffer, Dietrich. *Letters & Papers From Prison*. Collins Fontana, 1959.

Brown, Peter. *The Body and Society: Men, Women, and Sexual Renunciation in Early Christianity*. New York: Columbia University Press, 1988.

Buber, Martin. *I and Thou*. New York: Scribners, 1970.

Carveth, Donald L. "Four Contributions to the Theory of the Superego, Guilt and Conscience." In *The Canadian Journal of Psychoanalysis* 19 2 (2011) 349–60.

————. *The Still Small Voice: Psychoanalytic Reflections on Guilt and Conscience*. UK: Karnac, 2013

Cavey, Bruxey. *The End of Religion: An Introduction to the Subversive Spirituality of Jesus*. Oakville, Ontario: Agoraimprints, 2005.

Charles, Marilyn. *The Stories We Live: Life, Literature and Psychoanalysis*. Lanham, MD: Rowman and Littlefield, 2015.

Coakley, Sarah. *God, Sexuality and the Self: An Essay "On the Trinity."* Cambridge: Cambridge University Press, 2013.

Crabb, Larry. *Real Change is Possible if You're Willing to Start from the . . . Inside Out.* Colorado Springs: NavPress, 1988.

Dawkins, Richard. *The God Delusion.* New York: Houghton Mifflin, 2006.

Delay, Tad. *God is Unconscious.* Eugene, OR: Wipf & Stock, 2015.

Dinnerstein, Dorothy. *The Mermaid and the Minotaur: Sexual Arrangements and Human Malaise.* New York: Harper Colophon, 1976.

Enns, Peter. *The Bible Tells Me So . . . Why Defending Scripture Has Made Us Unable to Read It.* New York: HarperCollins, 2014.

Evans, Dylan. *An Introductory Dictionary of Lacanian Psychoanalysis.* London: Routledge, 1996.

Fairbairn, W. Ronald D. *Psychoanalytic Studies of the Personality.* New York: Routledge, 1952.

Farley, Margaret A. *Just Love: A Framework for Christian Sexual Ethics.* New York: Continuum, 2006.

Ferro, Antonino. *Mind Works: Technique and Creativity in Psychoanalysis.* New York: Routledge, 2009.

Foucault, Michael. *The History of Sexuality; Vol. 1: An Introduction.* New York: Vintage, 1990.

———. *The Use of Pleasure; Vol. 2 of The History of Sexuality.* New York: Vintage, 1990.

———. *The Care of the Self; Vol. 3 of The History of Sexuality,* New York: Vintage, 1988.

Freud, Anna. *The Ego and the Mechanisms of Defence.* London: Hogarth, 1954

Freud, Sigmund. *An Autobiographical Study.* London: Hogarth, 1925.

———. *Beyond the Pleasure Principle,* 1920.

———. *Civilization and Its Discontents,* 1927.

———. *The Claims of Psycho-analysis to Scientific Interest,* 1913.

———. *The Ego and The Id,* 1923.

———. *Further Remarks on the Neuro-psychoses of Defence,* 1896.

———. *The Future of An Illusion,* 1927.

———. *Instincts and Their Vicissitudes,* 1914.

———. *Moses and Monotheism,* 1939.

———. *Recommendations to Physicians Practicing Psychoanalysis,* 1912.

———. *Obsessive Actions and Religious Practices,* 1907.

———. *On Narcissism, An Introduction,* 1914.

———. *An Outline of Psychoanalysis,* 1940.

———. *Three Essays on Sexuality,* 1905.

———. *Totem and Taboo,* 1913.

Gay, Peter. *Freud: A Life For Our Time,* New York: Norton, 1998.

Gottlieb Zornberg, Aviva. *The Beginning of Desire: Reflections on Genesis.* New York: Schocken, 1995.

———. *The Murmuring Deep: Reflections on the Biblical Unconscious.* New York: Schocken, 2009.

Hays, Richard B. *The Moral Vision of the New Testament: A Contemporary Introduction to New Testament Ethics.* New York: HarperOne, 1996.

Hewitt, Marsha Aileen. *Freud on Religion.* Abingdon, UK: Routledge, 2014.

Holloway, Richard. *Leaving Alexandria: A Memoir of Faith and Doubt.* Edinburgh: Canongate, 2012.

Johnson, Eric. *Foundations of Soul Care: A Christian Psychology Proposal.* Downers Grove, IL: IVP Academic, 2007.

Kaplan, Louise. *Female Perversions.* New York: Anchor, 1992.

Kegan, Robert. *The Evolving Self: Problem and Process in Human Development.* Cambridge: Harvard University Press, 1993.

Kierkegaard, Søren. *Works of Love.* New York: Harper Perennial Modern Thought, 1962.

Klein, Naomi. *Macleans Magazine.* Sept. 10, 2007.

Kristeva, Julia. "About Chinese Women." In *The Kristeva Reader,* Edited by Toril Moi. New York: Columbia University Press, 1986.

Lacan, Jacques. *The Triumph of Religion.* Cambridge: Polity, 2013.

Laplanche, J. and J.B. Pontalis. *The Language of Psychoanalysis.* New York: W.W. Norton & Company, 1973.

Laplanche, Jean. *Between Seduction and Inspiration: Man.* New York: The Unconscious in Translation, 2015.

———. *Freud and the Sexual.* Translated by Jonathan House and Nicholas Ray, New York: The Unconscious in Translation, 2011.

———. *Life and Death in Psychoanalysis.* Baltimore: Johns Hopkins University Press, 1985.

Lear, Jonathan. *Open Minded: Working Out The Logic of the Soul.* Cambridge, MA: Harvard University Press, 1998.

Lemma, Alessandra. "The Prostitute As Mirror." In *Sexualities: Contemporary Psychoanalytic Perspectives,* edited by Alessandra Lemma and Paul Lynch, 189–204. London: Routledge, 2015.

——— and Paul Lynch. *Introduction: Let's talk about Sex . . . Maybe Not. . . .* In *Sexualities: Contemporary Psychoanalytic Perspectives,* edited by Alessandra Lemma and Paul Lynch, 1–16. London: Routledge, 2015.

Lewis, C. S. *The Chronicles of Narnia.* Fontana Lions, 1951.

———. "God in the Dock." In *The Collected Works of C.S. Lewis.* New York: Inspirational, 1970.

Loewald, Hans W. *Papers on Psychoanalysis.* New Haven: Yale University Press, 1989.

Mahler, Margaret S. "Symbiosis and Individuation—The Psychological Birth of the Human Infant." In *Psychoanalytic Studies of the Child* 29 (1974) 89–106.

Markson, Elliot R. "Depression and Moral Masochism." In *Int. J. Psycho-Anal.* 74 (1993) 931–40.

Martin, James. *The Jesuit Guide to (Almost) Everything: A Spirituality for Real Life.* New York: HarperOne, 2010.

Menninger, Karl. *Man Against Himself.* New York: Harcourt, Brace & World, 1938.

Miller, Alice. *The Drama of the Gifted Child.* Basic, 1996.

Miller, Michael. *Lacanian Psychotherapy: Theory and Practical Applications.* London: Routledge, 2011.

Mollon, Phil. "The Inherent Shame of Sexuality." In *Shame and Sexuality: Psychoanalysis and Visual Culture,* edited by Claire Pajaczkowska and Ivan Ward, 23–34. London: Routledge, 2008.

Moss, Donald. "Sexual Aberrations: Do we Still Need the Concept? If so, when and why? If not, why not?" In *Sexualities, Contemporary Psychoanalytic Perspectives,* edited by Alessandra Lemma and Paul Lynch, 177–88. New York: Routledge, 2015.

Muggeridge, Malcolm. *A Third Testament.* New York: Ballantine, 1976.

Nahum, Jeremy P. "The 'Something More' than Interpretation Revisited." In *JAPA* 53 (2005) 693–729.

Ogden, Thomas H. "Bion's Four Principles of Mental Functioning", *Fort Da* 14 (2008) 11–35.

Peterson, Margaret Kim, and Dwight N. Peterson. *Are You Waiting for the One? Cultivating Realistic, Positive Expectations for Christian Marriage.* Downers Grove, IL: IVP, 2011.

Reiner, Annie. *The Quest for Conscience and The Birth of the Mind.* London: Karnac, 2009.

Rizzuto, Ana-Marie. *The Birth of the Living God: A Psychoanalytic Study.* Chicago: The University of Chicago Press, 1979.

Rohr, Richard. *Falling Upward: A Spirituality for the Two Halves of Life.* San Francisco: Jossey-Bass, 2011.

Rollins, Peter. *The Divine Magician: The Disappearance of Religion and the Discovery of Faith.* Brentwood, TN: Howard, 2015.

———. *Insurrection: To Believe is Human; To Doubt, Divine.* Brentwood, TN: Howard, 2011.

Scarfone, Dominique. *The Unpast, Actuality of the Unconscious.* Presented to the Congress of French-Speaking Psychoanalysts. Montreal, 2014.

Schmemann, Alexander. *For the Life of the World.* Crestwood, NY: St. Vladimir's Seminary, 1963.

Shengold, Leonard. "Trauma, Soul Murder, and Change." In *The Psychoanalytic Quarterly* 80 (2011) 121–38.

Stein, Ruth A. "Unforgetting and Excess, the Re-creation and Re-finding of Suppressed Sexuality." In *Psychoanalytic Dialogues* 16 (2006) 763–78.

Stoller, Robert. *Perversion: The Erotic Form of Hatred.* London: Karnac, 1986.

Stolorow, Robert D., and George E. Atwood. *Contexts of Being: The Intersubjective Foundations of Psychological Life.* Hillsdale, NJ: Analytic, 1992.

Summers, Frank. *Self Creation: Psychoanalytic Therapy and the Art of the Possible.* New Jersey: The Analytic, 2005.

Target, Mary. *A Developmental Model of Sexual Excitement, Desire and Alienation.* In *Sexualities: Contemporary Psychoanalytic Perspectives,* edited by Alessandra Lemma & Paul E. Lynch, 43–62. New York: Routledge, 2015.

Ti.Po.Ta. https://www.youtube.com/TI.PO.TA.—Moonlight Avenue.

Torrance, Thomas F. *The Mediation of Christ.* Colorado Springs: Helmers & Howard, 1992.

———. *Reality & Evangelical Theology: The Realism of Christian Revelation.* Downer's Grove: InterVarsity, 1982.

Vitz, Paul C. *Sigmund Freud's Christian Unconscious.* Leominster, UK: Gracewing, 1993.

Volf, Miroslav. *Exclusion and Embrace: A Theological Exploration of Identity, Otherness, and Reconciliation.* Abingdon, 1996.

Walsh, Brian J., and Sylvia C. Keesmaat. *Colossians Remixed: Subverting the Empire.* Downer's Grove, IL: InterVarsity, 2004.

Winnicott, D.W. *The Maturational Processes and the Facilitating Environment: Studies in the Theory of Emotional Development.* London: Hogarth, 1965.

———. *Playing and Reality.* London: Routledge Classics, 2005.

———. "The Theory of the Parent Infant Relationship." In *International Journal of Psychoanalysis* 41 (1960) 585–95.

Wolf, Naomi. *The Beauty Myth.* Toronto: Vintage, 1990.

Wurmser, Leon. *The Power of the Inner Judge: Psychodynamic Treatment of the Severe Neuroses.* New Jersey: Aronson, 2000.

Yoder, John Howard. *The Politics of Jesus.* Grand Rapids: W. B. Eerdmans, 1971.

Žižek, Slavoj. *Interrogating the Real.* New York: Continuum, 2006.